Liberalism and Community

Liberalism and Community

STEVEN KAUTZ

CORNELL UNIVERSITY PRESS • ITHACA & LONDON

First published 1995 by Cornell University Press

Printed in the United States of America

♾ The paper in this book meets the minimum requirements of the American National Standard for Information Sciences— Permanence of Paper for Printed Library Materials, ANSI Z39-48-1984.

Library of Congress Cataloging-in-Publication Data

Kautz, Steven J.
    Liberalism and community / Steven Kautz.
        p.   cm.
    Includes bibliographical references and index.
    ISBN 0–8014–2979–X (alk. paper)
    1. Liberalism.   2. Community.   I. Title.
HM276.K258   1995
320.5'1—dc20   95–19672

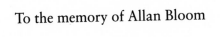

To the memory of Allan Bloom

Contents

Preface

The world of political theory has lately witnessed a remarkable revival of an old idea: the idea of community. This revival now takes an impressive variety of more and less radical forms—from traditional conservative to classical republican to social democratic to radical postmodernist—each somehow critical of the prevailing liberal individualism of our community. Liberalism, say its critics, is incapable of sustaining the civic virtue that is the foundation of a democratic community of free and equal citizens; it has impaired the moral lives of human beings by depriving us of certain goods that can be known only in communities (the comforts of "home," the pleasures of common action, the nobility of sacrifice); and it has confounded moral philosophers by encouraging them to undertake an unavailing quest for detachment or neutrality. In this book, I consider the consequences for liberalism of our growing attachment to the idea of community.

Here is our predicament: we love our privacy, and yet we long for community. We are all somehow liberals, but from modern rationalism and individualism, which have liberated or corrupted us, there is no easy escape, and no return to traditional community is quite imaginable. So we must ask: in the modern world, "after virtue," is it possible to revive moral community or republican citizenship without altogether abandoning our common sense that we are individuals, since this quality of the liberal soul is now inescapable, and even somehow admirable?

In this book, I defend a certain (classical) interpretation of liberalism against communitarian critics, and against critics who have been influenced by communitarian ideas. The liberalism that I defend is a cautious, conservative sort of liberalism, founded on the liberalisms of Locke and

Montesquieu. I argue that partisans of liberalism must now recover a prudent sense of the limits of liberalism, recognizing, with Locke and Montesquieu, its basis in a chastened disposition to take one's bearings from the great inhumanity of which human beings are somehow capable; and yet, Locke and Montesquieu reveal as well, I argue, that liberalism is an honorable doctrine, by which proud and spirited human beings vindicate their reasonable love of freedom. The liberal politics that I propose to defend is a politics of fearful accommodation among natural foes who somehow transform themselves into civil friends, by means of a sort of peace treaty that demands uncommon self-restraint or moderation ("liberal virtues") as the price we pay for public peace and private liberty: or, as Montesquieu says, it is the price we pay for "that tranquillity of spirit which comes from the opinion each one has of his security," where "one citizen cannot fear another citizen."

The communitarian critics of liberalism argue that liberalism is both morally and politically impoverishing. These arguments recall certain older "democratic" and "republican" assaults on the politics of liberty, assaults mounted in the name of equality, and of virtue. In order to defend liberalism, and even a rather sober interpretation of liberalism, against these more hopeful visions, I attempt in this book to locate the communitarian critique of liberalism in this larger context of enduring quarrels between liberals and republicans, and between liberals and democrats. And so I offer here several sustained accounts of various partisan quarrels between liberals (who love liberty), democrats (who love equality), and republicans (who love virtue). I argue that the case for liberalism against the communitarians has much in common with the case for liberalism against these earlier assaults. Beyond that, I contend that the unwillingness of contemporary communitarian critics of liberalism to embrace wholeheartedly the traditional arguments against liberalism manifests a revealing ambivalence toward liberalism. Perhaps the liberal vices that trouble communitarians are merely the natural and inescapable consequence of liberal achievements that even communitarians do not wish to repudiate.

Who are the communitarians? Perhaps one might say that communitarians, strictly speaking, are partisans of the idea of "constitutive" community: a community that wholly or substantially constitutes our identities, so that who we are is *principally* and *inescapably* constituted by our participation in the way of life of a particular community. From this point of view, Michael J. Sandel and Alasdair MacIntyre are perhaps our leading communitarian theorists. But in this book I examine a wider range of theorists, in an effort to reveal the effect of communitarian ideas on a variety of enduring ways of thinking about politics. Thus, although I discuss Sandel and MacIntyre in a few places, I focus here on three theorists who are perhaps not quite communitarians at all, or who are communitarians only with reservations: the *liberal* communitarian Richard Rorty, the *republican* communitarian Benjamin Barber, and the *democratic* communitarian Michael Walzer. Each of these theorists acknowledges that he is attracted by the idea of community, and each attempts to make use of that idea on behalf of more traditional (liberal, classical republican, and social democratic) ways of thinking about modern politics.

Walzer in particular is reluctant to be identified as a communitarian, and it is only fair to say that I have here offered a very partial portrait of his political theory, which is uncommonly rich and wide-ranging. And yet, the communitarian Walzer is a real Walzer too, and so I have chosen to confine myself to those texts that most reveal this communitarian aspect of his political thought. As for Rorty, who is a communitarian but not a critic of liberalism, I show that his postmodern bourgeois liberalism nonetheless signals the surprising encroachment of communitarian ideas within liberal theory itself. Perhaps the principal aim of the book, in fact, is to offer reasons why liberals should resist these encroachments. Finally, Barber's republican theory, which is the most formidable contemporary species of Rousseauian republicanism, reveals the influence of communitarian ideas within both politics and philosophy. As a consequence of his communitarianism, I suggest, Barber's republicanism is a greatly transformed republicanism whose aim is not virtue but moral comfort or warmth.

In Chapters 1 and 2, I introduce the main themes of the book: I describe the problem of community as it has emerged in recent years in the United States (which I shall call "America"), and I offer a first portrait of the liberalism that I propose to defend here. In Chapters 3 and 4, I defend this way of understanding liberalism against the erosions of postmodern liberalism, and thus consider the effect of communitarian ideas on liberalism directly. Chapter 3, an analysis of the liberal virtue of tolerance, includes a criticism of the understanding of tolerance advanced by Rorty and Sandel (among others). Chapter 4 is a discussion of Rorty's postmodern or communitarian liberalism, and in particular his repudiation of the liberal idea of "humanity." In Chapters 5 and 6, I defend the cautious, conservative way of understanding liberalism against two critics of liberalism, one democratic and one republican, who are also in some measure its friends, Barber and Walzer. Chapter 5, which is an analysis of Barber's account of republican citizenship, contains a more general discussion of the problem of self-government. Chapter 6, an account of various ways of thinking about the idea of patriotism, includes discussions of MacIntyre's and Walzer's views. The question of the status of patriotism is now as always a particularly revealing measure of the distance between liberalism and (democratic) republicanism. Finally, in Chapters 7 and 8, I consider a further battleground in the quarrel between liberals and communitarians and raise the question whether liberal reason can sustain the moral life of a community. Chapter 7 is an account of liberal virtue and liberal reason. Chapter 8 discusses Walzer's communitarian way of doing moral philosophy.

It is appropriate here to acknowledge that I do not discuss, in this book, a number of important issues that any full account of liberalism must confront. In particular, I do not address any of the issues, raised by both critics and friends of liberalism in recent years, associated with race, gender, the politics of recognition, multiculturalism, and so on. And I do not consider those questions associated above all with the old Left, concerning economic democracy and equality (another reason for the partial portrait of Walzer's thought). These are important sets of questions, and I regret the omissions. But here I seek to understand the relation between individualism and community from within the framework which had until recently dominated discussion of these issues (and which remains, I want to show, still useful): that is, by recalling the enduring quarrels between liberals, democrats, and republicans. I should add as well that I do not here discuss the political communitarianism, associated with the new journal *Responsive Community*, that has recently attracted popular notice. For that communitarianism seems to me mostly compatible with liberalism, and even with the cautious and modest liberalism that I defend in this book.

Friends and teachers generously offered encouragement and counsel from the beginning, and I am pleased to have this opportunity to acknowledge their good deeds.

It has been my good fortune to have had many fine teachers, at James Madison College of Michigan State University, and at the University of Chicago, and this work owes them much. Among these, I express my gratitude to Richard Zinman and Nathan Tarcov. From Richard Zinman, I first learned to take philosophy seriously; he revealed by his example that teaching and scholarship could be the heart of a pleasant and honorable way of life, at a time when I had other ends in mind. He remains for me the model of a dedicated teacher and scholar. Nathan Tarcov served on my dissertation committee; then and now, his friendly but skeptical criticism helped me to refine and enlarge my appreciation of the virtues of liberalism. I am among the many students who have profited from his example: his teaching and thinking are distinguished by a rare marriage of fearlessness and sobriety, the mark of a philosophic scholarship.

It is a great pleasure, though one mixed with sadness, to acknowledge my debt to the late Allan Bloom: a splendid teacher, a benevolent friend, and an indomitable champion of humane politics and freedom of thought. This book is dedicated to his memory.

Thanks also to many other generous friends and colleagues who read parts of the manuscript and offered helpful criticism: Shepard Barbash, Bob Bartlett, Fred Baumann, Walter Berns, David Bolotin, Ruth Grant, Harry Litman, Chris Nadon, Clifford Orwin, Jack Paynter, Jim Stoner. I wish that I had been able to respond more fully to their helpful suggestions; they deserve no blame for whatever foolishness remains, and praise for enabling me to avoid many mistakes in things small and large. I am especially grateful to Peter Ahrensdorf for his remarkable patience in discussions of these matters, for his incisive criticism, for his friendship and counsel over many years, and for much else besides; and to Richard Ruderman for his generosity of spirit and great good humor, as well as his thoughtful criticism of many parts of this book. Thanks also to the reviewers for Cornell University Press, whose judicious and generous advice enabled me to improve the book in many ways; to Roger Haydon, my editor at Cornell, for his friendly encouragement, thoughtful advice, and remarkable patience; and to Celia Carroll, my research assistant, for her meticulous work on the manuscript.

Richard Cordray has been a rare friend for many years, and among the many pleasures that I now associate with the writing of this book, none is greater than the memory of so many conversations with him about the ideas that animate it. To Peggy Cordray, who kindly shared her good judgment and perceptive criticism on innumerable occasions, I am grateful as well. Finally, it is a pleasure to acknowledge here the special debt that I owe to my parents, who know well that without their unstinting care and indulgence I would not have completed this project. For this, and for many other benefactions, I am grateful.

Thanks also to the Social Philosophy and Policy Center (Bowling Green State University), the John M. Olin Foundation, the Earhart Foundation, and the Lynde & Harry Bradley Foundation for generous research support during various stages of this project. A version of Chapter 3 was previously published in the *American Journal of Political Science* 37/2 (May 1993), by the University of Texas Press, and I thank the Press for its permission to incorporate a somewhat more extensive version of that essay here.

STEVEN KAUTZ

Atlanta, Georgia

Liberalism and Community

1

Liberals, Democrats, Republicans, Communitarians

Today, many of the most prominent critics of liberal politics are also partisans of the idea of "community." These communitarian political theorists are critics not only of the classical liberalism of John Locke, which greatly influenced the American founders, but also of the so-called Kantian liberalism of John Rawls and Ronald Dworkin, which is now prevalent in the academic world. They reject both the politics of liberalism and its moral psychology: liberalism, and especially classical liberalism, is said to be a doctrine of acquisitive individualism, one that is incapable of providing an adequate foundation for a democratic community of free and equal citizens; liberalism, and especially contemporary liberalism, is said to be based on an incoherent conception of the individual self, one that fails to recognize that our identities are partly or wholly constituted by our communal memberships, that there is no "I" before there is a "we." And so, liberalism is both politically and morally deficient, unable either to accommodate our intuitions about justice and equality or to acknowledge the moral depth of our attachments to other human beings.[1]

---

[1]For a variety of affirmations of a communitarian creed, see: Michael Walzer, *Radical Principles*, 12–13; Michael J. Sandel, *Liberalism and the Limits of Justice*, 173–74, 179–83; Benjamin R. Barber, *Strong Democracy*, 229–33; Barber, *The Conquest of Politics*, 199–211; Alasdair MacIntyre, *After Virtue*, 203–7; MacIntyre, *Is Patriotism a Virtue?* 8–11; William M. Sullivan, *Reconstructing Public Philosophy*, 159–62; Ronald Beiner, *Political Judgment*, 138–44; Roberto Mangabeira Unger, *Knowledge and Politics*, 184, 220–22; and Robert Paul Wolff, *The Poverty of Liberalism*, 184–85, 191–95. See, too, Richard Rorty, *Contingency, Irony, and Solidarity*, 44–69; and Rorty, *Objectivity, Relativism, and Truth*, 21–34, 175–210.

Communitarians are above all "antiliberals" who seek to establish a politics of the common good and thereby to tame the prevailing liberal politics of individual rights.[2] Beyond that fundamental antiliberalism, the communitarian "movement" is marked by a remarkable diversity of views regarding the nature of community itself, from traditional conservative to classical republican to social democratic to radical postmodernist—among many other communitarian parties.[3] Indeed, the idea of community is notoriously vague and indefinite. Besides, everyone admits that "community" names something good: who is not somehow a communitarian? So even liberals today (properly) seek to appropriate the idea of community, thereby lending a certain warmth to the cold liberal doctrine of individual rights.[4] It appears, then, that the revival of the idea of community reflects a profound dissatisfaction with prevailing liberal ways of life, so that even many liberals are prepared to seek common ground with these communitarian critics. So the question arises: How far can liberals, who seek to secure the rights of individuals, accommodate the idea of community? And, on the other hand, how far can communitarians, who seek to revive a politics of the common good, accommodate the rights of individuals? In this book, I consider these questions by recalling certain enduring democratic and republican arguments against liberalism. For the contemporary debate is in some measure a reprise of these old quarrels between liberals and republicans, and between liberals and democrats. And the revival of the idea of community is (at least in part) a somewhat ambivalent revival of these democratic and republican arguments in a novel hybrid form: marrying the older concerns about (democratic) equality and (republican) virtue yields the more or less novel idea of community.

But here I begin more generally, with a few remarks about the broad appeal of the idea of community in contemporary politics. I turn again in the sequel to the question of the place of communitarians in the partisan world of liberals, democrats, and republicans.

I

Talk about *community* is rife in contemporary scholarship; but it has also, more and more, become a feature of ordinary political discourse in America. Thus, Ronald Reagan often appealed to a "community of

---

[2]See Stephen Holmes, *The Anatomy of Antiliberalism*; and Peter Berkowitz, "Liberal Zealotry," a review of Holmes's book.

[3]For an account of the remarkable variety of communitarian views, see Robert Booth Fowler, *The Dance with Community*.

[4]See William A. Galston, *Liberal Purposes*; and Stephen Macedo, *Liberal Virtues*.

shared values," and especially to the idea of "family": "family and community remain the moral core of our society, guardians of our values and hopes for the future." And his Democratic opponents sometimes spoke as if they sought to make the whole community like a family: "we believe we must be the family of America"; "in our family are gathered everyone from the abject poor of Essex County in New York to the enlightened affluent of the gold coasts of both ends of our nation."[5] The growing popularity of the language of community in our political life reveals a growing dissatisfaction, on both Right and Left, with prevailing liberal individualism, which appears to emancipate mean-spirited greed and to encourage a selfish neglect of the duties of family and citizenship.

Democrats have recently been urged, by a leading communitarian theorist in the pages of *The New Republic*, to "learn the language of self-government and community"; in this, at least, liberals have something to learn from Reagan's conservatism, according to Michael Sandel.[6] Reagan's political achievement, Sandel argues, was his ability to bring together two kinds of conservatism: one of them individualistic, economic, libertarian, the other moral, religious, and communal. Indeed, Sandel suggests that the principal reason for Reagan's success was his appeal to our longing for community—his laments over the decline of traditional communities and his "evocations" of traditional moral and religious beliefs and sentiments. Moreover, this yearning for a renewal of community is, even in the conservative case, at the same time a plea for self-government and citizenship; for it is not federal judges, but local communities, the conservative citizen insists, who should make decisions about school prayer, pornography, and the rest.

But Democrats, Sandel argues, have so far been less successful in making an appeal to the idea of community, and this has hurt them. They have, surely, made attempts: Walter Mondale and especially Mario Cuomo spoke a rhetoric of community in 1984, calling for a nation

---

[5]The idea of community was a central theme in several of former President Ronald Reagan's most important speeches. The most notable example is his acceptance speech at the 1980 Republican National Convention. See *Vital Speeches of the Day* (15 August 1980): 642–46 ("community of shared values," 642). See, too, Reagan's 1986 State of the Union speech, *Vital Speeches of the Day* (1 March 1986): 290–93 ("the moral core of our society," 290); and his Second Inauguration Address, *Vital Speeches of the Day* (1 February 1985): 226–28. The idea of community has also begun to appear somewhat more frequently in the speeches of Democratic political leaders; the most famous instance is the keynote speech by Governor Mario Cuomo at the 1984 Democratic National Convention, in *Vital Speeches of the Day* (15 August 1984): 646–69 ("the family of America," 649; "our family," 647).

[6]See Sandel, "Democrats and Community," 21.

bound together by ties of compassion and love—a national community, but akin to a family. And more recently, the Clintons have sometimes been claimed to be adherents of a new communitarian "movement."[7] Nevertheless, such liberal appeals to community have generally been vitiated by the persistent nationalism of the Democratic Party: few thoughtful liberals really believe that the nation can be like a family, and most of us are frightened by the prospect of an effort to make it so. Indeed, the liberal appeal to national power has generally been a defense of individual rights and prerogatives against local community intolerance, and against private economic power, Sandel argues.

And yet, a communitarian politics of the Left, like that of the Right, must be a politics of local self-government, says Sandel. Above all, it requires an effort to decentralize the modern economy, which (rather than federal judges) is the real culprit in the decline of traditional communities: liberalism today requires a new debate about "the economic arrangements most amenable to democratic" politics and so to "self-government on a manageable scale." But Democrats must also leave room in our public life for moral and religious discourse, argues Sandel, if only to combat what he calls the "narrow moralisms" of the Right. These moral and religious impulses are simply too powerful to be restrained by liberal shackles. But it is in such cases that the old-fashioned liberal in Sandel sometimes makes an appearance: so, for example, "local control of schools" is desirable only insofar as it is "consistent with nationally assured rights to racial equality and a decent education for all citizens." In the face of such implicit concessions as this, a liberal might wonder whether a healthy politics today requires not the imitation of Reagan's communal conservatism, but its forceful repudiation, and a reaffirmation of the principles of a truly liberal politics.

Friends of liberty are properly somewhat skeptical of claims made on behalf of the idea of community, since "community" has so often been the slogan of intolerant or authoritarian parties. Even Sandel expresses such skepticism from time to time, as in his defense of rights to racial equality and a decent education. And so, praise of community today, especially on the Left, is sometimes tempered by a prudent recognition of the threats to liberty that might emerge within revitalized communities—and especially within the most natural, organic communities. Sandel im-

---

[7] That "movement" is associated with the journal *Responsive Community*, whose founding editor, Amitai Etzioni, is also the author of a programmatic communitarian text, *The Spirit of Community*. See, too, "The Responsive Communitarian Platform," which appears in Etzioni's book, 251–67.

plausibly asserts that "there is nothing intrinsically conservative about family or neighborhood . . . or religion." But partisans of the family are in practice almost always opposed, for obvious reasons, to certain kinds of liberation (especially sexual liberation), which are said to be incompatible with the sanctity of the family. And partisans of traditional religious communities are often enemies of another kind of freedom (of thought), which is said to be incompatible with faith. Thus, it is not surprising that the defense of family and religion often takes the form of conservative opposition to liberation: as in the condemnation of sexual liberation in its various forms (pornography, homosexuality, feminism), on the grounds that such liberation is destructive of the family; or as in the condemnation of so-called secular humanism in the schools, on the grounds that it is destructive of religion. Thus, our recent politics has sometimes been a contest between a conservative party that claims to speak for the family and traditional religious values and a party of liberation that claims to defend the individual against the strictures of these traditional communities.[8]

As a result, when those on the Left praise "community," they often refer especially to nontraditional communities that seek further liberation for their members. Such "communities" are typically based on ideology rather than locality: for example, the community of workers, or the gay community, or the black community, or the community of artists and intellectuals. Indeed, Walzer frequently speaks with some passion about the way of life of a community of comrades in a political cause, and wonders whether such a community can maintain its solidarity after the socialist cause has prevailed. Nevertheless, even nontraditional communities of the Left can surely pose threats to individual liberties. As a result, even the critics of liberal individualism seek to incorporate liberal political institutions, as safeguards of our liberties, into their portraits of the community of the future. This communitarian vision often takes the form of an imagined synthesis of the ancient polis, so to speak, with the modern liberal state, a synthesis that is said to be superior to either alternative; or, even more typically, it takes the form of more or less far-reaching amendments to the liberal state—small injections of fellowship and the rest that will cure us, it is hoped, of the most extreme symptoms of our solitude.[9]

[8]Sandel, "Democracy and Community," 20–23; and see, too, Sandel, "Morality and the Liberal Ideal."

[9]See Holmes, *Anatomy*, 180: "When striving to catch our attention, [the communitarians] regularly present their indescribable community as an *alternative* to liberal society.

Now not even the most strident individualist would deny that human beings, from time to time, find occasions to rub up against one another, and even to join into more or less permanent communities on the basis of certain more or less natural propensities to seek the company or assistance of other human beings. Nor are there many communitarians today who would insist that the individual human being does not exist outside of the community, or that solitary individuals are like hands without bodies, as Aristotle suggested. The debate between liberals and their communitarian critics, insofar as it is a debate about political institutions—or even about the place of such notions as the common good or virtue or equality in our public life—should be a relatively quiet controversy: a dispute among friends about where to draw the line between *my* rights and *our* vision of the common good, or how to reconcile the sometimes conflicting claims of liberty and equality, and so on. These are not quarrels about fundamental principles, for neither party altogether repudiates the idea of "rights" or the idea of the "common good." If nothing more than such marginal political issues is at stake, the communitarian critique of liberal political institutions soon "becomes indistinguishable from liberalism itself," as Christopher Lasch put it, especially since many liberals, too, are now eager to speak about "liberalism and the moral life."[10] A disinterested observer might perhaps be tempted to wonder what all the noise is about.

II

Begin again. We now live in the midst of "culture wars" pitting so-called (by the Left) fundamentalists against so-called (by the Right) cultural elitists in battles that concern a remarkable variety of moral, religious, and cultural issues: Murphy Brown and "family values"; flagburning and the "new patriotism"; gay rights and sexual decadence; evolution and religion in the classroom; and many more.[11] The tone of these disputes is remarkably nasty and bitter. Often, the partisans are almost speechless, for it is hard to speak—to give reasons—to those with whom one has so lit-

---

Once they succeed in attracting a sufficient number of critical onlookers, however, they . . . tend to retreat to the more modest position that community is merely a *supplement* to liberal society." See, too, Raymond Plant, "Community: Concept, Conception, and Ideology," a persuasive analysis of the half-hearted character of the contemporary longing for community, especially in its social democratic version.

[10]Christopher Lasch, "The Communitarian Critique of Liberalism," 72. See Nancy L. Rosenblum, ed., *Liberalism and the Moral Life*, for essays by liberals on the moral meaning of the liberal way of life.

[11]See, for example, James Davison Hunter, *Culture Wars*.

tle in common, so great is the chasm that has now opened between the cultural Left and the cultural Right in America. Partisan opponents are now regularly demonized in various ways: our enemies are not merely wrong but also wicked, "perverts" or "Yahoos."[12]

These cultural controversies between elitists and fundamentalists have their roots in certain enduring controversies regarding the nature of popular government. Such quarrels are a natural part of life in liberal democratic communities, for there will always be a culturally radical elite and a culturally conservative majority in such communities. This is an old story: Socrates was executed by democratic Athens for corrupting the youth. More generally, it is surely natural and ordinary for liberal democratic communities to lean right on moral, religious, and cultural issues and to lean left on economic issues: thus, populism is as naturally hostile to (artistic and other) intellectual elites as it is to economic elites. So human beings in self-governing communities are more or less naturally inclined to become adherents of certain natural political parties: liberals (who love liberty), democrats (who love equality), and republicans (who love virtue). And it is the principal business of the liberal community to tame the natural partisanship of democrats and republicans: or there will be "culture wars."

Because I will return, from time to time, to this portrait of popular politics, I propose to pause here to explain terms. Here and throughout, "liberalism" refers to the various philosophical defenses of *liberty* or the "rights of man," not to the political program of the moderate Left in American politics. "Republican" refers to any more or less popular politics that is based on *virtue*, wherein all citizens have an equal share in rule on the basis of common love of the republic. And "democratic" refers to any popular politics that is based on *equality*, wherein—as Aristotle put it—"all have an equal share [in rule] on the basis of number."[13]

To repeat, the communitarian revival of the idea of community might be understood as a revival of these republican and democratic arguments

---

[12]See Mary Ann Glendon, *Rights Talk*, 154: "It is only a slight exaggeration to say that the two main opinions in *Bowers v. Hardwick* make the case look like a battle between Yahoos and perverts."

[13]On republics, see Montesquieu, *The Spirit of the Laws*, bks. 2–8; Jean-Jacques Rousseau, *On the Social Contract*, 2.7–11, 3.12–15, 4.7–8; consider, too, the city of Plato's *Republic*. On democracy, see Aristotle's account in *Politics*, 1318a5–10, 1280a5–25, 1291b30–1292a35; and see Montesquieu, *Spirit*, 8.2. On liberalism, see John Locke, *Second Treatise*, in *Two Treatises of Government*, §§87, 123–33; and Montesquieu, *Spirit*, 11.5–6, 12.2.

in a somewhat novel hybrid form; for this reason, communitarianism is somewhat difficult to classify as a movement of either the Right or the Left: the language of community seems conservative at times and social democratic at times, depending on whether the republican (virtue) or democratic (equality) aspect of the idea of community dominates at any particular moment. Perhaps communitarianism is the newest replacement for failed Marxism; yet it lacks the moral intransigence, the love of justice understood as equality, that is inherent in socialism and social democracy. But if communitarians are less than wholehearted in their commitment to equality, they are at best halfhearted in their praise of virtue; the republicanism of today's communitarians lacks, as well, the moral intransigence of classical republicanism, which is marked by moralism, the abolition of privacy, and the unremitting self-sacrifice of citizens. So the hybrid is less demanding than either pure form. In republican moments, communitarians are tempted to excuse this or that (mild) policy of censorship, or to praise "family values," or to call for a renewal of moral education in the schools—but not at the expense of toleration or the rights of individuals, they invariably add. And in democratic moments, which are somewhat more frequent than the republican ones, communitarians are tempted to seek redistributionist policies designed to secure greater economic equality, and to call for the establishment of participatory institutions (e.g. "teledemocracy") designed to ensure a greater voice for the people in their collective capacity. But there is no question of abandoning liberal (free-market) economics, much less the goal of private prosperity; nor is there any question of abolishing representation (as Rousseau suggested) or any of the other liberal political institutions that filter the judgment of the people and so diminish the likelihood of folly or fanaticism.

And yet, from time to time these democratic and republican impulses can disrupt the liberal polity, for the exercise of the liberal freedoms is naturally obnoxious to partisans of equality and partisans of virtue; inequality and vice are among the natural consequences of freedom. Liberals therefore recognize that the "protection of different and unequal faculties of acquiring property" is the "first object of government," as Publius says; but "the possession of different degrees and kinds of property immediately results." Not inequality, but the freedom to acquire is the interest of liberals; but inequality is the natural consequence, and that is sometimes obnoxious to democrats, who love equality.[14] So too, liber-

---

[14]Alexander Hamilton, James Madison, and John Jay, *The Federalist Papers*, #10: 78. See Locke, *Second Treatise*, §50.

als often recognize that the freedom to write and to speak as one pleases, and more generally the right of privacy (as Justice Brandeis put it, "the right to be let alone—the most comprehensive of rights and the right most valued by civilized men"), is among the finest achievements of liberal politics; but where there is unfettered privacy, there will surely be sordid speeches and deeds. Not vice, but the freedom to choose a pursuit of happiness according to one's own lights is the interest of liberals; but vice is the natural consequence, and that is sometimes obnoxious to republicans, who love virtue.[15] So it is hardly surprising that both democrats and republicans from time to time resist liberal excesses, and sometimes press on even further; for this reason, the prudent liberal recognizes that it will often be necessary to achieve a kind of settlement, to keep the peace, between liberals and their democratic and republican enemies. Because such quarrels are natural in liberal democratic republics, so liberals must be ever vigilant in self-defense.

Harvey Mansfield argues, in *The Spirit of Liberalism*, that classical liberalism established a new and superior form of the mixed regime that has been the practical ideal of political philosophers from the beginning (since the pure or simple regimes are everywhere unjust or partisan). Liberal democracy is constituted by a *settlement* between the liberals ("men of ambition") and the democrats (those who "prefer a quiet, private life" with "security"), says Mansfield: "The democrats approve or tolerate ambition; the liberals have it." Thus the democrats can be brought to tolerate the practice of ambition in certain spheres of life as long as that ambition does not threaten their "quiet, private life"; and it may be that the pursuit of ambition yields certain public goods that profit the democrats too (e.g. prosperity). This Machiavellian mixed regime, a settlement between the rich and the poor, is more stable than the classical mixed regime, principally because it distracts the attention of the simple partisans from the fundamental ground of their quarrel: the partisan pride that gives rise to angry demands for equal (democrats) or unequal (oligarchs and other liberals) honors or rewards from the political community. In the liberal mixed regime, democratic pride is satisfied through political equality in a way that permits liberal (including oli-

---

[15]Justice Brandeis is the author of the famous definition of privacy, in dissent in *Olmstead v. United States*, 277 U.S. 438, 478 (1928). On freedom of speech, see Montesquieu, *Spirit*, 12.11–13; Benedict Spinoza, *Theologico-Political Treatise*, ch. 20, but cf. ch. 19; John Stuart Mill, *On Liberty and Other Essays*, 19–61; and cf. Locke, *A Letter Concerning Toleration*. On privacy more generally, see Montesquieu, *Spirit*, 12.4–6; Mill, *On Liberty*, 62–103; and Locke's *Letter*.

garchic) pride to be satisfied in the private pursuit of "unequal honors and wealth": or, in Mansfield's words, liberal democracy "has a dual advantage over the ancient mixed regime of a more democratic appearance and a more oligarchical reality."

Mansfield argues that the two most important groups of "liberals" in a liberal democracy are the "businessmen and intellectuals," and thus that the two most important liberal freedoms are "the right of acquiring private property" and "the right of free speech." A liberal community must therefore protect, above all, inequality in acquisition and heterodoxy in thought. Mansfield asks the important question: "Who benefits" from a liberal democratic community? He argues that it is the liberals, including above all the businessmen and the intellectuals, who "profit more from equal rights" than do the democrats, and he suggests that such liberals might properly be more grateful to the democrats for this more or less generous toleration of their private ambitions.[16] In this book, I endorse a similar settlement, or peace treaty, as the foundation of liberal politics, with one amendment—namely, the division of Mansfield's democratic party into two parties: the democrats and the republicans.[17]

Briefly, for now: democrats and republicans are not liberals, and so they are inclined to be intolerant of elitist liberal individualists. The republican believes that good citizenship requires virtue, which can only be achieved by means of public moral education and other modes of censorship; and so the republican despises the license that a politics of liberty makes possible. And the democrat believes that each citizen should share equally in the goods that belong to the political community, which can be achieved only where the people act collectively to vindicate this interest ("participatory" democracy) and where there is some measure of economic equality; and so the democrat despises the political and economic inequality that a politics of liberty makes possible. (See Chapters 3 and 5 for a more complete statement of this argument.) In the face of such partisan enmity, what is a liberal to do?

III

In Chapter 2, I present a portrait of classical liberalism, which is the sort of liberalism that is most likely, I argue, to achieve such a peaceful settle-

---

[16]Harvey C. Mansfield, Jr., *The Spirit of Liberalism*, 1, 9–15; see Machiavelli, *The Prince*, trans. Mansfield, ch. 9.

[17]The democrats and republicans are, to be sure, often allied: see Montesquieu, *Spirit*, 5.3–7.

ment with the democrats and republicans in the community.[18] In Chapters 3 and 5, I further describe the nature of these partisan disputes, and defend the settlement. Here, I propose to discuss the strategy for defending liberalism that I will advance throughout this book: liberalism as *peace treaty*.

One of the fundamental questions distinguishing contemporary neo-Kantian liberalism, such as the liberalism of Ronald Dworkin (among many others), from the sort of classical liberalism that I propose to defend here is this: are the interests of "liberals" best advanced *directly*, as Dworkin suggests, as through an effort to persuade citizens to embrace for themselves—in their hearts, so to speak—certain fundamental liberal ideas or values, including above all a certain understanding of equality (or, in other cases, autonomy)? Or is it, rather, more reasonable to defend those interests *indirectly*, by somehow carving out and then maintaining a space for liberals, for moral strangers to the community, in the naturally and thus permanently hostile environment that is the democratic polity, as through the sort of "settlement" among the parties of liberty, equality, and virtue that I describe and defend here?[19]

For Dworkin, liberal neutrality regarding the good life extends to every substantive moral opinion except a certain interpretation of equality according to which human beings are entitled to the "equal concern and respect" of the liberal polity. The liberal polity is properly constituted on the basis of a shared understanding of this liberal entitlement.[20] For the reasons already adumbrated, I have reservations about the prospects for success of this sort of ambitious liberal project. What is at issue is a strategic question, though, to be sure, one with broader implications: will "liberals" in a democratic polity be most secure where citizens are somehow persuaded to embrace the idea and the practice of autonomy itself (together with the corollary, a right to equal respect for those whose practice of autonomy is unorthodox), as a shared concep-

---

[18]That liberalism is a sort of hybrid of the liberalisms of Locke and Montesquieu. My understanding of liberalism has been influenced most by the recent scholarship of Nathan Tarcov, Thomas L. Pangle, Harvey C. Mansfield, Jr., and Judith N. Shklar. See Tarcov, *Locke's Education for Liberty*; Pangle, *The Spirit of Modern Republicanism*; Pangle, *Montesquieu's Philosophy of Liberalism*; Mansfield, *Spirit*; Mansfield, *Taming the Prince*; Shklar, *Ordinary Vices*; and Shklar, "The Liberalism of Fear."

[19]See Ronald Dworkin, *A Matter of Principle*, 181–213, 335–72; and Dworkin, *Taking Rights Seriously*, 240–78. I am grateful to Emily R. Gill, whose criticism of my "Liberalism and the Idea of Toleration" provoked these reflections. See Gill, "Liberty, Equality, and Liberal Toleration," manuscript, paper delivered at 1994 Annual Meeting of the American Political Science Association.

[20]Dworkin, *A Matter of Principle*, 190–91, 205–6, 364–72.

tion that constitutes a common enterprise? Or, rather, will they be more secure where they are persuaded to pay no attention to those other, peculiar folks who do care about autonomy—that is, in my terms, where the democrats are somehow persuaded to leave the liberals alone. Or again: is it more reasonable to aim to persuade our illiberal fellow citizens to become liberals themselves, or rather to persuade them to abide the presence of liberals (whom they might well despise) in their midst?

Here is the bottom line, in my view: liberalism is not natural; for individuals and especially for communities, liberalism is rare, and liberals are always threatened by enemies who are more powerful than they. Human beings more or less naturally find themselves members of certain political parties. The most important of these are the parties of liberty, equality, and virtue: the parties, respectively, of the liberals, the democrats, and the republicans (small *d*, small *r*). But the party of liberty, for reasons that I discuss in Chapter 3, is invariably weaker than are the parties of equality and virtue, especially in a democracy; for the interests, the passions, and above all the opinions, that draw human beings to embrace a politics dedicated to establishing equality or to inculcating virtue are more fundamental, more urgent or immediate, and perhaps above all more pleasing than are the interests, passions, and opinions that draw human beings to embrace a politics dedicated to securing liberty. So illiberalism (intolerance and the rest) is an unsurprising, natural and ordinary, tendency of democrats and republicans, who care more about equality or virtue than they care about liberty.

Let me offer a few examples to clarify my meaning. The liberal says: "I am not a Nazi, but I must defend the right of Nazis to march in Skokie; that is required by my devotion to 'liberty.'" Or: "I am not a pornographer, but I must defend the right of pornographers to express themselves as they please; that is required by my devotion to 'liberty.'" Or perhaps we need to consider harder cases, since Nazis and pornographers are not as respectable as democrats and republicans. Here is a liberal speaking to a democratic partisan of equality: "I am no friend of bigotry, but I must oppose hate-speech laws as a dangerous species of thought control; that is required by my devotion to 'liberty.'" And one final example, a liberal speaking to a republican: "I would not for my own part choose to have an abortion, but I must defend the right of others to make that choice; that is required by my devotion to 'liberty.'"

Now all of these are controversial arguments, and some liberals would refuse to embrace one or another of the positions invoked here, but nothing much rests on the particular examples, I think. The point I want to make here is simply this: that liberty is almost always a derivative or second-order political good, in a way that democratic equality and republican virtue are not. Attachment to liberty emerges only when we learn to recognize the dangers of partisan efforts to vindicate, or to defeat, our more immediate passions, interests, and opinions. But these dangers are often less obvious than our liberals sometimes seem to imply; and in any case the costs of acknowledging them are high, since respect for liberty often requires an uncommon self-restraint, a willingness to refuse to press a partisan advantage. Few human beings are naturally or spontaneously drawn to a politics of liberty for its own sake, but many human beings are drawn to a politics that aims to establish equality or inculcate virtue; and so, there will always be more democrats and republicans than liberals around, and they will ordinarily exercise the real power in any democratic polity. How do we establish a politics of liberty in the face of that fact? I should add that in my view the parties of equality and virtue are not only powerful, they are respectable, and liberals are obliged to respond to the arguments, as well as to the power, of their democratic and republican enemies. But I suppose that this further claim is not a necessary element of the underlying argument.

Orthodoxy is inevitable in a political community, and especially in a democratic community. The question is whether it is more reasonable to seek to *tame* and *moderate* that democratic orthodoxy, as I shall argue, or to seek to *supplant* it with a liberal orthodoxy—say, a shared conception of the good, including a shared devotion to a certain understanding of moral autonomy and a right to equal concern and respect—which seems to me a dangerous and ultimately futile enterprise. Acrimonious fights, now called culture wars, will be evaded only if liberals do the evading. It is mostly *our* responsibility, as liberals, to walk away, because our enemies will not walk away if we pick a fight (and, by the way, they are stronger than we are), and because we understand better than they do the reasons for evading cultural civil wars. It is a part of the task of the rest of this book to make the case for this strategy for defending liberalism.

IV

From democrats and republicans, let me now return to communitarians; the relation between communitarians and these older parties of equality and virtue will be clarified during the course of the book. Here, I discuss the manifest ambivalence toward liberalism exhibited by contemporary communitarian critics of liberalism. That ambivalence is also an important aspect of the analysis of communitarian politics in Chapters 5 and 6.

Many communitarian critics of liberalism are now also friends of liberalism, above all because they acknowledge that liberalism has proved to be an unexpectedly liberating doctrine, and that "liberation" is an important political good; but also because, as many of them now admit, the liberal welfare state has begun to reveal a surprising ability to provide for the "general welfare"—that is, not only to protect the property of the few rich, but also (more and more) to provide for the welfare of "successive waves of lower-class invaders" who were formerly "invisible," as Michael Walzer puts it. Indeed, the first of these liberal achievements ("liberation") is now more or less complete: Walzer, at least, is "doubtful" that "full liberation—equality under the law, career open to talents, moral and cultural *laissez faire*—will require radical changes in the structure of liberalism and capitalism," as he and others on the Left once thought; someday, perhaps rather soon, the "right of individuals 'to live their own lives'" as they please, without interference from repressive authorities, will be fully vindicated within liberal political communities. The "general welfare," by contrast, has so far been less completely achieved in liberal communities, according to Walzer; but here too the liberal principle—that the legitimacy of the "general welfare state" depends on its ability to include all of its citizens in the just and efficient distribution of the "welfare it produces"—has prevailed, more or less, and the struggle now consists only in securing the conformity of our practice to liberal principles. Thus, Walzer is again confident (but less so) that "one day, not soon, the welfare state will extend its benefits to all those men and women who are at present its occasional victims, its nominal or partial members."[21] And so, Walzer often concedes, "the achievement of liberalism is real even if it is incomplete." Indeed, the liberal state is for these reasons almost just, even "the most legitimate, rationally purposive, and powerful state that has ever existed."[22]

The attitude of contemporary communitarians (and socialists) toward liberalism is therefore often one of deep ambivalence: whatever its defects, liberal politics has by now proved to be the (more or less recalcitrant) instrument of leftist or egalitarian aspirations. Indeed, from time to time Walzer almost confesses an admiration for liberalism, in spite of his various criticisms of liberalism for its failure to provide adequately

---

[21]On the "unexpected" liberal achievement of liberation, see Walzer, *Radical Principles*, 3–30, esp. 23; cf. Walzer, "Liberalism and the Art of Separation," esp. 317–20; on the similarly surprising (but less complete) achievements of the liberal general welfare state, see Walzer, *Radical Principles*, 23–53, esp. 25–30.

[22]Walzer, "Liberalism and the Art of Separation," 320; Walzer, *Radical Principles*, 52.

for equality, democracy, and community.[23] Today's critics of liberalism are, in short, typically more moderate than those of the 1960s, less reliant on Marx than on Aristotle and Rousseau and Tocqueville and Hegel; they are not so much revolutionaries as reformists. Walzer himself is perhaps the most Marxist of these theorists, but his Marxism is, to say the least, quite restrained.[24] Nevertheless, the communitarian challenge to liberalism today still comes primarily from the Left; in some cases, the search for a radical alternative to Marxism is more or less explicit.[25]

And so, it is perhaps not necessary to overthrow liberalism, according to its new critics, but only to complete the liberal project of liberation— and then to ask, "What next?" Thus, the fundamental defect of liberal polities is their failure perfectly to fulfill the promise of liberation: we are at present liberated only "on the side," in our private or "cultural" lives, but are "still subordinate in the political and economic center" of our lives.[26] The liberal project of liberation has stalled, according to this argument, confronted by obstacles that are partly of its own making: the concentration of economic power in the hands of large and willful corporations that are increasingly beyond the reach of democratic politics; and the concentration of political power in the hands of a similarly irresponsible national bureaucracy. It is of course true that in the American experience many liberals have been admirers of both capitalism and the "national idea," and that such concentrations of power have sometimes been defended on more or less liberal grounds. But we must now recognize, the critics of American liberalism argue, that the very institutions that enabled us to secure our liberation from the old oppressors have given rise to new oppressors. Walzer makes this argument as follows, characteristically emphasizing the dangers of concentrations of economic

[23]Cf. Walzer, "Liberalism and the Art of Separation," where Walzer speaks of himself as a "leftist," not a liberal, and indeed opposes himself to "the liberals"; Walzer is here an admirer of the liberal "art of separation," but also offers a "leftist critique of liberal separation" (318–20).

[24]Walzer, *Radical Principles*, 4–6. See, too, Walzer's criticisms of the "New Left" (*Radical Principles*, 109–27, 139–56, 157–67) and of Marxist theory ("Liberalism and the Art of Separation," 317–20).

[25]See Unger, *Knowledge and Politics*, 10. See, too, Unger's account of "revolutionary reform," which is said to fall between "conservative reform" and "revolution," in Unger, *The Critical Legal Studies Movement*, 110. For a criticism of Unger's most recent and most radical version of his case for a "context-smashing" politics of "perpetual innovation," which is not revolution, but rather a "constitutionalism of permanent mobilization," see Holmes, *Anatomy*, 141–75.

[26]Walzer, *Radical Principles*, 12–14. For a somewhat different view, see Unger, *Critical Legal Studies*, 22–24, 40–42: Unger argues that the liberation is incomplete even, or especially, in our cultural or private lives, and most nearly achieved in politics, narrowly defined.

power: "As the institutions of civil society were protected from state power, so now they must be protected, and the state too, from the new power that arises within civil society itself, the power of wealth. The point is . . . to enlist liberal artfulness in the service of socialism." That is, Walzer is especially concerned to defend democratic citizenship against various threats from private powers, and especially private economic powers.[27]

Michael Sandel, in contrast, emphasizes the dangers, or rather the great frustrations, of our current "predicament" as citizens (so to speak) of a national "procedural republic": a republic that "made its peace with concentrated [political] power" but still lacks "a strong sense of national community." This "concentration of political power" was necessary in America, according to Sandel, in order to meet the threats posed to democracy by the "concentration of economic power." But the nationalization of power has not been accompanied by the emergence of a "strong sense of national community" capable of replacing our sentimental attachments to the "virtuous republic of small-scale, democratic communities" that once existed in America; indeed, it has now become clear that the nation is simply "too vast" to allow us "to cultivate the shared self-understandings necessary to community in the formative, or constitutive sense." Sandel argues that our national bureaucratic or procedural republic is now both "overly intrusive" and "disempowered": "individually and collectively, our control over the forces that govern our lives is receding rather than increasing," as the national republic more and more frequently frustrates the private purposes of citizens, but without effectively advancing any public purposes. We are increasingly impotent, says Sandel, both as (private) human beings and as citizens: our world seems to be "spinning out of control."[28]

As a result of this progress of liberal democratic politics, only a commitment to industrial democracy in the management of the workplace, and to participatory democracy in both local and national political life,

---

[27]Walzer, "Liberalism and the Art of Separation," 318; see also 320–22. The phrase "industrial democracy" in the next paragraph is also from this essay. On the concentration of economic power in modern liberal communities, see also Walzer, *Radical Principles*, 3–19, 23–53, 273–90; and Sullivan, *Reconstructing Public Philosophy*, esp. 23–55.

[28]Sandel, "The Procedural Republic and the Unencumbered Self," 91–95. On the concentration of political power, see Barber, "The Undemocratic Party System: Citizenship in an Elite/Mass Society," 34–49. For a defense of the "national idea," see Samuel H. Beer, "Liberalism and the National Idea," also cited in the Sandel article just mentioned; and see Beer, "The Idea of a Nation." For the claim that the world now seems to be "spinning out of control," see Sandel, "Democrats and Community," 20–23.

can now revive the liberal vision of a society of truly free and equal human beings, according to the new critics of liberalism. Friends of liberty must now also be advocates of unfettered democratic politics and of economic equality. Says Walzer, "Only a democratic and egalitarian community can accommodate liberated men and women"; today, "we can glimpse a consistent liberalism—that is, one that passes over into democratic socialism."[29] Or perhaps, as Benjamin Barber argues, "an excess of liberalism has undone democratic institutions"; nevertheless, "there is little wrong with liberal institutions that a strong dose of political participation and reactivated citizenship cannot cure."[30]

But these arguments imply that friends of liberalism today must be critics of the classical liberalism of John Locke and James Madison. Unlike their modern followers, those classical liberals thought that liberty might often be made most secure in less than perfectly democratic regimes (or in moderate democratic communities), and they accordingly argued that a well-ordered democratic political community would impose strict constitutional restraints on the power of the people. Moreover, those liberals counted the right to property among the most important of the individual liberties, its preservation the "great and *chief end*" of government, and they were willing to countenance significant economic inequality, both in order to protect the just accumulations of the "Industrious and Rational" and in order to "increase the common stock of mankind." Moreover, Madison (at least) suspected that this liberty and others would often be vulnerable, above all in a democracy, to unjust majorities or popular factions; that is, classical liberalism teaches that "an excess of democracy can undo liberal institutions."[31]

Thus, it sometimes appears that many contemporary political theorists are above all advocates of democracy and equality, rather than either liberty or community, and that these critics of liberal democracy seek not community but egalitarian democracy. Indeed, on these points many con-

---

[29]Walzer, *Radical Principles*, 13; and Walzer, "Liberalism and the Art of Separation," 323, 328.

[30]Barber, *Strong Democracy*, xi.

[31]Locke, *Second Treatise*, §§3, 34, 37, 132–33, 123–24. See, too, the discussion of property in *Federalist* #10, esp. 78. On the traditional liberal view of the property right, see also Marc F. Plattner, "The Welfare State vs. the Redistributive State." The attitude of the founders toward democracy is more complicated, but it is surely not satisfactory to contemporary advocates of unfettered participatory democracy. See, for example, *Federalist* #49, #50, #55, #63. And see below, Chapter 5, §§I–II. The last quote is Barber's characterization of Tocqueville's view (Barber, *Strong Democracy*, xi). See Tocqueville, *Democracy in America*, I.ii.5–9.

temporary defenders of liberalism (such as Rawls and Dworkin) are in agreement with its contemporary critics: today, almost everyone (including the most prominent liberals) agrees that the classical liberal conception of liberty, as divorced from equality and democracy, is deficient. But this aspect of the contemporary analysis of liberalism is merely a continuation of long-standing controversies (within liberalism) about the true meanings of democracy, equality, and liberty.[32] Is "liberty" primarily political liberty or private liberty, self-government or security? Is "liberty" genuine where many do not possess the economic means to effectively exercise their liberties? Is "equality" best understood in terms of rights or welfare, opportunities or conditions? Is the best "democracy" characterized by direct popular rule or by a limited government that is ultimately responsible to the people? Is democracy the partisan rule of the popular class or the nonpartisan rule of all citizens? But it is not obvious that it is necessary to refer to the idea of community in debates about these problems, which are problems within liberalism. These are surely important questions, and the contemporary communitarian political theorists make useful contributions to the debate, but these controversies do not reveal what is most distinctive about the communitarian critique of liberalism. In most of what follows, I focus on those aspects of the contemporary debate that explain why many theorists now claim to be partisans of community, above all, rather than partisans of egalitarian democracy.

The new communitarian critics of liberalism pose a more radical question: is liberation enough, they ask, even if fully achieved in a democratic and egalitarian political community? They argue that even in our cultural or private lives, where the project of liberation has largely succeeded, it is an unhappy liberation that our "individualism with a vengeance" has made possible. We are not only liberated from tyrants and masters, but are also deprived of any "common life" shared with fellow citizens, or even with family and friends, because liberalism attenuates the primitive self-knowledge that makes manifest the importance of these moral attachments in a complete human life. Thus, as Walzer puts it, our private lives are too often "bleak" and "frenetic" exercises in self-gratification, "grim parod[ies] of Jefferson's pursuit of happiness." Walzer captures this aspect of contemporary dissatisfaction with liberal culture with a characteristically compelling image of the moral poverty of mere liberation as a

---

[32]See Dworkin, "What Is Equality?"; and John Rawls, *Political Liberalism*, 289–371. See, too, Walter Berns, "Does the Constitution 'Secure These Rights'?" and Berns, "Judicial Review and the Rights and Laws of Nature," in his *In Defense of Liberal Democracy*, esp. 37–46.

way of life: "I imagine a human being thoroughly divorced, freed of parents, spouse, and children, watching pornographic performances in some dark theater, joining (it may be his only membership) this or that odd cult, which he will probably leave in a month or two for another still odder. Is this a liberated human being?"[33]

We have been taught by our classical liberal ancestors to think of ourselves as free individuals above all, rather than as children or parishioners or citizens, or as members of a racial or ethnic group—or, indeed, as members of any other communities. We do, of course, belong to such communities, though these memberships are less fundamental (morally and psychologically) than are our natural freedom and independence as individuals. But this idea of the free individual is based on a confusion, say its critics: one's deepest attachments to other human beings are not freely chosen, adopted, and then discarded like articles of clothing, but are given prior to such choices and "partly define the person I am," as well as many of one's obligations and prerogatives. Indeed, the human being who overcomes such "constitutive" attachments is not liberated, but is rather, says Sandel, "wholly without character, without moral depth"; an honorable human being must surely "feel the moral weight" of these primary loyalties, and will not fail to acknowledge the special duties and commitments that membership in any particular community imposes.[34]

All of this is doubtless partly true: the liberal idea of the free individual too often, in liberal practice, produces eccentric, passive, lonely individuals. But it is perhaps not exhaustive. Even for contemporary admirers of community, praise of the loyal and devoted citizen is commonly tempered by an awareness of the moral gravity of those who contributed to liberalism's past and present victories over intolerant and oppressive communities: moral freedom may require rebellion against moral community. Those free individuals who secured for themselves, and for us, the blessings of liberty, even at the price of rebellion against a father or a priest or a prince, are perhaps not wholly "without moral depth," but deserve both our admiration and our gratitude: the truly free human

---

[33]Walzer, *Radical Principles*, 6–8. Cf. Sandel, *Liberalism*, 179–83, 154–65, 54–59.

[34]See Sandel, *Liberalism*, 179, 149–50; and Walzer, "Liberalism and the Art of Separation," 323–26. See, too, Walzer, *Obligations*, which is a psychologically rich attempt to correct liberal consent theory by arguing that obligations arise not simply from the voluntary acts of individuals but also from a history, both personal and social, of memberships in social groups. Finally, see Walzer, "From Contract to Community," an admiring review of Sandel's book.

being possesses a moral dignity that at least rivals the dignity of a human life that is animated by love or piety or patriotism. But perhaps liberal politics today is incapable of reproducing the sorts of admirable human beings who were capable of founding a free politics, or even of preserving the free institutions that others constituted. The founders of liberal communities were, after all, the children of preliberal communities. But this implies, at most, that the achievement of freedom is possible only for those who somehow know the burdens of authority—it does not imply that we should repudiate the idea that freedom is an honorable way of life, and give that authority a new name: "community."[35]

Here too, the ambivalence that communitarian theorists feel toward liberalism is manifest. Today's critics of liberalism admit that an excellent human being is (of course) a free individual. Thus, Walzer writes:

> We [socialists] seek communities, then, of a certain sort, not of any sort. Our goal is not an ecstatic union of the faithful, or a band of brethren bound to some charismatic leader, or a hierarchy of benevolent masters and docile servants. Warmth can be had in all of these, but in none of them are the arrangements of the common life open to popular scrutiny and revision. In none of them do individual members share political responsibility. In none of them, indeed, is there room for the claims and counter-claims of members *who have learned to think of themselves as individuals*. Only a democratic and egalitarian community can accommodate liberated men and women.

We are, in this sense, all liberals, "rationalists of everyday life," who come together as individuals and "sign the social contract . . . , in order to provide for our needs." And so, liberals are unwilling to abide the various religious and ideological "mystifications" that provided the foundations of all communities of the past, which too often did not serve the genuine interests of their individual members. As Walzer admits, "it has been the great triumph of liberal theorists and politicians to undermine every sort of political divinity, to shatter all the forms of ritual obfuscation, and to turn the mysterious oath into a rational contract." Walzer, together with many other partisans of community, thus repudiates those visions of community that would require a renunciation of the acknowl-

[35]See Walzer, *Radical Principles*, 10; cf. 11–13. Even if contemporary liberal politics merits criticism on the grounds mentioned in the text, those criticisms would be very different from the communitarian criticism, which embraces the community, and so does not seek a way to make our freedom from community more secure.

edged achievements of liberal individualism and liberal rationalism.[36] Today's advocates of community do not, in general, seek to revive the ancient *polis* or the antiliberal republic of Rousseau and Montesquieu. Thus, for example, the radical legal critic Unger argues that the opposition of liberal democracy and "republican community" is a "false antithesis," and that (even) his radical program is only a "superliberalism" that perfects the internal ideals of liberalism itself; "community" does not require a "reversion to closed or hierarchical community life," but can be a "mode of association that somehow does justice to the goods of both autonomy and community."[37]

But, it turns out, "one of our needs is community itself: culture, religion, politics." "The community is itself a good—conceivably the most important good—that gets distributed."[38] We *are* individuals, but we need community: both rebellious moral freedom and devotion to moral community are aspects of human excellence, of "moral depth," according to this moral psychology.[39] Thus, the task of contemporary partisans of community is to constitute a political order that can satisfy the powerful human longing for unstinting attachments to other human beings, among the other moral advantages of community, and yet accommodate citizens who "have learned," from liberalism, "to think of themselves as individuals." Further, says Walzer, "political freedom . . . is an absolute value, for without that men and women with different ideas and interests cannot share a common life"; and yet, "individual liberty is meaningless until it is incorporated within particular forms of social life."[40] Thus, as Amy Gutmann has written: "the communitarian critics want us to live in Salem, but not to believe in witches."[41]

I have focused in these opening paragraphs on the odd combination of praise and blame of liberalism in the work of contemporary communi-

---

[36]Walzer, *Radical Principles*, 13, emphasis added, 25; and Walzer, *Spheres of Justice*, 64.

[37]Unger, *Critical Legal Studies*, 40–42; and Unger, *Knowledge and Politics*, 20. See, too, Barber's rejection of "the republican nostalgia of such commentators as Hannah Arendt or Leo Strauss" (*Strong Democracy*, 118). Finally, see Sandel, "Morality and the Liberal Ideal," 17.

[38]Walzer, *Spheres of Justice*, 64–65, 29, 31; see, too, Walzer, *Radical Principles*, 25–26.

[39]This combination of moral rebellion and communal obligation is perhaps most perfectly exhibited in a remarkable essay by Walzer, "The Obligation to Disobey," in his *Obligations*, 3–23, in which he argues that human beings sometimes possess communal obligations, derived from membership in subpolitical communities, to rebel against their political community.

[40]Walzer, *Radical Principles*, 12–13. Cf. Walzer, "Liberalism and the Art of Separation," 325–26.

[41]Amy Gutmann, "Communitarian Critics of Liberalism," 319.

tarian theorists, because it is an instance of a pervasive tendency in communitarian political thought: the desire to avoid the necessity of making choices among political goods. This tendency is manifested here in a complacent willingness to deny that liberty is a historically precarious possession, to deny that it is perhaps even today necessary to be vigilant in its defense against those who speak in the name of the community and justice, as well as those who speak in the name of democracy or equality. The preservation of liberty comes at a price, one that was once happily paid but has now come to seem an intolerable burden. Critics of liberalism, as well as its defenders, often repudiate this bargain too lightly, and sometimes even fail to recognize that it has been made. They may thus underestimate the danger, obvious to the naive or untutored understanding, that community is in some measure the enemy of liberty. In any case, the contemporary debate between the partisans of liberty and the partisans of community compels us to consider again what liberty is, as well as how it relates to democracy, to equality, and to community.

2

A Liberal Proposal

Classical and contemporary liberal teachings, in some uneasy combination, dominate our political discourse. America is still now, or perhaps now more than ever, somehow a liberal regime, dedicated to the preservation of individual rights and to the emancipation of reasonable self-interest. But today, thoughtful citizens must wonder whether liberalism can any longer serve as a "public philosophy," a common source of authoritative guidance on questions of political right. It is no longer clear how our choices about what is necessary here and now, choices that divide citizens along partisan or ideological lines, are related to any more comprehensive common understanding, or nonpartisan agreement, about the nature, purposes, and limits of our political community. Our liberal practice is no longer guided by a theoretical consensus about the meaning of liberalism; we no longer agree about what it means to "take rights seriously" or to pursue our "self-interest properly understood."

These disputes are first of all disputes within liberalism, but they have increasingly given rise to doubts about the adequacy of liberalism altogether as a public philosophy. The crisis of liberal public philosophy in America consists partly in this: we possess no shared vision, no common argument, that can serve as a philosophical defense, beyond mere partisanship, of our moral certitudes about rights. Certainly, very few now believe the classical liberal argument that human beings possess certain rights by nature, much less the view expressed in our Declaration of Independence, according to which we are endowed by our "Creator," or by the "Laws of Nature and of Nature's God," with certain inalienable rights.[1] But contemporary Kantian partisans of the idea of rights have not yet forged a new theoretical consensus, or public philosophy, to replace the consensus that emerged out of the founding period in America, even as they have contributed to the demise of that old liberal consensus. As a result, though everyone today *talks* about rights, we increasingly disagree about what our rights *are*, and whence they come.

Today, the academic debate about rights between their libertarian and egalitarian defenders often simply mirrors the political debate about interests between conservatives and liberals, and it therefore cannot provide a principled means of resolving or limiting these disputes. The leading libertarian theorist of rights is Robert Nozick, and the leading egalitarian theorists of rights are John Rawls and Ronald Dworkin; it has often been noted that these political theorists begin from very similar (or even almost identical) philosophical premises, and then argue to widely differing political conclusions.[2] A wide variety of other contemporary rights theorists offer arguments that echo the claims of political partisans across almost the whole of our political spectrum (the works of the lawyers Charles Fried and Bruce Ackerman are instructive in this regard). Such partisan diversity within liberal political theory constitutes a crisis for liberal theory today, for one cannot help wondering whether that partisan diversity is not in fact more fundamental than the apparent consensus regarding principles of political right. But that would imply that we no longer possess a nonpartisan consensus that transcends partisan diversity, a public philosophy that can guide us and moderate our disputes; it would imply, that is, that *party* is now more authoritative than *community*.

A public philosophy makes it possible to tame partisan squabbling about secondary questions by means of an appeal to a nonpartisan consensus about fundamental principles; a public philosophy keeps the peace, by reminding citizens that what unites them is more fundamental than what divides them. But today, *rights* are themselves often a matter of partisan debate, and these debates are often barely disguised quarrels about *interests*. Indeed, nonpartisan consensus about our rights has been

---

[1] See Carl L. Becker, *The Declaration of Independence*, for a classic statement of prevailing doubts about the validity of the principles of the Declaration. Cf. Fred Baumann, "Historicism and the Constitution."

[2] See, for example, Sandel, *Liberalism*, 66–103; see, too, on the divergences between these new liberal political theories and earlier liberal constitutionalism, Clifford Orwin and James R. Stoner, Jr., "Neo-Constitutionalism? Rawls, Dworkin, and Nozick."

replaced, to a troubling degree, by debates in which different parties, or factions, express very different understandings of those rights: we no longer possess a shared understanding of these matters. Everywhere in our politics, today, one hears only the language of rights; but "rights" is no longer the name of a common resource. So the Right appeals to a right of property and the Left speaks of economic welfare rights; the Right condemns affirmative action as an infringement of individual rights, while the Left praises affirmative action for vindicating the collective rights of disadvantaged minority groups; the pro-life movement contends that abortion deprives a child of the right to life, but its pro-choice opponents see, rather, the right of privacy of the mother; some feminists contend that pornography violates the civil rights of women, but civil libertarians respond that it is necessary to protect the free-speech rights of the pornographers; and the list could be extended almost at will. This is not to say that each of these "rights" is merely an "interest" in disguise (although, as it happens, most of these, it seems to me, *are* properly understood as interests, not rights), but I do say that this unprecedented proliferation of rights claims signals our growing inability to tell the difference, or even to say how one *might* tell the difference, between a true right and an ersatz right.[3] Indeed, says Walzer, "the effort to produce a complete account of justice or a defense of equality by multiplying rights soon makes a farce of what it multiplies"—this, at any rate, has happened in our own politics.[4] And so our confusion about the idea of rights makes it necessary, as many have argued, to attempt to reconstitute our public philosophy, the liberal public philosophy of rights.

But perhaps it is not the idea of rights that is defective, as Walzer suggests, but rather our unfortunate tendency to multiply them, which might be resisted on the basis of a more adequate (or at least more generally accepted) argument about the foundations of our rights—that is, I will here argue, through a restoration of the reasonable sobriety about rights evinced by the earliest liberals. These classical liberals taught human beings that it would be necessary to lay down their more or less unbounded natural rights in order to constitute a community that would secure certain quite limited civil rights to all.[5] A reasonable regime of rights must

[3]On the often dangerous tendency to translate interests into rights, see Berns, "Taking Rights Frivolously," esp. 59–60, 62–64; see, too, Tarcov, "A 'Non-Lockean' Locke and the Character of Liberalism," 131–34, for a somewhat different view of the relation of rights and interests.

[4]Walzer, *Spheres*, xv.

[5]On this distinction between "natural" and "civil" rights, see Mansfield, "The Revival of Constitutionalism," esp. 219–22.

limit the class of favored civil rights to a very few fundamental rights, on this view, in order to enable the community to secure these rights, which are so terribly insecure where there is no civil peace.[6] But a too-long list of civil rights might tend to undermine civil peace, for two reasons. First, respect for rights is a form of self-restraint: when we respect a right, we restrain a natural impulse to tell other people what to do. Because such respectful restraint is demanding, only a reasonably short list can secure the enduring consent or allegiance of the people, and thus encourage the people to refrain from indulging the natural temptation to renounce this or that civil right in a moment of passion—or even, perhaps, in a moment of exasperated incomprehension: "How can that be a 'right'?!"[7] Consent, in this arena, is a means to peace: peace is most secure where citizens consent to restrain themselves, where they understand the very good reasons for this self-restraint, and where they are (as a result) rarely surprised to learn what counts as a right. So rights must be intelligible to citizens and not only to judges and philosophers, or citizens will soon cease to respect them.

Second, if a regime of rights acknowledges conflicting rights claims, as now often happens, it might often exacerbate natural animosities among individuals, by transforming them into moral quarrels between parties, thereby justifying moral indignation. But such angry partisan quarrels disturb the peace. A human being who is deprived of his "rights" (and not merely of some interest), as when one loses in a moral struggle where

---

[6]See, for example, Locke, *Second Treatise*, §§4, 6, 13, 87, 95–99, and 123–31 (esp. 128–31). Although I say "civil rights" here, Locke actually speaks, more modestly, of limits on legislative power (§§123–24, 131, 134–42). In the language of the argument in the text, Locke's "short list" of the rights that individuals retain against their government is very short indeed, so short that it is hard to name one (but cf. §§136, 139, 142). To be sure, the people retain a right of opposing the rebellion of their government, but that is a collective right of the people, not an individual right; and so Locke is prepared almost to excuse the "Oppression of here and there an unfortunate man" (§230). (On this point, Montesquieu is somehow more solicitous of the rights of individuals: see *Spirit*, 12.1–13; but cf. 12.19, approving bills of attainder.) As for property rights, here too the matter is complicated, for Locke admits that in entering civil society each individual "submits to the Community those Possessions, which he has, or shall acquire" (§120): property rights belong to individuals by a prudent grant of the community (cf. §§138, 140), except for the popular (not individual) right of 'no taxation without representation' (see §142). For a judicious attempt to offer a (short) list of liberal rights that is suited to the American liberal experience, see Tarcov, "American Constitutionalism and Individual Rights."

[7]See Chapter 3 for a full defense of this suspicion. Here, consider the current controversy concerning federal funding of obscene and blasphemous art; this too is understood, in some quarters, as a question of "rights." What is perhaps also worth mentioning is the notorious reluctance of Americans to endorse even the provisions of the Bill of Rights when questioned by public opinion pollsters.

rights conflict, is not only hungry, so to speak, but also insulted: his pride is wounded and he may, when the time is ripe, fight back (using violence, as Hobbes says, "for trifles, as a word, a smile, a different opinion"). A debate about "rights" can never be quite peaceful: and where rights are everywhere, everyone feels these wounds.[8]

In this chapter, I offer a portrait of a more modest, or more conservative, liberalism, one that has its roots in the classical liberalism of Locke and especially Montesquieu. Montesquieu raised from "within the liberal tradition certain penetrating notes of skepticism as regards the political wisdom—and even, to some extent, the moral soundness—of an unmitigated stress on the rights of the individual," argues Pangle.[9] (Set against contemporary liberals, Locke himself appears to share some of this skepticism, as noted earlier.) Here, I propose to outline the reasons for a more cautious liberalism; I am aware that the liberalism described here is too spare not only for critics of liberalism but even for many contemporary liberals. So I propose to defend this liberalism against such critics in the next several chapters. In Chapters 3 and 4, I defend this way of understanding liberalism against an important new strand of liberalism, sometimes called "postmodern liberalism." Postmodern liberalism (most forcefully advanced in Rorty's recent work, especially *Contingency, Irony, and Solidarity*) is the species of liberalism that has been most influenced by communitarian ideas regarding the nature of community and of the self; because the influence of postmodern liberalism is now rather widely felt in the world of liberal political theory more generally, this is a fruitful place to begin an inquiry regarding the effect of communitarian ideas on liberal politics and society.[10] And in Chapters 5 and 6, I defend the conservative species of liberalism against Barber and Walzer, two democratic and republican critics of liberalism who are also in some measure friends of liberalism. In each of these chapters I take the opportunity to further characterize the liberalism that I defend, focusing in turn on these new themes: toleration, humanity, citizenship, and patriotism.

---

[8]Thomas Hobbes, *Leviathan*, ch. 13. See Berns, "Taking Rights Frivolously," 54–63 (struggles among "moral claimants," especially judicial struggles, are "zero-sum" games, and are thus more dangerous than struggles among economic interests, which admit compromise more readily). See, too, Berns, *Taking the Constitution Seriously*, esp. 147–80, 214–41; and Berns, "The Constitution as Bill of Rights," in his *In Defense of Liberal Democracy*, 9–18, 24–28.

[9]Pangle, "The Liberal Critique of Rights in Montesquieu and Hume," 31.

[10]In addition to Rorty's book, see Joseph Raz, *The Morality of Freedom*; Raz, "Multiculturalism: A Liberal Perspective"; and Rawls, *Political Liberalism*.

I

Why is "community" a problem for us, here and now? The short answer is: liberalism. The political philosophy of liberalism, its critics and friends agree, is in some sense *our* political philosophy: we are all somehow liberals. Liberalism, and even a rather morally debilitating interpretation of liberalism, has prevailed in this century in America, overwhelming those elements of the American political tradition that once tamed our individualism and materialism. If liberal America once found needed moral sustenance in various religious and republican traditions of virtue that have long since been abandoned, as many argue, then it must now find a way to reconstitute those indispensable moral supplements to the material comforts that liberal politics provides—or somehow to supply the defect from its own resources.[11]

It should not be surprising, even to partisans of liberalism, that a world dominated by liberal individualism has given rise to longings for lost community. Classical liberalism is a doctrine of acquisitive individualism, and teaches that man is by nature solitary and selfish, not political or even social: the most powerful natural passions and needs of human beings are private. Human beings are not friends by nature. This harsh moral psychology is, at any rate, *the* fundamental teaching of classical liberalism. As a result, the idea of community is always somewhat suspect, for thoughtful liberals. Liberals are inclined to view partisans of community as either romantic utopians or dangerous authoritarians. If there is no natural common good, beyond peace and security, then invocations of the spirit of community are either foolish or fraudulent, impossible dreams or wicked ideologies. This is perhaps especially true in today's world, where enlightenment and individualism have so undermined traditional communities that the attempt, now, to reconstitute community seems to require a willful or fanatical disposition to impose novel and alien ways on intractable subjects.

These suspicions are the legacy of familiar classical liberal doctrines about human nature and the political community. Aristotle had argued that human beings "strive to live together even when they have no need of assistance from one another"; human beings are in some measure friends by nature. This is not, to be sure, the most important reason for *political* community, according to Aristotle, partly because this natural

---

[11]See John P. Diggins, *The Lost Soul of American Politics*; J. G. A. Pocock, *The Machiavellian Moment.* And see, further, Wilson Carey McWilliams, *The Idea of Fraternity in America*; and Christopher Lasch, *The True and Only Heaven.*

inclination to associate with other human beings by itself brings them together only into the household, and partly because such natural strivings
do not lead human beings to choose republican *political* communities as
opposed to one or another form of "mastery." Aristotle certainly recognizes the importance of the need for law, and perhaps even fear, as an origin of political community. Nevertheless, he would surely argue as well
that liberal moral psychology is too simple, and that it underestimates, if
it does not altogether forget, both gentler and harsher motives for seeking "community": love of honor, which sometimes inspires tyranny; the
impulse to make speeches about "the just and the unjust," which arouses
partisanship but also animates free politics; and the aspiration to "live
nobly," which gives rise to a love of virtue.[12]

Classical liberals, on the other hand, seem to believe that we could be
content to live alone, because there are no natural bonds among human beings, and so there is no truly natural community. Indeed, the family is not
simply natural, according to some of the founders of liberalism. And even
if there were certain natural passions or sentiments that might, in favorable
circumstances, bring human beings together in a natural community, these
passions are overwhelmed, in most circumstances, by the strongest human
passion, the desire to preserve oneself and to live in tolerable comfort in a
world of human enemies (among other hardships) that does not readily
provide for our preservation and comfort. In short, the most urgent human
good, which is the object of the most powerful human passion, is the security of our bodies; this is a private good, not a common good. And where
there is no common good that stands above all private goods, there can be
no true community, no community that can inspire unwavering loyalty or
that can rightfully demand significant sacrifices, let alone the greatest sacrifices, from its individual members. Liberalism simply cannot accommodate longings for such a community. I repeat: our classical liberal teachers
have taught us that human beings are in the decisive respect friendless by
nature, and we have constructed a world on the basis of this understanding. It is not surprising that we feel lonely, now and then.[13]

Liberal politics is, as a result, a politics of fearful accommodation
among natural foes who somehow reconstitute themselves as civil friends;

---

[12]Aristotle, *Politics*, 1253a1–40; but see, too, Locke, *Second Treatise*, §101; and especially Montesquieu, *Spirit*, I.2. And see *Politics*, 1278b15–30, 1266b30–1267a15,
1278b15–1279a22, 1280b5–1281a10; and Wayne H. Ambler, "Aristotle's Understanding
of the Naturalness of the City."

[13]Locke, *Second Treatise*, §§ 7–13, 16–21, 87, 123–28; Montesquieu, *Spirit*, 1.2–3; and
cf. Hobbes, *Leviathan*, ch. 13.

that is, liberal politics is no more, but also no less, than a quest for "that tranquillity of spirit which comes from the opinion each one has of his security," where "one citizen cannot fear another citizen."[14]

Since human beings are by nature solitary and selfish, querulous and untrustworthy competitors for scarce and often fragile private goods, prudent individuals will learn to attend to the mostly private acquisition of the tools necessary to provide for their mostly private welfare—above all, liberty and property—and then to defend these gains. The acquisition of property, especially, must be a mostly private pursuit, since even a well-ordered civil society can only mitigate, but not abolish, the harsh natural conditions and the querulous traits of our human natures that make it necessary to treat our fellows with abiding suspicion, as "Quarrelsom and Contentious" competitors for scarce goods, who (as Tarcov puts it) "so love power and wealth, that a condition that makes it in their interest to be unjust will likely find them unjust." So it is the principal business of political community to arrange "conditions" so that the acquisition and maintenance of liberty and property is protected, as against the "Fancy or Covetousness" of incipient aggressors, by means of policies that aim to show such aggressors that injustice is not in their "interest"—thus by means of harsh criminal laws and economic policies that yield a broad prosperity, which benefit even those who have not yet learned to be "Industrious and Rational."[15] Liberty, too, is in the last resort in need of private defense: that is what is meant by the liberal commonplace that free citizens must be ever vigilant in defense of their liberties; indeed, liberals defend a right of resistance against usurpation and tyranny as the last resort of a people that has reason to doubt the security of their liberty and property. Only a fool would rely altogether on other human beings, or on a beneficent government, to provide the liberty and property that are the prerequisites of preservation and comfort.

Much of this is doubtless overstated, and requires some qualification. Thus, the liberal defense of private property is, of course, compatible with public regulation of private property: but only toward the end of general prosperity or the common good (understood in a liberal way: "to secure every ones Property," as Locke put it), and only by means that are consistent with the preservation of a regime of private property that encourages industry. The acquisition of property is properly only an indirect object of

---

[14]Montesquieu, *Spirit*, 11.6; cf. 1.3, 12.2; Locke, *Second Treatise*, §§21, 87, 127–31, 134–35; and cf. Hobbes, *Leviathan*, ch. 17.

[15]Locke, *Second Treatise*, §34; Tarcov, "A 'Non-Lockean' Locke," 134.

public concern: liberal political communities provide only the public *conditions* of prosperity, including civil order as well as the emancipation of free labor, within which private individuals can seek to acquire.[16]

The case of liberty is somewhat more complicated, for liberty *is* properly the direct object of public concern in well-ordered communities in ordinary circumstances, in a way that the acquisition of property is not. There is no reason for individuals to renounce their private control over the acquisition of property, which is a mostly peaceful activity, but permitting private individuals to defend their own lives and liberties with force would surely be too dangerous (precisely to our security and comfort), except in extraordinary circumstances. Thus, Locke argues that the human being who enters liberal society "wholly *gives up*" the executive power that belongs to him in the state of nature; but he only gives up the natural legislative power "so far forth as the preservation of himself, and the rest of Society shall require." By the same token, the policeman is a liberal state official, but the businessman is not. And the way of life of the businessman is only the most prominent among many other private ways of life, available in a liberal community, that enable human beings substantially to retain their natural freedom to "order their Actions, and dispose of their Possessions, and Persons as they think fit, . . . without asking leave, or depending upon the Will of any other Man." So we must renounce our natural executive powers, but not our natural acquisitive faculties, when we enter the liberal political community.[17] Furthermore, the defense of liberty, even in extraordinary circumstances, against "Great Robbers," can never quite be an individual activity, but must be undertaken by the "people" or even by a party, in opposition to a tyrannical government.[18] This is suggested, for example, even by the Second Amendment to our Constitution, the language of which appears to protect a right of the "people" to bear arms, not a private right of individuals to do so.

Liberalism does, of course, contain an account of the nature and purpose of political community, as well as an idea of the common good and

[16]Locke, *Second Treatise*, §§131, 123–24, 135, 138, 26, 28, 32–35, 41–42, 45, 48–51; and cf. §§72–73. On classical liberalism and private property, or capitalism, see Marc F. Plattner, "American Democracy and the Acquisitive Spirit"; Plattner, "The Welfare State vs. the Redistributive State," 28–48; and Plattner, "Capitalism."

[17]Locke, *Second Treatise*, §§4, 129–30; and see §§8–13, 18–20.

[18]See Locke, *Second Treatise*, §176 (a remarkable passage that immediately concerns unjust conquerors but might as well apply to usurpers and tyrants); and see §§208, 230. See Tarcov, "Locke's *Second Treatise* and 'The Best Fence against Rebellion'"; and Tarcov, "American Constitutionalism," 103.

even an idea of virtue. According to classical liberals, the political community is surely not natural: man is not by nature a political animal. Still, there can be no doubt that membership in a peaceful and stable political community accords with the interests of almost all individual human beings. Thus, the liberal political community, which seeks above all to secure this peace and stability, is an artificial rational construction, established by a "social contract" among free individuals; it is not a natural organism, a whole to which the individual is related as the hand is related to the body. Aristotle had suggested that "the city is . . . prior by nature to the household and to each of us." The liberal believes, on the contrary, that "each of us" is somehow independent of, or prior to, the political community. Or again: we constitute our (political) communities; they do not "constitute" us.[19]

The natural condition of human beings, in the absence of a common judge who can enforce common judgments about political right, is one of suspicion and hostility, an incipient war of all against all. But this is an unstable situation, one that almost inevitably leads to the establishment of tumultuous and illiberal political communities that do not make peace their overriding objective, where petty warfare is soon replaced by partisan warfare—often between rich and poor, sometimes among religious sects or other parties animated by one or another of the bizarre opinions contrived by the imaginations of men. Liberal theorists and politicians fear partisan (class, religious, ethnic, ideological) warfare above all, not simply the relatively petty quarrels of individuals (crime is ugly, but it is not, after all, civil war). There is, indeed, a kind of communitarian logic about war: human beings at war seek allies because they have enemies. And alliances, sects, and parties will soon conceive the ideologies or dogmas that are necessary to justify oppressing the others, thus arming the warlike passions by civilizing them. (Peaceful persons could remain solitaries, except that they are compelled to join parties to defend against the warlike partisans, who are not content to live and let live.) In the absence of a "social contract" that secures peace by guarding individual rights, says the classical liberal, political communities will surely arise out of partisan or sectarian warfare, with some party or sect for a time imposing its views on the others. "Community" is inevitable, given the insecurity of the state of nature; but the most likely or natural path to political community is not a social contract, but a partisan struggle, because the

---

[19]Aristotle, *Politics*, 1253a19–20; on "constitutive" community, see Sandel, *Liberalism*, 150–54 and context; and cf. Walzer, *Spheres*, 6–10, 68–83.

passions (which suggest war) are more powerful than reason (which suggests peace), in the beginning.[20] Thus, says Locke, "the imagination is always restless and suggests variety of thoughts, and the will, reason being laid aside, is ready for every extravagant project; and in this State, he that goes farthest out of the way, is thought fittest to lead, and is sure of most followers: And when Fashion hath once Established, what Folly or craft began, Custom makes it Sacred, and 'twill be thought impudence or madness, to contradict or question it."[21]

It follows, say liberals, that there is no natural political community, but only this choice: we may endure life in one of those unhappy communities that transform the natural war of all against all into the more sanguinary and civilized wars of party against party or sect against sect; or we may construct a rational and peaceful political community on the basis of a social contract among free individuals who promise mutual self-restraint, or *moderation*. This liberal moderation consists above all in the willingness of citizens to forgo public efforts to vindicate controversial (moral, religious, and ideological) opinions, since these spirited public debates might disturb the peace, or inspire the "Folly or craft" of potential masters. The "legislative power" properly extends, on the liberal view, only to the preservation of security, property, liberty, and the like; liberals do not quarrel about gods, or even about happiness or virtue, at least not in public. Liberal moderation also restrains the exercise of "executive power": liberals express their anger at criminals only through the considered judgments of the community; this enables "calm reason" rather than "passionate heats" to prevail.[22]

And so, in establishing a liberal community, we must understand that the only truly common goods are peace and the means to peace (above all, private liberty and prosperity, as well as habits of public moderation), since peace is the necessary condition of security in the possession of all private goods. All other speeches about so-called "common goods" are merely the (foolish or fraudulent) ideologies or dogmas of this or that party or sect. Peace or security is most easily achieved where private, par-

---

[20]Cf. Montesquieu, *Spirit*, 1.2–3; Locke, *Second Treatise*, §§10, 104–12, esp. 108–9; and Hobbes, *Leviathan*, ch. 13. And see Locke, *Second Treatise*, §176: "Great Robbers punish little ones, to keep them in their Obedience, but the great ones are rewarded with Laurels and Triumphs, because they are too big for the weak hands of Justice in this World." For a further development of war, see Richard Cox, *Locke on War and Peace*.

[21]Locke, *First Treatise*, §58.

[22]Locke, *Second Treatise*, §§3, 123–24, 134–42. See, too, Locke, *Letter*, esp. 26–28 (on the "Care of Souls"), and 53–56; and see Montesquieu, *Spirit*, 12.4–6, 11–13; 25.9–13; 24.22–23. On executive power, see Locke, *Second Treatise*, §§8, 130.

tisan, and sectarian opinions about more substantial common goods are not admitted into political debate, excluded for example by means of various constitutional gag rules (such as the religion clauses of the First Amendment, which announce that certain political arguments are presumptively illicit). In a liberal world, high-minded moral and political aspirations have their proper place only outside the sphere of common deliberation and common action of citizens. Liberals must therefore admit that the political way of life is not an end in itself: politics properly attends above all to the manifestly instrumental questions of security and prosperity, because debates about these matters admit compromise and encourage moderation; and so, the ways of life of citizens and statesmen are soon deprived of their former dignity—statesmen are supplanted by bureaucrats, citizens by entrepreneurs. Liberal politics, in short, is boring (or so it is hoped): we refrain from more exciting or inspiriting political and moral partisanship, because we worry that such quarrels are often merely more or less quiet modes of civil war—cold civil war, so to speak. When the political community steps beyond these bounds, it invites civil strife, interrupted only by the more or less enduring conquests of whatever party happens to possess, for a time, the greater force.[23]

Our passions do not by themselves bring us together in political communities, other than by way of war for the sake of partisan or private advantage, and the liberation of the passions from the constraints of reason cannot bring peace to existing political communities; but prudent men and women can nevertheless be taught that "we can know a good in common that we cannot know alone"—namely, peace. These are the concluding words of Sandel's *Liberalism and the Limits of Justice*. But Sandel has something nobler in mind than peace. That he does is at least in part because his book is more or less silent regarding the possibility of war, not only because Sandel denies that the body is *the* principle of individuation (and therefore an ordinary source of conflict among individuals), but also because of a remarkably optimistic view of the goods (or passions) of the soul. For Sandel, as for many recent advocates of community, it appears that the goods of the body are trivial and (besides) easily satisfied, and that the goods of the soul are principally common goods, not private goods. Ambition or the love of glory, for example, does not emerge as a problem in Sandel's book; nor does partisan intolerance, which is often inspired by an honorable love of the common

<hr />

[23]See Mansfield, "Hobbes and the Science of Indirect Government"; and Mansfield, "Modern and Medieval Representation."

good (based on an opinion about virtue or salvation, say). There is therefore no good reason for human beings to go to war, or so it appears.[24]

Reason understands, says the classical liberal, what the (more warlike than sociable) passions do not feel, that there is a common good. Peace is good, to repeat, because it is the necessary condition of all private pursuits of happiness; and peace is a *common* good, even requiring common deliberation and common action, because it cannot be made secure in the absence of various forms of civility and self-mastery. Here is the origin of the liberal virtues.[25] To secure peace, the citizens of a liberal political community must be persuaded to acknowledge that it is their duty to respect the rights of their individual fellow citizens; they must recognize that their private, partisan, and sectarian opinions have no place in political debate; and they must hire police officers in order to assist each other in common defense against those villains who would take advantage of the general peace in order to commit particular crimes in safety, or who would destroy the general peace in the name of partisan ideals. Mutual respect of individual rights, the political self-restraint of parties and sects, and a willingness to enlist the force of the community in support of this liberal moderation: these are the core virtues of liberal politics. Most men and women will, of course, still be motivated by private (as well as partisan or sectarian) concerns. But a well-ordered liberal polity can so order social conditions and political institutions that private interests and common obligations are not, or not much, in competition.[26] And then, where peace is secure because rights are respected and habits of moderation observed, human beings are liberated to engage in their various private pursuits of happiness, privately defined.

And so, as Walzer says, the liberal community "is an instrument and not an end in itself." The liberal view of the political community implies a radical diminution of the dignity of the political life: liberalism has turned the "political order into an administrative agency" that seeks to provide a plentiful and secure world, within which men and women can safely "turn away from public to private life, to business and family, or to religion and self-cultivation." As Walzer says, in the liberal welfare state, "the policeman and the welfare administrator will be the only public persons":

[24]Sandel, *Liberalism*, 183; and see 80, 50–63 (esp. 62–63), 147–65.
[25]Thus, Hobbes: "Peace is Good, and therefore also the way, or means of Peace, which (as I have shewed before) are *Justice, Gratitude, Modesty, Equity, Mercy,* & the rest of the Laws of Nature, are good; that is to say, *Morall Vertues*" (*Leviathan*, ch. 15).
[26]See Tarcov, "A 'Non-Lockean' Locke," 132, 134.

Liberal theorists of the welfare state have always claimed to know what we want. . . . People want pleasure, but such pleasure as cannot be shared or does not depend on any form of sharing—individual delight, egoistic satisfaction. . . .

In the heat of battle, goals have sometimes been suggested that elude or transcend the liberal definition of human desire. Wild hopes for equality and fraternity have been proclaimed. But each success has turned out to be a further triumph for what might best be called political utilitarianism. If we or our ancestors or our comrades in this or that struggle have sought the actuality of freedom and love, we have settled readily enough for the pursuit of private happiness—so readily, indeed, that it would be difficult to deny that private happiness is all we ever wanted.

Walzer is here, as always, ready to praise the "enormous achievements" of liberal "welfare politics." And yet, he is not quite ready to believe, what he admits is "difficult to deny," that private happiness is really altogether satisfying for almost all human beings. We must want something more: but "whatever the nature of our past demands, what we want *next* is not on any of the liberal lists."[27]

Neither the participating citizen nor the statesman has much of a place in liberal theory, and neither way of life has (in general) proved to be attractive enough, in liberal practice, to lure liberal "citizens" away from their various private pursuits—in families, churches, schools, businesses, and so on. In part, this situation obtains because the very questions of politics have been greatly transformed: we quarrel endlessly about how to provide, efficiently and justly, the instruments that are necessary (or so it is said) for every private pursuit of happiness; but we are forbidden to raise, in the political arena, questions about happiness itself, which is after all the end of human life, if we have not actually forgotten the questions. So, the matter of political debate and the arena of political action now seem less dignified. Political life no longer provides many opportunities for statesmanlike displays of excellence or great benefactions, the possibility of which might (in a prior time) have tempted the most ambitious human beings to vie to be honored and to rule in their political communities. (Indeed, the place of the statesman in the political community is neglected not only by liberals, but also by today's communitarian theorists, who speak only of citizens.) And, for the same reason, we liberal citizens are now also largely deprived of some of the greatest joys of political association, including above all the

[27]Walzer, *Radical Principles*, 28–29, 24–25.

sometimes agreeable but often dangerous business of common deliberation about what is a good and just and happy human life, and about how the political community can bring such human beings into being; perhaps it is pleasant to consider together how we should order our lives together, but this is a pleasure that liberals cannot know, at least in politics.

Thus, the manifestly instrumental questions of economic policy now dominate our political life: politics today is concerned primarily with the largely technical problem of how to ensure prosperity, secondarily with questions about the distribution of this prosperity (including not only the adjudication of conflicting claims made by economic interests, but also debate about the appropriate extent of communal provision or welfare). Indeed, it is possible that liberalism implicitly favors commercial ways of life, and associated conceptions of the good, over other private ways of life, as well as over public life.[28] These are not trivial questions, but they can hardly inspire citizens or statesmen to great public deeds. To be sure, liberalism has not yet abolished war and enemies, so that the urgent and exhilarating questions of foreign policy are still with us and, from time to time, provide suitable tasks for liberal citizens and statesmen. But foreign policy too is manifestly instrumental: everyone knows that war is a means to peace. Besides, the citizen at war is the soldier, and in the regime whose end is the security of the bodies of its members, the way of life of the soldier often seems merely perverse, or at best a necessary evil. So the liberal understanding both of peace and of war diminishes the dignity of the political ways of life. In a time of crisis, a prudent human being might accept the burdens of political life, but not happily, and not if other capable hands can be counted on to perform the necessary tasks. But in quiet times, politics is best understood as an arena in which individuals, or groups of individuals, pursue their (primarily economic) interests: liberal politics is interest-group politics. So it is perhaps not surprising that we have turned many of these questions over to bureaucrats and experts, for these technical and instrumental problems are just the sorts of necessary burdens that a free human being will eschew, and leave to his public "servants." The real action lies elsewhere.

II

This account of liberalism may seem a caricature; today, many friends of liberalism seem to doubt that "self-interest, even self-interest 'rightly understood,' " is capable of sustaining a civilized liberal politics. These new

[28]See Berns, "Taking Rights Frivolously," 59–60, 62.

liberals are inclined to attempt to reconstitute liberalism on the basis of a novel moral psychology, one that makes a place for "the liberal virtues" and other liberal moral qualities, including "that honorable determination which animates every votary of freedom to rest all our political experiments on the capacity of mankind for self-government"; political virtue and honorable pride must do the work that reasonable self-interest cannot do alone. This view implies, according to Galston, that liberals today must reject "any comprehensive egoism."[29] And so I want to explain my inclination to emphasize that those liberals who seek security in political communities are engaged in a reasonable pursuit of self-interest. To be sure, prudent liberals must cultivate certain social virtues in order to secure the peace; and these virtues, however modest they might be, do not arise spontaneously in the souls of human beings. Beyond that, a proud love of liberty must animate the public lives of those liberals who establish, maintain, and defend such liberal communities.

And yet, these virtues and that pride are among the habits and dispositions of reasonable human beings, as Tarcov demonstrates in *Locke's Education for Liberty*: "Locke, however, constructs modern moral virtues, including civility, liberality, justice, and humanity, on the basis of his egoistic and hedonistic psychology." Certainly, a full account of liberalism must rely upon all three sorts of moral argument: self-interest properly understood, honorable pride, and the liberal virtues all have a place in the classical liberal argument. Lockean liberals are not the "naive" rationalists they are sometimes supposed to be. A reasonable liberal easily admits the necessity of cultivating certain more-than-reasonable (passionate or sentimental) habits and dispositions. Hard times will surely come: and then the naturally illiberal passions, which might well counsel an imprudent practice of vice or a submission to mastery, may overpower the liberal reasons that counsel virtue or pride, since these reasons are most evident and most instrumental in calm times. In anticipation of hard times, a liberal moral education is required: it is simply reasonable to cultivate habitual, sentimental, and passionate supports for reasonable liberal judgments, so that passion can be made to counteract passion, in support of reason, when the necessity arises. But is this not yet a "comprehensive egoism"? Or must the liberal who recognizes that even a liberal polity must cultivate certain moral virtues repudiate the founding liberal idea: the idea of a reasonable pursuit of

---

[29]Galston, "Liberal Virtues," 1281. For "that honorable determination," see *Federalist* #39: 240.

happiness? Here, I want to suggest that the case for liberal politics must finally be submitted to the private judgments of individuals, who must decide for themselves whether it is reasonable for a self-interested human being to choose to be a citizen of such a community: liberal virtues must be reasonable virtues; proud liberal freedom must be a freedom that is guided by reason.[30]

Tarcov has argued that the "contemporary political dissatisfaction with liberalism and the historical search for non-Lockean elements in the American tradition rest in part on the dominant interpretations of the moral vision of Lockean liberalism, which attribute to Locke a mean-spirited selfish materialism." He argues, further, that this view of Locke is misleading and deprives us of access to the "broader, deeper, and loftier liberalism" suggested by more careful attention to Locke's works. The dominant interpretations of classical liberalism today surely do not inspire a lofty moral vision, and cannot serve as a public philosophy for those human beings who hope (in various ways) for a more civilized or honorable political life: "not everyone can be satisfied by an understanding of man as an asocial individual dedicated solely to the unlimited accumulation of property and by an understanding of society as an aggregate of such individuals and an arena for the pursuit and compromise of their interests." It is not surprising that where such an understanding of political life is dominant, people talk about community, among other absent moral goods that might be imagined. Not only the critics of liberalism, but also a growing number of its friends, now sometimes express such doubts about contemporary liberal politics.[31]

Nevertheless, we are all still somehow liberals, in spite of our various complaints about the dominant interpretations of liberalism. (I have already emphasized the ambivalence even of radical critics of the prevailing liberalism.) Why? In what does our continuing attachment to liberalism consist? We are still liberals, it seems to me, just so far as we remain, in Walzer's words, "rationalists of everyday life" who have "learned to think of [ourselves] as individuals." Whatever else might trouble us about liberal politics, most of us will not now repudiate this aspect of liberal rationalism: we insist that we must be permitted to see for ourselves—and not only to be told by the authorities—what is good for us. So any communitarian (or new liberal) alternative to the prevail-

---

[30]Tarcov, *Locke's Education*, 210. On liberal virtues, see Hobbes, *Leviathan*, ch. 15; on liberal freedom and reason, see Locke, *Second Treatise*, §57.

[31]Tarcov, "A 'Non-Lockean' Locke," 130, 138. See, too, Don Herzog, "Up Toward Liberalism"; and Galston, "Liberal Virtues."

ing liberal interpretations of contemporary liberal politics must some-how accommodate the continuing vigor of this liberal rationalism. Even today, the liberal community is almost invariably measured first by its ability to provide for the welfare of its individual members. We demand that the political community serve our needs; and we refuse to admit that individuals are subordinate parts of an "organic" whole, or that cit-izens owe service and loyalty to their community even when it does not provide for their welfare and security. In this respect, we are the uncom-promising heirs of the classical enlightenment liberals. Today, even par-tisans of community do not often deny these liberal orthodoxies. A liberal "community," if it is to exist at all, must be a community that reasonable human beings would choose, free of the various mystifica-tions of tradition.[32]

We constitute the community through our voluntary acts, says the lib-eral; no community "constitutes" our identities in ways that we can "nei-ther summon nor command," as Sandel says. Indeed, liberal freedom is above all this moral (or perhaps it is a "metaphysical") freedom from the "constitutive" power of one's community.[33] If such freedom is not possi-ble for human beings, then neither is political freedom, for in that case politics would everywhere authorize the (more or less nasty) tyranny of those partisan authorities who write the founding ("constitutive") myths of the community. And so, classical liberals must argue that reasonable moral freedom from community is possible for (many) human beings, who can learn the law of nature or "*Law of Reason*" and so consent to establish or to join a liberal community—in this, classical liberals must oppose the philosophical communitarianism of much of contemporary political theory. (Consider, for example, Locke's response to communi-tarian objections to his doctrine of consent.) Otherwise, it is not clear how human beings could be said to be the authors of their communities, rather than merely the texts written by those communities; for only those who are able to think for themselves are truly able to choose for them-selves. As Locke says, "The *Freedom* then of Man and Liberty of acting according to his own Will, is *grounded on* his having *Reason*, which is able to instruct him in that Law he is to govern himself by."[34]

---

[32]See Walzer, *Spheres*, 64–65 (in the chapter on "Security and Welfare"). And see Walzer, *Radical Principles*, 23–30, 13–15.

[33]See Sandel, *Liberalism and the Limits of Justice*, 179; cf. 139–54, 80–82.

[34]Locke, *Second Treatise*, §63; on the communitarian objections to the consent doctrine, see §§100–22; and see Locke's account of the rise of children to moral freedom, under a law of reason, in §§55–63, a passage whose emphasis on reason as the ground of freedom is truly remarkable, given the context ("parental power"). For "*Law of Reason*," see §57.

"Rationality," says Tarcov, "enables and entitles us to be free, whether from political tyranny, as in the *Two Treatises*, or from intellectual superstition and authority, as in the *Essay*."[35] And the latter freedom is the foundation of the former freedom, as Walzer and Locke agree: political freedom is possible only where we somehow liberate ourselves from "every sort of political divinity."[36]

And so, the problem for friends of liberalism today is to find a way to show that it is *reasonable*, on liberal grounds, not to become "mean-spirited selfish materialists," among other liberal vices. That is, what is now needed is a way of thinking about liberalism that not only overcomes the widespread objection that Lockean liberalism is politically and morally impoverished, but at the same time preserves this crucial moral achievement of liberalism: its vindication of a way of life that is both *reasonable* and *free*, or that is free *because* it is reasonable.[37] Otherwise, we liberals will be compelled to choose between reason and virtue, so to speak: and it is still hard to see why a liberal, or any other human being, should choose to be virtuous, in such a case. But it is not obvious that it is necessary to make such a choice: who says that it is reasonable to live a nasty, slavish, lonely life? It would be a rank caricature of liberalism to suggest that (naturally selfish) liberal rationalists, who seek peace above all—because peace is the necessary condition of private pursuits of happiness—are unable to think reasonably about virtue, community, character, and the rest.

Liberals strive to lead a truly reasonable way of life, one that requires them to establish reasonably moderate and peaceful communities. And that is a rather lofty aspiration. For a freedom that is not guided by reason is too often mere folly: human beings are free but miserable in the state of nature; they have not yet studied the law of nature, which is the law of reason. And if loyal or dutiful membership in a community is *not* reasonable for a human being, then citizenship or virtue is really a more or less gentle form of slavery to some authority within the community or to the community as a whole, and why should we choose that? So-called

---

[35]Tarcov, *Locke's Education for Liberty*, 211 (the last words of the book).

[36]Walzer, *Radical Principles*, 25. For Locke, the principal form of illiberal political authority arises from the political abuse of paternal power (*Second Treatise*, §§1 [summarizing *First Treatise*], 74–76, 104–12); and this political authority of fathers or kings, Locke says almost in passing, had a religious foundation: " 'tis certain, that in the Beginning, *The Father of the Family was Priest, as that he was Ruler in his own Houshold*" (§76).

[37]For a moral psychology that suits this reasonable liberal way of life, see Tarcov, *Locke's Education*. As the title suggests, Tarcov often emphasizes the liberal's love of liberty, not only the liberal's obedience to a law of reason.

virtue must be measured, says the liberal, according to the rules of reasonable self-interest that are given to us by our natural reason. But there is little reason to think that virtue and community, properly understood, are not reasonable. It is surely reasonable, for example, to recognize that various forms of moral self-mastery are necessary for human beings who seek any goods that require one to be vigilant in their pursuit, especially when it is necessary to pursue these goods in common with more or less recalcitrant companions.[38] Further, it is surely reasonable to seek to live among human beings who might bring one benefit rather than harm: wicked or wretched companions are threatening, and public-spirited concern not only with one's own character but also with the character of one's fellow citizens in a community is (at least in some measure) reasonable.[39] Finally, it is reasonable to love freedom, and to defend it with vigor. As Locke says: "Reason bids me look on him, as an Enemy to my Preservation, who would take away that *Freedom*, which is the Fence to it."[40] So even a "comprehensive egoism" teaches human beings to cultivate those habits and sentiments and virtues, as well as the liberal sciences of politics and economics, that enable liberal citizens to choose well how to govern themselves as individuals and as a community. But it would surely be a great mistake for liberals to repudiate the rationalism in politics that is their finest achievement, in the quest for imagined moral goods—such as community, or virtue. But this is what many of today's partisans of community—and some liberals too—would have us do. I discuss this communitarian assault on liberal rationalism in later chapters, especially Chapter 4 and Chapter 5 (and, from a different point of view, in Chapter 8).

III

Classical liberalism is a sober understanding that can sustain only an austere politics. Liberal *politics* is about peace and prosperity, which make possible the private "pursuit of happiness"; it is, therefore, not about happiness itself, which we must pursue alone, or at most in the company of a few kindred spirits. But human beings care about their happiness above all, not peace and prosperity: liberal communities therefore demand a kind of *public* moderation, which enables prudent liberals to acknowledge their public responsibilities as citizens even when those duties

---

[38]See Tarcov, *Locke's Education*, 129–83, esp. 132–37; cf. 86–93.
[39]Cf. Plato, *Apology of Socrates*, 24c-26a.
[40]Locke, *Second Treatise*, §17.

seem (at first) to be at odds with their private aspirations as human beings; more narrowly, liberals must learn to refrain from uttering their controversial opinions about happiness or the good life in the political arena, even though these opinions concern what is most important to them, in order to secure certain more urgent (if less ennobling or pleasing) goods—peace, privacy, prosperity. (This is the classical liberal's version of the prevailing neo-Kantian liberal case for "neutrality" regarding opinions about the good; but classical liberal neutrality is both more and less far-reaching than contemporary liberal neutrality, for reasons that will be clear presently.) Liberals need not, of course, renounce such opinions altogether; and yet, not every opinion about the good life can be reconciled with the liberal demand of public moderation.

Moderation is a liberal virtue: it is the reasonable habit of taming those natural passions that might bring civil strife, and especially the political expressions of those passions in partisan opinions. Thus, moderation is above all a virtue of liberal public *speech*. A liberal politics is incompatible with certain kinds of license or immoderation: prudent liberals are moderate, in public speech as well as (or more than) in private deed, whenever a failure of self-control would be too likely to provoke partisan anger, and thereby to arouse the spirited opponents of a certain way of life or political opinion. Perhaps the most important task of liberal theory is to persuade or remind citizens that it is necessary, in order to secure the peace that makes possible the pursuit of happiness, to moderate our almost natural temptation to turn to politics, or to parties ("comrades") or sects (the "righteous"), for (more than minimal) public assistance in our various pursuits of happiness. The liberal community enables us to pursue happiness at home; it does not teach us the meaning of happiness, much less guarantee that government will make us happy, and we must not ask it to do so.

But what if this vision of the liberal political community proves to be morally unsatisfying? In that case, liberals argue, when human beings have the luxury of pursuing putatively more satisfying goods than security and comfort (a luxury that exists, for most human beings anyway, only in well-ordered or liberal political communities), these goods must be made the objects of private pursuits of happiness, in family and church and school and business, or perhaps in solitude. Liberal *politics*, in any case, is not about happiness.

As liberal politics is not about happiness, so it is not about justice, or God. If justice requires something more than respect for the rights that are a means to peace—roughly, if "justice" means "distributive justice"—then a public life that seeks to "establish Justice" must also somehow establish certain authoritative philosophical (or religious) opinions (about equality, moral desert, and moral responsibility, for example). Such theories of human nature are at the foundation of the various partisan moral opinions about distributive justice. But these opinions are (naturally, so to speak) matters of dispute among human beings—often angry dispute. For this reason, the "neutrality" of classical liberals is somewhat more far-reaching than the "neutrality" of such theorists of distributive justice as Rawls and Dworkin, among others.[41]

As Plato suggests (in the conversation between Polemarchus and Socrates in the *Republic*, and elsewhere), ideas of distributive justice always depend upon certain naturally controversial opinions: about what the "goods" are that are to be distributed; about who the "friends" are to whom these goods properly belong in common; about how one judges what is owed to this or that particular friend or fellow citizen, or what is due to them. Walzer also emphasizes the diversity ("pluralism") of opinions about "goods" (as well as the diversity of opinions about "distributive principles" and about "membership"), and he even insists (against Plato) that there are in principle no means of resolving disputes about these goods. In so doing, Walzer appears to concede that many partisan controversies about distributive justice cannot be settled by philosophy or reason.

But Walzer does not much worry about the dangers of warlike partisanship that this theoretical impasse might seem to invite. Plato and especially Aristotle suggest, more moderately, that there are often no practical measures that can resolve such disputes in a manner that is altogether consistent with what we can know about justice; but since we can in principle know something about what is good for human beings, and something about justice, a prudent statesman might from time to time achieve some measure of distributive justice by recognizing the compromises with false prevailing opinions that might be productive in a particular time and place. (Such compromises with injustice are also justified in part by an almost liberal recognition of the importance—for decent politics—of peace or security.) But war, or the conquest of partisan ideas (tyranny), is not necessary in principle, however ordinary it might be in practice; ideas of justice are not in principle partisan. The question of "friends" is more complicated,

[41]For an example of the ambition of contemporary liberals to defend a particular (egalitarian) account of distributive justice, see Dworkin, *A Matter of Principle*, 181–213; and especially Dworkin, "What Is Equality?" See, too, Rawls, *A Theory of Justice*, esp. 60–83, 100–108, 151–83, 258–332.

but Plato's discussion raises the same kinds of issues that are raised by Walzer in his discussion of "membership" and in his discussion of alternative "distributive principles." To whom do we owe "good," however understood, as a "friend" or fellow citizen? And how do we know how to distribute these "goods" among those to whom we somehow owe such debts? These questions, which must be answered by partisans of any idea of distributive justice, will of course be answered differently by the various partisans in most political communities, and especially in "pluralist" political communities (as Walzer seems to admit), once it becomes possible to ask them in public forums.[42] For this reason, classical liberals are even more modest than Plato and Aristotle, and do not seriously aim to achieve distributive justice; indeed, distributive justice, although a very important case, is merely a special case of the more general argument for moderation set forth earlier.

And so, if liberal politics aims at peace above all, it can "establish Justice" only by assigning to "justice" a simple, minimal, and uncontroversial meaning (respect for rights, performance of contracts, punishment of criminals, and the like). But ideas of *distributive* justice are always more or less controversial, above all because, by their nature, they fail to acknowledge the proud sense of equality that persuades almost every human being that no one knows better than he does what is "fitting" for him, but also because they sometimes fail to recognize the necessity of accommodating the similarly proud sense of merit that persuades some human beings that they deserve their unequal station.[43] These opinions about justice and equality are naturally controversial, chiefly (but not only) for the following reason, which is revealed in Aristotle's account of the partisan controversy between democrats and oligarchs. Aristotle argues that ideas of distributive justice depend upon controversial opinions about equality, opinions that have their roots in certain natural and ineradicable psychological and moral differences among human beings. Distributive justice demands equality for equals and inequality for unequals; it reaches further than the more limited kind of (equal) justice that is appropriate in markets and courts of law. But then, the political community that seeks to "establish (distributive) justice" must judge (in an authoritative way) who are equals and who are not, among other things. Certainly, this cannot fail to arouse the anger of those partisans

[42]On these points, see Walzer, *Spheres*, chs. 1–3.

[43]For this paragraph and the next, see Aristotle, *Politics*, esp. 1280a5–1284b35; and see Aristotle, *Nicomachean Ethics*, bk. V. See, too, Machiavelli, *The Prince*, ch. 9; and, finally, see Hobbes, *Leviathan*, ch. 15, on "distributive justice" and "equity."

who are morally wounded by the community's judgment. This is true even if the conquering opinion is an altogether egalitarian one, since the opinion that all human beings are equal is itself a partisan opinion that will offend those human beings who deny this natural equality, or who deny that natural equality in every case sanctions a civil equality. Aristotle elaborates this argument, that ideas of distributive justice are naturally contentious, by emphasizing the prevalence of certain more or less natural parties in many political communities. Political life is a struggle among natural parties that advance competing opinions about distributive justice: above all, the party of property, the party of freedom, and the party of virtue.

Classical liberals seek to evade these partisan disputes about equality and distributive justice. More precisely, liberals affirm the natural equality of human beings in a (moderate) manner that does not offend prudent partisans of natural inequality: liberal equality is only the natural equality (in freedom) that exists in the state of nature and the consequent civil equality (in rights) that is established by a social contract. Similarly, liberals interpret justice as requiring no more than what is required by the kind of (equal) justice that is appropriate in markets and law courts, which is not "distributive" justice. But beyond this fundamental equality (equal protection of the laws) and simple justice (fairness in markets and contracts), liberals permit the contest between proud egalitarians and proud inegalitarians to be won or lost in many private spheres of life without the intervention of the community—with its moral (and other) force—in support of any party's understanding of justice.

More generally, liberals achieve nonpartisan agreement about the meaning of naturally controversial moral ideas (e.g. equality, goods, friends, justice) by reducing these ideas to noncontroversial fundamentals (e.g. natural freedom and consent, peace and prosperity, fellow social contractors, and respect for civil rights, respectively). Liberals hope to preserve the peace in this way, by permitting more controversial opinions about these matters to emerge only in private: no partisan moral opinions can be permitted to prevail in public. But this implies that liberals do not seek to "establish (distributive) justice" by political means. And so, the idea of distributive justice has no place in classical liberal politics, which forbids the partisan imposition of philosophical opinions about justice, just as it forbids the partisan imposition of religious opinions about the "Care of Souls."[44] Thus, there is no account of distributive jus-

---

[44]Cf. Hobbes, *Leviathan*, ch. 15, esp. on "distributive justice."

tice in Locke's *Second Treatise*. Liberal politics demands not only moderation in the partisan advocacy of any understanding of happiness or the good life, but also moderation in the partisan advocacy of moral and religious causes, which are founded on diverse and controversial opinions about justice and virtue, or on similarly diverse opinions about gods.

Even the liberal idea of rights, insofar as rights have a moral ground that is somehow independent of their ordinary necessity as a means to peace, must sometimes (not always or usually) give way before the classical liberal imperative: "seek peace." Prudent men and women must from time to time be prepared to endure deprivations of their putatively just deserts; further, the liberal community may from time to time be obliged to deprive citizens of their surely just rights, whenever that is necessary to preserve civil peace and comity: in the face of perverse and obstinate partisan enmity, or when the security of the community is threatened in some other manner. Thus Montesquieu even offers a defense of bills of attainder, on the grounds that it is from time to time necessary to draw "a veil . . . over liberty"—even for the "freest peoples that ever lived on earth." This is an especially revealing case, since the liberal Montesquieu is generally a rather uncompromising defender of individual security against those who emphasize the necessity of subordinating the claims of the individual to the requirements of civil peace. It is also, happily, an extreme case.[45]

IV

Perhaps the most striking failure of contemporary liberal thought is its inability to speak to the sort of liberal portrayed here, who insists that he must be permitted to see for himself what goods belong to human beings (by nature), and so to choose a way of life (a "pursuit of happiness") that is founded on an idea of his own. It is not enough, says this liberal, to hear the speeches of political and moral authorities about what is good or just; even the authority of tradition, or of a constitutive community, is somehow oppressive. Indeed, the authority of tradition or community can be more oppressive than the authority of particular rulers, here and now. For it is always possible to appeal, in thought if not in deed, from today's rulers to the higher authority of the community itself and its enduring principles, as Lincoln appealed from Justice

---

[45]Montesquieu, *Spirit*, 12.19. Cf. Montesquieu's mild rebuke of Machiavelli, in 6.5. See Lincoln's defense of the arrest of Vallandigham, in *Speeches and Writings*, 701–7. And see Pangle, "The Liberal Critique of Rights."

Taney to the Declaration and the Constitution; but it is much harder to appeal from the authority of the community and its principles altogether. In all of this, the sort of liberal I here portray is akin to the Glaucon of Plato's *Republic*, who undertakes a daring search for "what any nature naturally pursues as good." Such a liberal would never be deterred from this quest by those spokesmen for the community and its laws who, like so many of our preachy liberal theorists, tell him only what the prevailing authorities have agreed about justice, but offer no good reasons for *his* obedience to these agreed rules—as when Rawls reports on the "overlapping consensus" of citizens or parties in our democratic community, and calls this agreement "justice." What is the difference, from the point of view of the classical liberal, between the "compact" that Glaucon despises and the agreements about justice that have been reported by our liberal theorists?[46]

For it is now everywhere admitted, even by the most respectable liberal theorists, that moral freedom from the authority of community is not possible for human beings. Moral reasoning is simply the more or less creative "interpretation" of our shared moral horizon, or of an "existing morality" that "is authoritative for us because it is only by virtue of its existence that we exist as the moral beings we are."[47] Or, it is the more or less faithful reading of an "overlapping consensus" among the prevailing parties in our community, an inquiry that proceeds from "basic intuitive ideas" or "settled convictions" to a "congenial" conception of justice, by "shaping" these notions into a coherent public doctrine; it goes without saying that this "tolerant" appeal to the consensus of the community accommodates only those who affirm "doctrines likely to persist and to gain adherents" in our sort of "democratic society."[48] Or, perhaps moral reasoning is an essentially rhetorical enterprise, a mode of propaganda that enables partisans of liberalism to "outflank" their opponents through the use of artful "metaphors" and "redescriptions" (not "arguments"), which are designed to make their enemies "look bad"; such "postmodernist bourgeois liberals" defend "the institutions and practices of the rich North Atlantic democracies" (or "our common European

---

[46]*Republic*, 358b-362c; Rawls, *Political Liberalism*, esp. 89–172; cf. Walzer, *Spheres*, 6–10, 64–83, on the conventional character of all "goods."

[47]Walzer, *Interpretation and Social Criticism*, 20–21; see, too, Walzer, *Spheres*, xiv, 29, 313–14. For further discussion of this communitarian account of moral reasoning, see Chapter 8.

[48]Rawls, "Justice as Fairness," 224–31; and see Rawls, *Political Liberalism*, esp. 133–72; and Rorty, *Objectivity*, 175–96. See Orwin and Stoner, "Neo-Constitutionalism? Rawls, Dworkin, and Nozick."

project") on the basis of solidarity alone, without appeal to the universal reasons of the Enlightenment liberals.[49]

Such liberal theorists can of course preach only to the converted. They will persuade only those many (orthodox) citizens who have already implicitly agreed—in their hearts, so to speak, if not with their voices—to respect the principles of political right that liberal philosophers now say they discern in the jumble of our shared intuitions. But our theorists can offer no good reasons for obedience that will persuade the ambitious, daring, courageous (or merely foolhardy) few who may not be eager to submit to an agreement of this sort, and who may not listen to the (moralizing) spokesmen for the democratic community. Such a liberal expects more from the philosophic partisan of justice (or equality, or virtue) than a report about the agreement that constitutes the community, and that calls whatever is approved by this moral compact "justice." For any such agreement or community, says our liberal with Glaucon, may "pervert" nature to "honor equality," or to honor virtue.[50]

Postmodern liberalism in particular suffers from this inability to offer good reasons for liberal principles and practices, a fact that Rorty admits and even celebrates: the postmodern liberal believes that "cruelty is the worst thing we do"; yet he knows that "there is no answer to the question 'Why not be cruel?' " The postmodern liberal is distinguished above all by the courage to "face up" to the contingency of this most fundamental liberal belief without falling into despair. Indeed, the proper pose of the postmodern liberal is playful "irony," says Rorty. But the classical liberal suspects that the cheerful courage of the liberal ironist depends upon finding or creating human beings who are "never quite able to take themselves seriously," as Rorty says. There is something frivolous, or so it has appeared to a number of Rorty's critics, about this sunny disposition in face of the loss of permanent sources of meaning. At the least, "facing up" to contingency should be hard. From the Left, it appears that Rorty's playful ironist is content to abandon his love of justice and of humanity, and so to become the easygoing tool of the prevailing authorities in his community. From the Right, it appears that the ironist is content to trivialize community, treating it as an "experiment," an arena for play, and not as the deepest ground of the duties, loyalties, and aspirations that ennoble the lives of human beings.[51]

---

[49]Rorty, *Contingency*, 44; and see xiii–xvi, 44–95; Rorty, *Consequences*, 172–73; and Rorty, *Objectivity*, 197–202; see, too, 21–34, 203–10; and cf. Sandel, *Liberalism*, 149–53, 168–83.

[50]Plato, *Republic*, 359c; cf. Rorty, *Contingency*, 189–98, xv, 74, 82–94.

[51]Rorty, *Contingency*, xv, 73, 45.

Because these are real losses, it is hard to know what to make of the cheerful, not-to-worry pose that Rorty and kindred partisans of postmodern liberalism sometimes adopt. In a splendid essay, Elshtain speaks of the "unbearable lightness of [Rortyian] liberalism."[52] For some, it will be hard to resist the suspicion that the "death of God"—for that is what is at stake here, the loss of what most human beings have always held most dear—must soon diminish humanity. Indeed, Rorty is prepared to concede that our liberal democratic societies "have no higher aim than what [Nietzsche] called 'the last men'—the people who have 'their little pleasures for the day and their little pleasures for the night.' "[53]

In Chapters 3 and 4, I defend classical liberalism against its postmodern liberal critics, especially Rorty; his is the species of contemporary liberalism that has been most influenced by communitarian ideas regarding both the nature of community and the nature of the self (e.g. the "contingency of community," the "contingency of the self"). In Chapter 3, I further elaborate the classical understanding of liberalism, focusing on the liberal virtue of tolerance. I argue that the classical account of liberalism provides a more certain foundation for the liberal virtues than does the postmodern account of liberalism. And in Chapter 4, I consider Rorty's postmodern liberalism itself, and especially his repudiation of the liberal idea of "humanity."

---

[52]Jean Bethke Elshtain, "Don't Be Cruel: Reflections on Rortyian Liberalism," 200.
[53]Rorty, "Posties," 12.

3

Liberalism
and the Idea of Toleration

Tolerance is a liberal virtue: it is among the most honorable of the respectable habits of liberal citizens. Here is the noble promise of our "enlarged and liberal policy" of toleration, in President Washington's famous words: that among us "every one shall sit in safety under his own vine and fig-tree, and there shall be none to make him afraid"; that here the community will give "to bigotry no sanction, to persecution no assistance" (Letter to the Hebrew Congregation of Newport, 1790). This is a splendid portrait of a truly liberal community.

But today, these lofty words ring hollow, not only because bigotry has not yet vanished from our public life, but also because the policy of toleration has now been exposed. From the Left, it is sometimes said that toleration is not the "enlarged and liberal policy" of a free people, but rather the cramped and even "repressive" policy of reactionary parties, against which "authentic liberals," who are enemies of "institutionalized inequality," must struggle. This suspicion, that the liberal idea of toleration is a fraud perpetrated by apologists for reactionary oppressors, persists among postmodernist social critics; it may also be reflected in some of the recent controversy concerning "political correctness" in the academy.[1] And from the Right, it is sometimes said that toleration is the indiscriminate and overindulgent policy of a dissolute people, against which the

---

[1]Herbert Marcuse, "Repressive Tolerance," 81–84; and see Paul Berman, "Introduction: The Debate and Its Origins," in his *Debating P.C.*, 1–26, on the relation between postmodernism and "political correctness." On p. 6, Berman writes, of postmodernism, "It was a revolt *against* liberal humanism. It said, in effect: Liberal humanism is a deception. Western-style democracy, rationalism, objectivity, and the autonomy of the individual are slogans designed to convince the downtrodden that subordination is justice."

friends of republican government, who are troubled by a decline of civic and moral virtue, must struggle. Thus, neoconservative social critics now argue that an indiscriminate practice of tolerance causes and excuses our public neglect of "character" and family. Liberal society has long been "living off the accumulated moral capital of traditional religion and traditional moral philosophy," writes Kristol; but now that we have expended that moral capital we have proved ourselves unable to supply the defect from our own resources.[2]

Perhaps these competing assaults on the liberal policy of toleration are not so dissimilar as first appears. At any rate, both sets of critics seem to be animated by a certain moral indignation (even "residual puritanism") regarding these ordinary and predictable consequences of freedom: inequality and vice. Moreover, the strange and surprising alliance of feminists and conservatives against pornography suggests that there may be an unsuspected affinity between "virtue" and "love of equality" in our democratic community.[3] However that may be, the policy of toleration evidently requires liberals to tame both species of moral indignation, to crush the natural love of equality and virtue of democrats and republicans: the price of toleration is inequality and vice.[4] But if we can now see that the liberal idea of toleration is simply the apology of exploiting or wicked elites, and no more, why should the partisans of virtue, or of equality, listen?

In this chapter, I propose to reconsider certain aspects of the liberal case for toleration, in light of such doubts; for friends of liberalism must now fear that as we forget the good reasons for our policy of toleration we will, sooner or later, lose the respectable habits of tolerance as well.

I

"Classical" liberals admire a certain sort of human being: the free and rational individual, who is capable of self-government but seeks neither to rule others nor to gratify them. Such a liberal will stand alone, if need be: one human being against a multitude in defense of a certain conviction or way of life. This proud liberal individualist seeks above all to liberate

[2]Irving Kristol, *Two Cheers for Capitalism*, 65–66; see, too, 137–38; and see Kristol, *On the Democratic Idea in America*, 22–47.

[3]See Elizabeth Fox-Genovese, *Feminism without Illusions*, 87–95, 107–11, for a temperate and somewhat ambivalent discussion of pornography that contains elements of both criticisms of the policy of toleration (for the phrase quoted in the text, see 88). See, too, Berns, *In Defense of Liberal Democracy*, 119–42. On the affinity between "virtue" and "love of equality," see Montesquieu, *Spirit*, 5.2–7; cf. 7.8–12.

[4]See Mill, *On Liberty*, 66–77, 85–90.

himself as far as possible from every sort of authority, and so to choose a way of life "untrammeled alike by old and new," by hoary tradition or glittering fashion.[5] And yet, such individualists, who love liberty, eschew dominion: as they would not be slaves, so they would not be masters. (For a classical liberal portrait of the free and rational individual, see Nathan Tarcov's analysis of a liberal education of human pride, which is an education in self-mastery, in *Locke's Education for Liberty*.)[6]

Classical liberals do not seek rule or mastery, but are content to live and let live, because they have somehow learned that it is reasonable to consent, for their own private good, to the constitution of a peaceful and moderate political community, where rights and privacy are respected. They recognize that peace or security can be established only on the reasonable basis of the practice of certain liberal virtues, including tolerance. And they know that peace is the fundamental condition for security in the possession of all private goods—including, perhaps above all, the sorts of happiness that are pursued by those individualists who, from time to time, dissent from the prevailing opinions in their own communities. So liberal individualists, who are somehow able to stand apart from community, are among the principal beneficiaries of the liberal peace that tolerance (among other virtues) makes possible: for they might be among the first casualties of civil war. Such liberals, who are no moral slaves to the community, can yet be made to recognize that there can be no security, even in private pursuits of happiness, unless every human being quits some part of the common natural freedom and assigns it to the community, thus submitting in some measure to its authority.[7]

Thus, the classical liberal philosophers imagined a new sort of human being, one who would unite in one soul the proud independence that makes possible moral freedom from authority, and a prudent regard for the "*Law of Reason*," which reveals that "*where there is no Law, there is no Freedom*," as Locke put it. Liberal theorists sought to educate pride and to confine independence, and so to cultivate such virtues as tolerance and civility (among other species of "self-mastery"), precisely in order to

[5]W. E. B. DuBois, *The Souls of Black Folk*, 81–82. Further, on this "higher individualism," "there must come a loftier respect for the sovereign human soul that seeks to know itself and the world about it; that seeks a freedom for expansion and self-development; that will love and hate and labor in its own way, untrammeled alike by old and new. Such souls aforetime have inspired and guided worlds" (81–82). See, too, 38–42, 61–67.

[6]Tarcov, *Locke's Education*, 77–211; see, too, Mill, *On Liberty*, 21.

[7]See Locke, *Second Treatise*, §§21, 87–89, 123–31 (esp. §87); cf. Hobbes, *Leviathan*, chs. 13–18.

secure a sphere within which individuals might be free to follow their private demons, unconstrained and indeed almost unnoticed by the liberal community. But they also sought to provide for the sustenance of an honorable "love of liberty," so that the liberal social contract would not be transformed into merely another partisan mystification—an instrument, say, of repressive tolerance. Without proud self-assertion we would soon be slaves; without moderate self-restraint we would hope to be masters.[8] So, the liberal policy of toleration is one strategy (among many) for accommodating as well as taming the natural pride of the free and rational individualist, who might otherwise seek to rule: it is not only, then, the apology of the wicked. By granting toleration, the liberal community honors such individuals; by asking no more than toleration, the liberal individualist respects the reasonable claims of the community.

But perhaps this liberal image of a proud but moderate citizen was always only a dream; at any rate, there is also a liberal nightmare. Beginning with Rousseau, even more or less friendly critics of liberal politics have wondered: what is the real effect on the souls of human beings of the practice of the liberal freedoms? Today, do liberal citizens commonly display the complementary virtues of independence and civility that liberal philosophy commends?[9] Perhaps it is now necessary to admit that our so-called freedom is nothing more than a taste for thoughtless or merely willful idiosyncrasy, and that our so-called moderation is simply an excuse for thoughtless or slavish conformism.

Here then is a "liberal" who must be despised, the corrupt cousin of the liberal one might pray for. Walzer offers a "glimpse of our liberated future," a future, we can now see, that will bring unprecedented toleration in all spheres of life (including, for example, "liberty and *laissez faire* in sexual life," such as "our recently won right to watch 'live sex acts' on stage"). Will we not then, he asks, confront a "bleak vision"? Recall Walzer's powerful portrait: "I imagine a human being thoroughly divorced, freed of parents, spouse, and children, watching pornographic performances in some dark theater, joining (it may be his only membership) this or that odd cult, which he will probably leave in a month or two for another still odder. Is this a liberated human being?" Such a "liberated" way of life, made possible by an indiscriminate policy of tolera-

---

[8]Locke, *Second Treatise*, §57 (emphasis in original); Tarcov, *Locke's Education*, 210–11; cf. Hobbes, *Leviathan*, ch. 15 (including on "pride").

[9]See Rousseau, *First Discourse*, 4–7, "Preface" to *Narcissus*, 96–111, and *Second Discourse*, 167–99, in *The First and Second Discourses*; and see Arthur Melzer, *The Natural Goodness of Man*, 49–85.

tion, is surely a "grim parody of Jefferson's pursuit of happiness."[10] Similarly, Fox-Genovese worries that liberals are no longer able "to distinguish between liberty and license," so that now "the liberty of the individual inexorably becomes license."[11] Such worries regarding the psychological and moral effects of liberation foster a growing suspicion that the admirable qualities of our imaginary liberal are somehow the residue of vanishing preliberal communities, against which our modern liberal imprudently rebels.

But the problem we confront today is not only that the choices we make about how to conduct our private lives are often contemptible. That is the ordinary price of freedom, and it may be that it is still a price worth paying. It is more troubling that our indiscriminate theory and practice of tolerance has made many liberals uneasy in principle about all attempts to distinguish between what is good and bad, honorable and dishonorable. Is it possible that tolerant ("wet") liberals today, as Rorty says, "have become so open-minded that our brains have fallen out," and that we are beginning "to lose any capacity for moral indignation, any capacity to feel contempt"?[12] On the prevailing view, tolerance is somehow justified by liberal openness or neutrality: intolerance is unreasonable because moral opinions are subjective, or (at least) must be admitted to be so for political purposes. Here is the source of many of our vices. Where the practice of indiscriminate tolerance that is authorized (or demanded) by liberal openness does *not* give rise to perverse idiosyncrasy or groundless "self-creation" (what troubles Walzer and amuses Rorty), it may often produce an uncritical conformism, as well as a "new breed of intolerance—a lazy, easygoing loutishness" associated with conformism, as Melzer puts it. Toleration understood as openness may become another excuse for thoughtless acceptance of one's own way of life, one of the many techniques now available to liberals who wish to evade self-criticism; for if all ways of life are worthy of equal respect in a liberal community, it follows that my way of life in particular merits the (un-

[10]Walzer, *Radical Principles*, 6, 8. It may be that Walzer was somewhat too confident that liberal toleration (what Walzer calls "moral and cultural *laissez faire*") would soon be more or less unlimited. Compare Walzer's discussion (in the text cited) of the religious use of the drug peyote with the recent Supreme Court decision on the same issue in *Employment Div'n, Dep't. of Human Resources v. Smith*, 494 U.S. 872 (1990). As for our right to watch live sex acts on stage, cf. *Barnes v. Glen Theatre, Inc.*, 501 U.S. 560 (1991).

[11]Fox-Genovese, *Feminism*, 111; cf. 87. On the other hand, Rorty and other postmodern liberals admire the capacity of liberal communities to accommodate (and even to celebrate) such diversity. See, generally, Rorty, *Contingency*, 3–43, 96–137.

[12]Rorty, *Objectivity*, 203.

earned) respect of my fellow liberals. Such openness may also give rise to
a thoughtless hostility to alien or eccentric ways of life and opinions; for
the now respectable habits of uncritical conformism will sooner or later
excuse indifference to whatever is not one's own, and so undermine the
"principled openness" that enables liberal citizens, as Melzer says, "to
stand up to the intolerance of others, and to the intolerance within themselves." In the absence of tolerably clear good reasons for self-disciplined
moderation and for the self-critical quest for autonomy, most human beings will pursue this easier course: they will choose uncritical self-expression rather than a self-critical quest for genuine autonomy; and they will
choose uncritical conformism (and easygoing intolerance of strangers)
rather than moderate loyalty to a reasonably civil political community.[13]

Beyond this, we may now be witnessing the emergence of a "new
strain of intolerance" (the rise of "cults"), an irrationalist and dogmatic
response to the "debilitating effects of diversity" itself, as Melzer says.
Liberal relativism may even become a "seminary of intolerance," argues
Leo Strauss, in spite of "its roots in the natural right tradition of tolerance." For the relativist must admit that intolerant ways of life possess
a value "equal in dignity" to tolerant ways of life. Some human beings
will be impressed by the superior quality of the "genuine choice" or
"deadly serious decision" of the intolerant, as compared to the frivolousness or indifference of liberals.[14] Nor is this response to today's
"widespread indifferentism" altogether discreditable: it is not hard to
despise (for example) the comfortable piety of certain liberals whose
"religious relativism . . . leads to the belief that 'one religion is as good
as another.' " Though such religiosity may be politically salutary, it too
often seems a petty and tiresome alternative to dogmatic orthodoxy or
dogmatic atheism.[15]

---

[13]Arthur Melzer, "Tolerance 101," 11; and see Orwin, "Welfare and the New Dignity";
Orwin, "Civility"; Allan Bloom, *The Closing of the American Mind*, 25–67, 157–240; and
Mansfield, *Spirit*, 16–27.

[14]Melzer, "Tolerance," 11; Strauss, *Natural Right and History*, 5–6.

[15]Pope John Paul II, from an encyclical issued in translation by the Vatican under the
title "The Church's Missionary Mandate," as quoted in *The New York Times*, 23 January
1991, A2. Eugene Genovese, in "Pilgrim's Progress," on liberal theology: "For if God is a
socially conscious political being whose views invariably correspond to our own prejudices on every essential point of doctrine, he demands of us no more than our politics require. Besides, if God is finite, progressive, and Pure Love, we may as well skip church
next Sunday and go to the movies. For if we have nothing to fear from this all-loving, all-
forbearing, all-forgiving God, how would our worship of him constitute more than self-
congratulation for our own moral standards? As an atheist, I like this God. It is good to
see him every morning while I am shaving."

Here, then, is the liberal nightmare: that the liberal way of life is too often marked not by the proud practice of freedom, but by grim dissipation, or careless self-satisfaction, or "loutish" conformism, or desperate self-expression, or dogmatic irrationalism.

II

Republicans are intolerant. It almost goes without saying that republican political communities depend on the virtue of patriotic citizens to a higher degree than do other forms of government.[16] But since such virtue and patriotism do not emerge naturally or spontaneously, partisans of republican politics have always argued that a more or less "repressive" moral and civic education, including censorship among other species of intolerance, would be required in order to bring into being a virtuous republican citizenry.

Prone as we are by nature to arrogance and envy, to license and dominion, to avarice and ambition and corruption and partiality, we must recognize that a civilized common life is possible for human beings only where our naturally lawless and warlike appetites are somehow controlled: government is required. And so, humane and public-spirited political philosophers, ancient and modern, have taught that where there is no law, there can be no freedom, no prosperity, no privacy, no virtue, no equality—but only poverty, civil war, tyranny. "For just as man is the best of the animals when completed, when separated from law and adjudication he is the worst of all," says Aristotle; "a Government without Laws is, I suppose, a Mystery in Politicks, unconceivable to humane Capacity, and inconsistent with humane Society," says Locke.[17] Liberty without law is invariably license; humanity demands that liberty be subordinated to law. Even the liberal political community is fundamentally an order constituted by law (a "Government").

Republican government differs from other species of humane government in this, above all: here, we must give to ourselves the laws that restrain our partisan and immoderate appetites. Republican politics therefore depends on the "virtue" that makes possible such self-mastery. The people in a (democratic) republic, according to Montesquieu, "are, in certain respects, the monarch; in other respects, they are the subjects." Indeed, this is the meaning and the problem of self-government: the

---

[16]See *Federalist #55.*

[17]Aristotle, *Politics*, 1253a30–35 (and see 1281a10–35, 1292a1–35, 1295a25–1296a20, 1302a20–1302b35); and Locke, *Second Treatise*, §219 (and see §§1, 8, 11, 13, 16, 19–20, 57, 87–88, 124–29, 172, 176, 199). See, too, Hobbes, *Leviathan*, ch. 13.

rulers and the ruled are the same human beings. In a republic, the people as a body must rule itself; the people as a body is not ruled by a sovereign or a prince, and so it is not restrained, when it must be restrained, by fear. Thus, as Montesquieu says, a republic differs from a monarchy or despotism: "the force of the laws in the one and the prince's ever-raised arm in the other can rule or contain the whole. But in a popular state there must be an additional spring, which is VIRTUE."[18]

What, then, is republican virtue? Virtue in a republic is "love of the laws and the homeland," says Montesquieu; it requires "a continuous preference of the public interest over one's own"; it is "a renunciation of oneself"; it is a "feeling," akin to the love of a monk for his order, which attaches the citizens to "the very rule that afflicts them" and "deprives them of everything upon which ordinary passions rest." Virtue is the disposition of the citizen to "love" the community, says Plato, which rests on a belief that "the same things are advantageous to it and to himself"; refusing to distinguish between "my own" and "not my own," the citizen instead holds that all things, indeed all pleasures and pains, belong to the citizens in common. Thus, as Rousseau argues, the legislator of a republic must somehow transform "each individual, who by himself is a perfect and solitary whole, into a part of a larger whole from which this individual receives, in a sense, his life and his being."[19]

Now republican virtue does not arise spontaneously in the souls of human beings. It must be forced into being by a political community that restrains the private interests and appetites of individuals, which are naturally so potent. Thus, Plato argues that the root of all injustice and vice in a republic is privacy, which divides citizens into families and parties or reduces them to solitary individuals: the citizens must possess "nothing private but the body," and even that privacy must somehow be tamed. Montesquieu too insists that privacy must be strictly limited in the republican community, where (for example) "private crimes are more public" than they are in other communities. (To be sure, Montesquieu is less ambitious than Plato in this respect.) Moreover, it is evident that "the full power of education" must be brought to bear in order to achieve virtue, "which is always a very painful thing"; otherwise, human beings will naturally incline toward a gentler way of life. Thus, among other hard-

---

[18]Montesquieu, *Spirit*, 2.2, 3.3; cf. Hobbes, *Leviathan*, chs. 14, 17; and Machiavelli, *The Prince*, chs. 9, 17. For a more thorough account of this problem of self-government, see below, Chapter 5, §I.

[19]Montesquieu, *Spirit*, 4.5, 5.2–3; Plato, *Republic*, 412c–e, 462a–465d; and Rousseau, *Social Contract*, 2.7.

ships, "there must be censors in a republic where the principle of government is virtue," in order to anticipate the emergence of those small "seeds of corruption" that will inevitably evade the laws. Finally, a love of equality and frugality will be necessary in a republic, for without these, citizens might soon be animated by envy or arrogance. Each citizen must enjoy "the same happiness and the same advantages"; and so it is necessary to establish by law an equality not only of wealth but also of talents—"middling talents" are to be encouraged and "superior talents" thwarted. It would surely not be surprising if, after all of this, some humane friend to liberty were to object (as Montesquieu does) that "even virtue has need of limits."[20]

Democrats are intolerant, too, for less honorable yet still respectable reasons. The principle of democratic politics is equality; and the love of equality is also a potent root of popular intolerance. Democrats err, says Aristotle, in supposing that "if they are equal in a certain thing, such as freedom, they are equal generally." The truth is, says Aristotle, that "justice is held to be equality, and it is, but for equals and not for all." As a result of this error, democrats tend to be intolerant of every species of inequality. Above all, democrats and their partisans are easily annoyed by economic inequality; thus, the fundamental problem of democratic politics is to manage the natural quarrel between the rich and the poor. Where an immoderate people rules, the democrats will often use "force" and "distribute among themselves the things of the wealthy," mostly with disastrous consequences for themselves.[21]

Any claim of inequality (or even eccentricity) is likely to be offensive, and so perhaps intolerable, to the democrat. Thus, democrats are often inclined to be hostile to the impious or freethinking, who openly disrespect the moral and religious orthodoxies of the community—as when the democratic city of Athens executed Socrates for not believing in the gods of his city, or perhaps for acting the impudent part of gadfly to the sleeping city. Even today, fundamentalist democrats and freethinking liberals often trade hatred for contempt. (Thus, "republicans" and "democrats" will frequently be united in hostility toward certain kinds of dissenters, but on different grounds.) Beyond this, as Aristotle says,

[20]Plato, *Republic*, 457c–465e (and see 376e–379a, 414d, 416c–417b); and Montesquieu, *Spirit*, 3.5, 4.5, 5.19, 5.3, 11.4 (and see 5.5–7, 7.2–12, 12.23). See also Strauss, "On the Intention of Rousseau"; and Orwin, "Civility," 554–55 ("the one thing that Athenians do *not* tolerate is immersion in private life").

[21]Aristotle, *Politics*, 1280a10–25, 1281a10–40 (and see 1295a25–1296a40, 1291b30–1292a35, 1304b20–1305a10); see, too, *Federalist* #10.

democrats are often hostile to preeminence and ambition altogether, because they fear that any form of inequality will sooner or later yield dangerous "political strength" for the enemies of equality: "democratically run cities enact ostracism for this sort of reason."[22] Or, what is more clever and moderate, democrats may seek to turn such preeminence to their own advantage, by offering sufferance only in exchange for flattery, or by channeling superior talents and ambition toward ways of life that serve the democratic community.[23] But democrats and their partisans are not willing to tolerate any mode of preeminence that permits a proud or extraordinary human being to remain wholly outside the democratic community, because such an individualist stands apart as a living reproach to the ways of life of orthodox or ordinary democratic citizens: scolds are tiresome. Whatever democrats cannot comprehend, they are likely to hate or despise. Even today, (ordinary) democrats from time to time manifest a certain impatience with (elitist) liberal speakers who denounce the vulgarity or stupefaction that marks (or so it is said) the ways of life and moral concerns of ordinary citizens. They sometimes rightly detect, in such speeches, an uncivil note of scorn, as in our recurring controversies concerning traditional family values, the place of religion in the schools and in our public life, flag-burning and the pledge of allegiance (the new patriotism), and federal funding of offensive art. It is certain that "democracy has a problem: it is good for the growth of the ordinary man, not so good for that of the extraordinary man."[24]

Intolerance is not, to be sure, a peculiarly democratic or republican phenomenon. The natural roots of intolerance are manifold, and its practice nearly ubiquitous: it is fun to rule. It is enough to recall the case of Rushdie, or the civil strife in nations emerging from Communist rule, or the periodic revival of nativism in American public life, to see that intolerance serves many causes: "so natural to mankind is intolerance in whatever they really care about," as Mill says.[25] But for us, I suppose, the greatest and most honorable of these natural temptations are republican virtue and democratic love of equality. And so, it is still necessary today for proud liberals to make peace with their republican and democratic fellow citizens. Their injustice and immoderation may have been tamed,

---

[22] Aristotle, *Politics*, 1284a5–35. Barber seems to approve: see Barber, *Strong Democracy*, 240; and esp. Barber, "Neither Leaders nor Followers," 124.

[23] See Mansfield, *Spirit*, 1–15; and Mansfield, *Taming the Prince*.

[24] Mansfield, "Dewey, All-Out Democrat"; and see Plato, *Republic*, 558b–565c.

[25] Mill, *On Liberty*, 12 (see, too, 17–19, 29–32).

but those many hidden motives for intolerance will surely endure, always at hand for partisan use in a moment of intemperance.

III

Liberals are tolerant. But what a profound transformation of human nature is required before the liberal polity can be established: for it is first of all necessary to crush those natural passions that give rise to the habitual intolerance of republicans and democrats, together with the other natural roots of intolerance. Only where these naturally warlike passions—love of equality, virtue, ambition—have somehow lost their grip on the souls of partisans and patriots and princes can sober and reasonable human beings (who have learned the "Law of Nature") begin to construct a peaceful and moderate political community, where rights and privacy are respected. For the "Studier of that Law" will be silenced, his pleas "thought impudence or madness," wherever "the Phancies and intricate Contrivances of Men" have instituted illiberal governments: "when Fashion hath once Established, what Folly or craft began, Custom makes it Sacred."[26] It is sometimes said, and it is true, that liberal politics builds on low but solid ground: what could be more natural than a politics that is based on the almost irresistible desire for comfortable preservation, and that is devoted to providing for the "security" of its citizens?[27] And yet, it seems that liberals must often undertake a kind of excavation, to strip away the ordinary (and perhaps "imaginary") moralisms and vanities that blind most human beings to their true natural desires. Drive out the love of justice (or virtue, or ambition) with a pitchfork: yet she still will hurry back.

Classical liberals suppose that human beings are by nature illiberal, and thus intolerant. Hobbes argues that "the Lawes of Nature (as *Justice, Equity, Modesty, Mercy,* . . .) of themselves, without the terrour of some Power, to cause them to be observed, are contrary to our naturall Passions, that carry us to Partiality, Pride, Revenge, and the like." Agreeing with Hobbes in part, the classical liberals hope to impose a "Law of Reason" on these naturally lawless and warlike passions, and so

---

[26]Locke, *First Treatise,* §58; *Second Treatise,* §12. Further: "Thus far can the busie mind of Man carry him to a Brutality below the level of Beasts, when he quits his reason. . . . He that will impartially survey the Nations of the World, . . . will have Reason to think, that the Woods and Forests, where the irrational untaught Inhabitants keep right by following Nature, are fitter to give us Rules, than Cities and Palaces, where those that call themselves Civil and Rational, go out of their way, by the Authority of Example" (*First Treatise,* §58).

[27]But cf. Aristotle, *Politics,* 1252b25–1253a30, 1280b30–1281a10; and see Machiavelli, *The Prince,* ch. 15.

to secure civil peace, but without needless recourse to "the terrour of some Power." In its way, this liberal project is almost as improbable as the republican hope that such passions can be governed by virtue: "Knowledge makes men gentle, and reason inclines toward humanity," says the liberal Montesquieu; but reason is also, unhappily, too often silent in the face of prejudice, intolerance, and even savagery.[28] And yet, here is the liberal idea: that enlightened self-interest can somehow do the work of republican virtue or Hobbesian fear, and thus cure the natural disease of lawless and immoderate passions. We may dispense with republican and other foundations of law and order, or of civil peace, says the liberal—but only so far as reasonable self-government or self-mastery is possible. This is the genius of liberal politics: it shows a reasonable way between the natural and discreditable intolerance of lawless partisans and the less natural but more honorable intolerance of republican communities. Thus, a liberal community is more civil and just than any partisan (e.g. democratic) community, but it is also more natural and humane than any republican community. Nevertheless, it is not surprising that this liberal moderation is (like every species of moderation) vulnerable from every side: "enlightened" liberals are at once too corrupt for the republicans, too elitist for the democrats, and too conventional for radical or postmodernist liberals.[29]

Human beings are not friends by nature: this is the fundamental teaching of classical liberalism. We are by nature selfish, querulous and untrustworthy competitors for scarce and insecure goods. So liberal politics is properly a politics of fearful accommodation among naturally selfish and acquisitive individuals. Mutual respect for privacy and rights, self-restraint of parties and sects, and a willingness to employ the force of the community against those villains who would take advantage of the general peace in order to commit particular crimes in safety, or who would destroy the general peace in the pursuit of partisan aims: these are, in sum, the fundamental moral habits required by a liberal politics.

Now this liberal moderation requires, above all, that citizens forgo public efforts to vindicate controversial (moral, religious, and ideological) opinions, since these spirited public debates might disturb the peace by arming demagogues and parties and sects. Classical liberals do not quarrel about piety, or even about happiness or virtue, at least not in

---

[28]Hobbes, *Leviathan*, ch. 17; Montesquieu, *Spirit*, 15.3 (see, too, Preface and 1.2–3, 4.6–8, 12.1–6, 15.4–12, 25.13). See, too, Locke, *Second Treatise*, §§4–21, 57, 87, 123, 135, 172, 176.

[29]Cf. Mansfield, *Spirit*, 16–27, 52–71.

public. Yet, as they may not pursue happiness (or establish justice, or serve God) through partisan or sectarian political activity in common with kindred spirits, liberals are encouraged to undertake such pursuits in private, in liberal "society"—at home, in churches, and in other private associations. It is prudent for a liberal community to tolerate such pursuits, however idiosyncratic and whatever their quality, so long as they remain altogether private. The liberal policy of toleration is a kind of safety valve; it assists those citizens who seek to calm their natural desire to vindicate private opinions about the good life by imposing a way of life on their "corrupt" neighbors.[30] Toleration enables natural enemies to live together in peace.

Imagine a liberal who is challenged by a nosy republican or democratic interloper to justify his or her private choices, with the community as the tribunal. Here is that liberal's proud but moderate speech: "Mind your own business." Now, what is the meaning of this speech? Such a liberal refuses to admit the right of the community or its meddling agents to interfere (by threatening public sanctions) with private pursuits of happiness. But this liberal speech is not merely an angry outburst, for it contains a second thought, a dignified but friendly peace offering: as I do not need your permission, says the liberal, so I do not ask your blessing. Moderation often requires liberals to rest content with toleration or "permission," and not to seek in addition "praise" or respect, for their private ways of life. Often enough, democrats and republicans are willing to abide liberal individualists in the community, so long as their heterodoxy remains obscure, and so unthreatening. But the liberal who seeks not only permission but also praise, or who asks to be treated with "equal concern and respect," sometimes overreaches. In seeking the "respect" of the community, the dissenter implicitly admits that private choices are indeed the "business" of the community; such an anxious liberal is not happy to be left alone, and is not willing to leave others alone. He does not "mind his own business." Once the right to equal concern and respect becomes a political entitlement, its vindication requires (no less than republican moralism or democratic prejudice) that the community undertake to teach each citizen, and especially the quiescent democrats and republicans, what to think: "sensitivity" is the new liberal cousin to republican "virtue." That is surely an imprudent as well as an

---

[30]And so, a liberal might say: "The public realm is beyond repair, but there is after all a private realm. It is a realm in which we can tend to the salvation of our souls; its existence makes corruption voluntary to an appreciable degree" (Werner J. Dannhauser, "Ancients, Moderns, and Canadians").

illiberal project, capable of waking the sleeping partisans and rousing them to anger. Even *Newsweek* and *Time* have recently noted certain comic instances of this threat to civility, in the theory and practice of "political correctness," which often trivializes the real achievements of the liberal policy of toleration, besides giving it the odor of republican moralism. Anyway, for this reason liberals must learn again to "distinguish between permission and praise," however "fragile" that distinction now seems to many theorists.[31]

IV

For many political theorists today—liberal and communitarian alike— the case for toleration rests upon a certain account of the "contingency of the self" and of the origins of self-esteem. Endorsing the arguments of "historicist, including Marxist, critics of 'liberal individualism,'" Rorty argues that "there is nothing to people except what has been socialized into them": "socialization," he claims, "goes all the way down, and who gets to do the socializing is often a matter of who manages to kill whom first." It follows that "there is no such thing as *inner* freedom": what human being can stand alone against a multitude if there is "nothing deep inside each of us, no common human nature, no built-in human solidarity, to use as a moral reference point" in a lonely quest for freedom from community?[32] Sandel, too, argues that the self is "radically situated" in constitutive communities, from which we acquire "loyalties and convictions whose moral force consists partly in the fact that living by them is inseparable from understanding ourselves as the particular persons we are—as members of this family or community or nation or people, as bearers of this history, as sons and daughters of that revolution, as citizens of this republic." He, too, concludes that we must abandon the foolish liberal hope for moral freedom: "To imagine a person incapable of constitutive attachments such as these is not to conceive an ideally free and rational agent, but to imagine a person wholly without character, without moral depth."[33]

Now, it is not my purpose here to dispute this communitarian account of the nature of the human self. Rather, I propose to consider applications of this doctrine to the problem of liberal toleration. According to Rorty and Sandel, the roots of self-esteem (as well as self-knowledge) are

[31]Sandel, "Morality and the Liberal Ideal," 15.
[32]Rorty, *Contingency*, 177, emphasis in original, and 185.
[33]Sandel, *Liberalism*, 179; and cf. Rorty, *Objectivity*, 200.

communal or social. There is no such thing as inner freedom: there is no reasonable ground of self-esteem beyond the community, as liberal rationalists once supposed; the old liberal idea of the rugged individualist is a myth. It is therefore a great error to distinguish between "permission" and "praise" in the practice of toleration, for this distinction implies that self-respect need not rest upon the respect of the community, or that there *is* such a thing as inner freedom. But, as we now know (according to Rorty and Sandel), that is wrong: communal praise is a basic human need. For this reason, the most impressive achievement of the liberal policy of toleration is that it has enabled us, as Rorty says, "to extend our sense of 'we' to people whom we have previously thought of as 'they' ": we have learned to praise more widely.[34] Thus, it is an error, or at least it is living in the past, to conceive of the liberal community as constituted by a politics of fearful accommodation among naturally lawless human beings who prudently submit themselves to the law of reason in order to preserve, as far as possible, natural freedom: that brand of individualism is too rugged. Rather, we should conceive of the liberal community as quite properly taking guidance from its "agents of love," who teach us to esteem ways of life that formerly seemed not only unfamiliar but even contemptible or hateful: an anxious need for love (not a prickly demand for freedom) is now the psychological root of tolerance.[35]

Sandel argues that liberals are no longer able to "distinguish between permission and praise" with a good conscience: above all, liberals are now "too often" relativists, he says, and relativists have no good reason to prefer tolerance to intolerance. Such liberals are sometimes tolerant, but only because they are now so lacking in spirit or judgment that nothing is able, any longer, to move them to anger or contempt; or, if liberal relativists somehow retain these moral passions, they may then become intolerant, because they no longer remember the reasons for their habitual self-restraint. Relativism, in any case, is surely not an adequate basis for liberal tolerance, which now (in the absence of good reasons) appears to be either petty indifference or foolish timidity. Sandel argues, moreover, that the more substantive ("minimalist" and "voluntarist") arguments for liberalism, and so for tolerance, are also defective. Any account of liberalism that "ties toleration to autonomy rights alone" will yield

[34]Rorty, *Contingency*, 192. See, too, Rawls, *Theory*, 440–46, 542–48 ("perhaps the most important primary good is that of self-respect," which Rawls identifies with self-esteem in the next sentence [440]); and Walzer, *Spheres*, 272–80.

[35]Rorty, *Objectivity*, 206–8. I further elaborate this argument in my "Postmodern Liberalism and the Politics of Liberal Education," forthcoming.

only a "thin and fragile toleration," he says. Thus classical liberal toleration, which grants permission but may withhold praise, is simply
"demeaning." Unless we abandon the empty language of rights ("permission") for the more potent language of the good ("praise"), we will
never achieve the "deeper respect" for diversity and dissent that would
make toleration valuable to the anxious human being who seeks a
"home" here, and not merely to be left alone. Tolerance is satisfying only
if it is accompanied by praise. For this reason, Sandel is obliged to affirm
the "naive" view that, for example, "the justice or injustice of laws
against abortion and homosexual sodomy may have something to do
with the morality or immorality of these practices"—for we cannot
praise what we must condemn (as immoral). He acknowledges that it
may be "reckless" to tie toleration to the praise of the community in this
way: if we must be prepared to praise what we permit, then we may soon
grow stingier with our permission. Nevertheless, Sandel insists that the
classical liberal alternative is not satisfactory, since liberal moral freedom
is imaginary (and so, permission alone will not yield self-esteem), and
since each citizen is somehow bound to recognize the moral authority of
the "constitutive" community (and so, the community may not even
grant permission to those moral strangers who are not yet thought of as
"we").[36] Permission without praise is not enough, or it is too much.

　　Rorty goes further. Liberal tolerance (or, rather, "solidarity," since
mere tolerance is too stingy) implies a loving acknowledgment of the private poetry, or unique dignity, of every human life. Since there is no
" 'objective truth' about what the human self is *really* like," according to
Rorty, the most admirable (or at least the most interesting) human beings
are those who "experiment," who seek "to invent a self rather than to
play out a role embedded in ordinary forms of life." In the end, says
Rorty, "we praise ourselves by weaving idiosyncratic narratives—case
histories, as it were—of our success in self-creation, our ability to break
free from an idiosyncratic past"; and "we condemn ourselves for failure
to break free of that past rather than for failure to live up to universal
standards." What is most admirable about the liberal community is that
it permits such individualists to "try out their private visions of perfection in peace." But such a community will be populated by many different sorts of "oddballs" (not only the usual suspects), for self-creation is
not constrained by any moral or prudential rules. Rorty even speaks of

---

[36]Sandel, "Morality," 15–17; and Sandel, "Moral Argument and Liberal Toleration:
Abortion and Homosexuality."

"the private poem[s] of the pervert, the sadist, or the lunatic: each as richly textured and 'redolent of moral memories' as our own life." As a result, the liberal community must somehow ensure that those "who have a taste for sublimity will have to pursue it in their own time, and within the limits set by *On Liberty*." But is Rorty's hope a reasonable one? What will thwart the ambition or cruelty of those whose "private poems" do not respect the ordinary folks who are the democratic or republican community? More precisely, in the absence of liberal reasons for self-restraint on the part of both creative individualists and ordinary citizens, how will it be possible to keep the peace between them? Anyway, it is hard to see why most human beings, both ordinary and creative, would not (in time) learn again to listen to their natural passions, which teach (as Hobbes says) "Partiality, Pride, Revenge, and the like," rather than to those "dreamers" who preach peace and love, but for no good reason.[37]

Classical liberal individualists, who are sometimes moral strangers even at home, do not abuse their welcome in tolerant liberal communities by using the occasion of that tolerance to needlessly offend their generous fellow citizens, who are typically more ordinary or conventional, and who are not individualists or moral strangers to the community. But is such self-restraint consistent with self-esteem? That liberal politics protects such moral strangers is one of its most splendid achievements; the generosity of more ordinary liberals, who tolerate moral strangers even though they do not understand or admire them, is one of the most agreeable liberal virtues. It is only a small act of gratitude, and one surely conducive to civility and peace, for the individualists in the liberal community to refrain from demanding more than tolerance (such as approval or praise) from their more conventional fellow citizens. They thus honor those ordinary citizens who leave them alone, by refusing to repay this respectable generosity with contempt.

Just as tolerance might seem to be cowardice or meekness to those who do not understand its reasons, so this reticence might seem to be hypocrisy or slavishness. But that is a confusion, against which liberals must guard, for the liberal's self-effacement is an expression of self-respect. Moral strangers in the liberal community are, so to speak, "rugged individualists," who do not need, and therefore do not seek, kudos from fellow cit-

---

[37]Rorty, *Objectivity*, 193–94, emphasis in original (and see 203–10); Rorty, "Posties"; Rorty, *Contingency*, 33, 38 (see, generally, 23–43, 73–95); Rorty, "The Philosophy of the Oddball"; and Hobbes, *Leviathan*, ch. 17.

izens. (They may seek praise in their private worlds, from friends and family.) Liberal individualists make a deal with their more ordinary fellow citizens, in the name of civility or peace: tolerance in exchange for discretion. Too often, today's partisans of freedom immoderately express not only the desire to be left alone, to choose and practice a private way of life, but also the desire to be esteemed in this choice by the community, and even to win this applause against the will, so to speak, of the fans. Thus, their demand for tolerance rests on their ability to persuade the community that their activity is estimable; but that is surely imprudent. There is here, then, hidden beneath the rhetoric of freedom and tolerance, an elitist demand that ordinary citizens recognize the higher "poetry" (in Rorty's language) of the ways of life of alienated individualists and other moral strangers to the community. But this is an elitism that cannot abide the solitude of rugged individualists—who are grateful to be left alone and so do not demand applause from those who are unwilling, and putatively unworthy, to give it.

V

Here then is a liberal strategy for managing the natural and ordinary tendency of human beings, including republicans and democrats, to be intolerant of dissenting ways of life. Following Montesquieu, the classical liberal recognizes that it will often be necessary to harmonize provocative liberal demands for rights and respect with hostile democratic and republican passions or prejudices.[38] The uproar concerning federal funding of offensive art is only the most recent example of the tumult that is sometimes caused by liberal overreaching. When liberal individualists (here, artists) forget that they "stand properly and necessarily in a certain opposition to the civil societies in which they live and work," they may be tempted to extend their just demand for permission until it becomes a provocative plea for praise (e.g. taxpayer support). Barber, a democratic theorist who is also an advocate for such liberals before the democratic community, argues that "the only inviolable obligation a democracy has is to leave its artists alone"; it has no further obligation "to underwrite rather than just to tolerate assaults on its conventions, its law, its institutions and its mores."[39] If, as I have argued, a moralizing impatience with oddballs, ironists, strong poets, eccentrics, and individualists (and others, including the wealthy and the intellectuals) is one of the natural popular

---

[38]Mansfield, *Spirit*, 1–15.
[39]Barber, "Letter from America"; see, too, Robert Hughes, "Art, Morals, and Politics."

vices, then the lovers of liberty who are also partisans of popular government are obliged to explain how it may be possible to tame popular passions and prejudices without abandoning popular politics.

What is more, a sober liberal might even be obliged to admit that angry democrats and republicans also offer good reasons, from time to time, for resisting liberal claims. Unlike the republican, the liberal knows, as Montesquieu says, that "even virtue has need of limits." But the republican knows, what the liberal sometimes forgets, that self-government (even "liberal" republicanism) presupposes "virtue" more than other forms of government do. Thus, those liberals who are also republicans must be prepared to answer their more wholehearted republican friends, who will from time to time be heard worrying that the toleration of this or that practice of liberal freedom undermines the civic or moral virtue that is required for self-government. So, too, democratic love of equality, which is sometimes at odds with the liberal practice of freedom, often reflects a public-spirited, and so respectable, concern that necessary habits of self-government may be threatened by obnoxious forms of inequality.[40]

Today's friends of liberty, on the contrary, are too often reduced to sneering at popular ignorance and prejudice. These liberals thus altogether fail to respect either the sometimes honorable motives for popular intolerance or the often formidable power of that intolerance. What is required, it seems to me, is a strategy for teaching democrats and republicans the value of tolerance, and liberals the value of moderation. But when liberals speak to republicans today, their tone is frequently sermonizing and patronizing, as may be appropriate when speaking to "Yahoos." Perhaps this is just; surely it is imprudent. And when republicans speak to liberals today, their tone is frequently uncomprehending and angry, as may be appropriate when speaking to "perverts."[41] Such failures of respect and communication in today's quarrels between liberals and republicans (as well as in quarrels between liberals and democrats) are at the root of our so-called "culture wars." I propose to conclude, then, with some remarks about how it might be possible today to reconstruct a respectful conversation among these partisans.

---

[40]Montesquieu, *Spirit*, 11.4; *Federalist #55*; Glendon, *Rights Talk*, 109–44.

[41]Speaking of the unimpressive opinions in a recent (1986) case concerning the privacy rights of homosexuals, Glendon writes: "It is only a slight exaggeration to say that the two main opinions in *Bowers v. Hardwick* make the case look like a battle between Yahoos and perverts" (*Rights Talk*, 154). Indeed, as I argue in the text, it seems to me that this would be an accurate description, today, of almost every controversy between our liberals and our republicans and democrats.

Liberal republicanism is founded on the idea that a politics dedicated to securing individual rights can be established without destroying the virtues and other habits of good citizenship that make self-government possible. Since virtue (or the good life) can no longer be a direct object of public concern in the liberal community, it is necessary to ensure that there will be respectable private arenas for thinking and talking about civic and moral virtue, as well as for the practice of virtue. Even as we speak the liberal language of rights in our public life, we must not fail to speak the democratic and republican language of the good in our private lives.[42] And we must of course remember that it is usually necessary to reserve such speeches for our homes and churches and other private associations. For this reason, among so many others, the liberal political community thrives only where there is a robust "civil society"; elsewhere, such a recourse to a private moral world will not be satisfying to many democrats and republicans. This combination of public tolerance, which is always at risk of becoming private frivolousness, and private strength of conviction, which is always at risk of becoming public intolerance, is a hard one: it is an instance of the liberal dream of a human being who would be neither slave nor master.

Liberty, says the classical liberal Montesquieu, "consists in security or in one's opinion of one's security." That security is threatened "principally" by criminal prosecution: "the citizen's liberty depends principally on the goodness of the criminal laws"; indeed, "knowledge . . . concerning the surest rules one can observe in criminal judgments, is of more concern to mankind than anything else in the world." For Montesquieu, then, the most important discovery of the new liberal "science of politics," which Hamilton praises for showing how republican government can be made moderate, is not separation of powers, or representation, or checks and balances, or even the independent judiciary, although each of these impressive innovations was devised or improved by Montesquieu; rather, the most important new "knowledge" concerns the nature of good criminal laws. Above all, the criminal laws must not be arbitrary; and they must be moderate.[43]

In a series of remarkable chapters, Montesquieu offers a humane account of the fitting "proportion" or "moderation" of criminal laws in a liberal community. Here is the fundamental principle of a liberal regime of criminal law: "It is the triumph of liberty when criminal laws

---

[42]Glendon, *Rights Talk*, 1–17, 40–46, 98–144.
[43]Montesquieu, *Spirit*, 12.1–2.

draw each penalty from the particular nature of the crime." Thus, the punishment for crimes against religion directly, such as simple sacrilege, "should consist in the deprivation of all the advantages given by religion," including "deprivation of the society of the faithful for a time or forever," and even "execration." Where the harm is to God only, and not to civil "tranquility or security," there is "no criminal matter": "it is all between the man and god who knows the measure and the time of his vengeance." Unlike the republican, the liberal will not "arm" the zealous by permitting them to make use of the criminal laws to vindicate the cause of virtue or piety. Similarly, the punishment for crimes against mores, and especially sexual mores, properly consists only in "deprivation of the advantages that society has attached to the purity of mores," including "public infamy." Here, too, Montesquieu, unlike the republican, refuses to place the arms of the criminal law into the hands of those puritans whose zeal might become a threat to the liberty or security of citizens. So, too, "thoughts" and "indiscreet speech" and even "writing" are not criminal acts, under a liberal regime of criminal law, unless the speech somehow accompanies or incites a criminal act— that is, only if it threatens civil peace or the security of citizens, and not if it merely flouts conventional opinions about religion or (sexual) mores.[44]

In the spirit of Montesquieu, the liberal holds that criminal punishments are not fitting sanctions for thoughts, speeches, writings, or even ways of life that do not immediately threaten civil peace or tranquillity. And yet, Montesquieu respects the liberal distinction between permission and praise: he does not disapprove of the various "natural" social sanctions ("execration," "public infamy") for the lesser "crimes." Here, Montesquieu differs from later liberals, such as Mill, who is troubled as much by the "social stigma" attached to "eccentricity" or "individuality" as by criminal sanctions for wayward opinions or ways of life, and who seeks a political cure for this kind of social intolerance. In this, Mill's concern is misplaced, it seems to me, above all (but not only) because he fails to recognize that it is necessary to accommodate the republican and democratic enemies of liberal individualists. Social ostracism and similar penalties are indeed pernicious, and liberals should seek private ("natural") remedies of their own for this disease; but to impose a public remedy for the unhealthy opinions of democrats and republicans,

---

[44]Montesquieu, *Spirit*, 12.4–13 (esp. 12.4–6); on the republican view of criminal law, see 7.1–3, 8–12.

however foolish or wicked those opinions might be, is itself an intolerable excess of zeal. "Social tyranny" can be cured only by social means.[45]

Consider a recent extension of this sort of Millian argument. Dworkin argues that the liberal community properly rests on a certain interpretation of equality—and not, therefore, on unqualified moral neutrality or moral skepticism. Liberal politics does, however, require political neutrality regarding "the good life"; liberal neutrality, then, extends to every substantive moral opinion except a certain interpretation of equality. Liberals are committed to the view that each of us is "entitled" to be treated with "equal concern and respect" by the government. In order to treat people as equals in this sense, the community may "impose no sacrifice or constraint on any citizen in virtue of an argument that the citizen could not accept without abandoning his sense of his equal worth." Thus, a liberal community must weigh "all preferences on an equal basis on the same scales"; and so, "the majority's moralistic preferences about how the minority should live" must be excluded from political deliberation as incompatible with equal respect.[46]

Dworkin argues that the principle of equal respect requires liberals to oppose political "moralism," for the following reason: "No self-respecting person who believes that a particular way to live is most valuable for him can accept that this way of life is base or degrading. No self-respecting atheist can agree that a community in which religion is mandatory is for that reason finer, and no one who is homosexual that the eradication of homosexuality makes the community purer." Now, if we strip this statement of its rhetorical excess, it is clearly false. It is not at all hard to imagine a self-respecting atheist or homosexual who believes not only that his or her way of life is an honorable one but also that a "fine" community may choose to forbid that way of life, because it is easy to imagine an admirable community within which the good of the individual is in some measure at odds with the good of the community. Such a community would obviously not be a liberal community.[47] And yet, it is still

[45]Mill, *On Liberty*, 8–11, 36–38, 73–75, 83–103; and cf. Mansfield, *Spirit*, 104–14.

[46]Dworkin, *A Matter of Principle*, 190–91, 205–6, 364–72.

[47]Dworkin, *A Matter of Principle*, 206; see Plato, *Republic*, 402d–403c. As for the atheist, consider the following excerpt from a splendid letter of Edmund Burke: "I do not know whether the dissenters will hereafter think me their wellwisher: But whether they think it or not, I am so. I am naturally inclined to those who do not command. My opinion is, that they will always be found very *weak* when they put their Cause upon a *Trial of Strength*; and that, to carry their point, they must change their whole plan. That they must cease to *alarm* the Church establishment; which many people believe (and I among the rest) to be connected, in its safety or danger, with many *other* establishments which form parts of our con-

easier to imagine a self-respecting atheist or homosexual who believes not only that his or her way of life is an honorable one but also that a "fine" and "liberal" community can offer no more than grudging tolerance and not equal concern and respect—especially in light of the compensating pleasures of vanity often available to individualists. I do not say that any liberal democracy must behave in this balky manner; still, such a community is imaginable, and it is consistent with self-respect though not a right of equal respect.[48]

The authentic or original liberal reason for a policy of toleration that permits the community to withhold its collective "respect" is that the liberty of dissenters or nonconformists is naturally vulnerable to challenges from orthodox (democratic or republican) citizens, so that it is only (and not even always) possible to wring from the conventional a concession that there are good reasons to tolerate those they despise. In some cases, these ordinary citizens simply cannot be brought to believe that the ways of life they despise may for some (perhaps good) reason be valuable or respectable in themselves, and that they therefore merit more than permission but also praise.

But perhaps there is another reason for this policy of grudging toleration. It may be that liberals have underestimated the necessity of certain kinds of limits to what can be held respectable in a healthy liberal community. It may be, in other words, that liberals are now obliged to admit that certain ways of life and moral opinions that are in themselves unobjectionable or even admirable are more corrosive, politically and morally, than was once thought; it would follow that what may be privately tolerable and even admirable cannot be wholeheartedly praised by the community. Thus, for example, it is possible that even a liberal community might from time to time profit from the prevalence of religious belief. And this may be so even if there is no true religion. To say that the liberal community must tolerate every sort of religion (and even irreligion) is not to say that each of these opinions is equally respectable, or that the liberal community should never be permitted to choose sides in contests

---

stitution. They will consider the Church, as a *jealous* friend to be *reconciled*, and not as an *adversary* that must be *vanquished*." Burke, letter to John Noble, 14 March 1790, in *Selected Letters of Edmund Burke*, 158; and see, generally, 128–59.

[48]See, too, Charles Taylor, *Multiculturalism and "The Politics of Recognition."* Consider Taylor's account of the "Politics of Recognition": on one hand, "our moral salvation comes from recovering authentic moral contact with ourselves" (29); on the other hand, "due recognition is not just a courtesy we owe people. It is a vital human need," so that a failure to "recognize" or esteem alien private choices "can inflict harm, can be a form of oppression" (25–26). See, generally, Taylor, *Multiculturalism*, 25–44.

among religions or between religion and irreligion. A law that forbids certain religious opinions or practices would surely be illiberal; but a law that expresses public support for religious institutions, or that confers benefits on those who practice religion, might be defensible on the view that I am advancing—as an expression of the collective judgment of a certain people, and without thereby offending the self-respect of liberals. Similarly, the law at issue in *Bowers v. Hardwick* is surely illiberal; but it does not follow that every failure of respect on the part of the community would be illiberal, even if these failures were to find their way into some of the laws of the community. A thoughtful consideration of this issue requires reflection not only about the respectable private qualities of homosexual ways of life, but also about the political and social effects of open moral indifference toward such choices.[49]

There are doubtless occasions when concessions to perverse and obstinate partisan enmity would pose a greater threat to peace and security than would a resolute defense of liberal rights and even respectability, since tyranny or oppression sometimes pose a greater threat, even to security, than does civil strife. But these occasions are perhaps more rare than many liberals today seem to think: not every concession to intolerance, even unjust or nasty intolerance, puts the liberal community on a slippery slope to tyranny. Of course, neither does every angry partisan dispute give rise to civil tumult; but I am inclined to think that liberals are now too quick to raise the specter of tyranny, and often forget that partisan enmity and civil strife may also undermine limited government and ultimately threaten privacy and rights. Thus, liberals must cultivate a reasonable disposition to restrain their anger in such cases, together with a prudent sense of when to display that anger. Such liberals love peace before they love justice, even (or especially) when they are judges in their own cases. Prudent liberals know that it is reasonable and necessary to cultivate a habitual insensitivity to moral slights and even injustices.

This is the beginning of the argument, not the end; but contemporary formulations of the liberal argument often foreclose debate about these kinds of accommodations between the needs of the community and the claims of liberal individualists. I do not say, again, that liberal concessions to democratic prejudice or republican moralism are always required by liberal prudence. Whether, in any particular case, the liberals

---

[49]See Glendon's thoughtful and balanced discussion of the decisions in *Bowers v. Hardwick* in her admirable recent book, *Rights Talk*.

should prevail can be revealed only by an inquiry, which I have not here undertaken, into the quality of the public goods and the strength of the prejudices that are threatened by this or that liberal claim. Moreover, the form and substance of these settlements will vary from time to time and from place to place: there is no escaping the need for prudent statesmen and citizens. What is certain, it seems to me, is that every party in our liberal community would now profit from the renewal of respectful conversations about such issues. The liberal who denies this may be too optimistic in two respects: first, that habits of tolerance will endure in the face of popular distaste for liberal ways of life; and second, that indiscriminate toleration is compatible with a decent politics.

VI

Liberals, democrats, and republicans have long lived together in uneasy harmony in our community. That is an impressive achievement, considering that the natural hostilities that divide the parties of liberty, equality, and virtue are so deep and abiding, and have so often inspired civil tumults and even tyrannies. We live in an uncommonly civil polity that accommodates and even honors many of its liberal individualists (with academic freedom, artistic freedom, economic freedom, religious freedom); and yet, it also respects the arguments and prejudices of democrats and republicans, who may worry that the practice of tolerance merely excuses inequality and vice, with unhappy consequences for the community as a whole. That settlement is today under fire, from every party: liberals today are sometimes troubled by the stingy limits of our collective tolerance and respect; republicans are worried that excessive tolerance gives rise to corruption or vice both in our public life and in our private lives; democrats are troubled that tolerance is a fraud that enables elites to rule unnoticed. Each party must be reminded of the good reasons for the original settlement: that peace and security, which is the fundamental condition of any civil politics, is permanently threatened by the naturally immoderate passions of human beings.

So republicans and democrats must be made to admit that the security of individuals, to which they are not naturally committed, serves the real needs of the community, even the democratic or republican community: what good is virtue or equality, if life and liberty are insecure? And liberals must be reminded that obnoxious forms of inequality may be intolerable in a democratic community, and that certain sorts of heterodoxy or nonconformity may always be disreputable in a republican community, for reasons that are sometimes honorable and sometimes not. Anyway, the liberal settlement does provide homes for ambition and private virtue (as well as mere eccentricity) in a democratic republic that is not naturally hospitable to such uncommon ways of life, and that is a notable achievement.

4

Rorty's
Postmodern Liberalism

Richard Rorty is one of the principal architects of a new way of thinking about liberalism. He calls his way "liberal ironism": this is a postmodern liberalism, lacking Enlightenment rationalism, lacking the hopeless and finally enervating aspiration to discover an ahistorical philosophical foundation ("natural rights") for liberal principles and practices. The postmodern liberal ironist, unlike the classical liberal rationalist, "faces up to the contingency of his or her own most central beliefs and desires," says Rorty, including the characteristic liberal belief that "cruelty is the worst thing we do." Such postmodern liberals frankly admit the apparently unhappy consequence of that essential "contingency," that "there is no *neutral*, noncircular way to defend" liberal ways, no good argument (but none is needed) to deploy against "Nazi and Marxist enemies of liberalism."[1]

Postmodern liberalism is no strategic retreat, according to Rorty; this is not the embattled liberal grudgingly conceding that Enlightenment rationalism has by now been so thoroughly discredited that friends of liberalism must seek a more up-to-date, philosophically modest, way of defending liberalism. Rather, says Rorty, we now see that "the vocabulary of Enlightenment rationalism, although it was essential to the beginnings of liberal democracy, has become an impediment to the preservation and progress of democratic societies." We have progressed beyond the need for Enlightenment rationalism, which was so useful when the enemies of freedom, priests and others, spoke a language of more-than-rational authority. For now the enemies of freedom have ap-

[1]Rorty, *Contingency*, xv, 53, 197.

propriated the formerly liberating language of reason and nature, Rorty argues, crushing the poetry in our souls, those self-creative impulses that enable human beings to liberate themselves from inherited, tired, used ways of life. So a new vocabulary, the vocabulary of liberal ironism that "revolves around notions of metaphor and self-creation rather than around notions of truth, rationality, and moral obligation," is more suited to today's progressive liberalism than is the inherited language of inalienable rights, self-evident truths, and the rest. And a new "conception of the self," which makes " 'community constitutive of the individual' " and yet at the same time honors idiosyncratic self-creation more than knowledge of our common humanity, "in fact comport[s] better with liberal democracy than does the Enlightenment conception of the self" as having "an intrinsic nature" that justifies certain moral understandings. So postmodern liberal ironism is even a strategic advance over classical liberal rationalism, says Rorty: the liberal ironist describes prevailing liberal principles and practices more faithfully than the liberal rationalist; and he is as well more confident in defense of liberal ways, because less troubled by the skepticism that is always the flip side of the rationalist coin.[2]

To be sure, Rorty's strategy does not permit a defense of the old, robust liberalism of natural rights. We now know that our attachment to liberal democracy is a historically contingent faith, one among many such fighting faiths, and that liberal political principles are in no sense in "the common interest of humanity." We are, says Rorty, "postmodern bourgeois liberals," products of the "institutions and practices of the rich North Atlantic democracies," tolerably comfortable (both physically and morally) with our way of life but lacking the cultural arrogance of our ancestors: we are ethnocentric, but we do not insist on the superiority of our ways. After all, what is wrong, asks Rorty, with "the attempt to fulfill the hopes of the North Atlantic bourgeoisie"? If we must indeed abandon the naive hope of those starry-eyed early liberals, to vindicate by our example the *rights of man*, of human beings qua human beings, so what? Will *we* not still live comfortably as liberals, and even be able to defend our liberal way of life with, as Rorty says, "unflinching courage"?[3]

In this chapter, I discuss Rorty's postmodern liberalism, in particular with a view to the question whether this new species of liberalism can

[2]Rorty, *Contingency*, 44, 35; and Rorty, *Objectivity*, 178.
[3]Rorty, *Objectivity*, 198; and Rorty, *Contingency*, 47 and context.

sustain the practice of the humane liberal virtues.[4] Here is the problem: if a human being can be attached to the liberal community only in an ethnocentric or contingent spirit, why should he or she not choose to embrace a more exhilarating commitment than the commitment to humane liberal virtues? Liberals all somehow agree that peace is good, that liberty is good. But there remains a question: how do decent and honorable folks persuade the many fools and the few fanatics who do not yet see that liberal principles and practices are (self-evidently) good? The classical liberal recognizes the necessity of *transforming* human beings, who are naturally warlike, into peaceful liberals. Thus, the core of liberal political psychology is the need to tame the fanatics, the ideologues, the ambitious, the "committed," in order to enable the people to follow their (hidden) natural inclination toward moderation, no longer blinded by the "Folly or craft" of demagogues and priests. But the liberal taming can be achieved only where human beings, both ambitious and moderate, are taught a certain account of human nature or the good: that all choiceworthy ways of life depend upon conditions of civil peace or felt security. If liberals abandon this account of the good, do they not also abandon the strongest psychological motive for choosing liberalism over a more exciting politics that seeks to satisfy more extreme passions? In emancipating and even praising idiosyncratic commitment and self-creation, Rorty seems to risk a nasty, illiberal rebellion (" 'Thus I willed it' ") against gentle liberal virtues.[5] Can one really put these self-creative impulses in the service of the humane liberal virtues? In the absence of a reasonable argument for moderation, and especially if there are forms of political fundamentalism that are more fun than liberalism, will not most human beings choose a more pleasing immoderation than extremism in defense of liberty?

I

Rorty describes himself as a new kind of liberal—a "postmodernist bourgeois liberal," or perhaps a "pragmatist" or "ironist" liberal.[6] In any case, Rorty clearly understands himself to be a friend of liberalism.

---

[4]I discuss Rorty's moral psychology, or the account of privacy that is the companion to his account of liberty community, in my "Privacy and Community," forthcoming; and see my "Postmodern Liberalism and the Politics of Liberal Education."

[5]Rorty, *Contingency*, 29; and see 35–38, 83–85, 96–121 (esp. 99, 111).

[6]On "postmodernist bourgeois liberalism," see Rorty, *Objectivity*, 198–99; Rorty, "Thugs and Theorists: A Reply to Bernstein"; Rorty, *Contingency*, 63–65; and Rorty, *Essays on Heidegger and Others*, 175–76. See, too, on "liberal ironists," Rorty, *Contingency*, 73–95.

Moreover, he sometimes opposes himself to certain contemporary partisans of community: those who repudiate liberal pluralism in the name of "an old-timey *Gemeinschaft*," or who despise the frivolous sorts of human beings (the "last men") that liberal culture is said to engender, or who argue that liberal principles of justice presuppose an incoherent philosophical account of human nature or the self. Rorty appears to be a liberal critic, then, of the communitarians.[7]

Thus, Rorty is an admirer of those liberal "connoisseurs of diversity" who teach the rest of us to enlarge our "capacity for sympathy and tolerance" of other ways of life; and yet, he also admires the liberal "moral narcissist," whose private self-absorption is made possible by liberal institutions and principles of justice. In defense of these disparate moral dispositions, Rorty criticizes MacIntyre's wistful longing for community "in the strong approbative sense of 'community' used by critics of liberalism"; such a community would foster an intolerable (and intolerant) homogeneity of opinion about "who counts as a decent human being and who does not." The homogeneity of MacIntyre's community of virtue is at odds with both the insular moral narcissism of creative human beings and the ecumenical love of diversity of more ordinary spectators. Liberal pluralism, in contrast, protects privacy and idiosyncrasy, and thereby sustains an admirable variety of distinctive ways of life. A truly liberal community nurtures idiosyncrasy, and then teaches the rest of us to enjoy the spectacle. And so, Rorty defends the "Western liberal ideal of procedural justice" against those who seek the kind of "fraternity" that depends upon the cultivation of some common substantive ideal of a good and moral way of life. He even imagines a liberal utopia, a fit home for both connoisseurs of diversity and moral narcissists: our "agents of justice" would protect each of us equally, according to (Rawlsian) principles of procedural justice that respect our privacy and so permit us to attend to our idiosyncratic pursuits. But we would also be taught by our "agents of love" (the "anthropologists," above all) to see formerly "invisible" or despised persons ("drunken Indians") as very much like the rest of us, and so admirable. Soon, we would learn to open "the doors of procedural justice to people on whom they had been closed." The liberal politics that Rorty admires is a politics of "solidarity": we liberals should "try to extend our sense of 'we' to people whom we have previously thought of as 'they.' "[8]

---

[7]Rorty, *Objectivity*, 209; and Rorty, *Essays*, 158–63.
[8]Rorty, *Contingency*, 192; Rorty, *Objectivity*, 203–10.

But perhaps it would be better to say that this is a liberal nightmare. Rorty's so-called liberal utopia would merely harmonize two ordinary corruptions, not virtues, of the liberal moral personality: our narcissistic obsession with trivial private miseries and pleasures; and our thoughtless inability to feel contempt for what is contemptible—since we have, as Rorty puts it, "become so open-minded that our brains have fallen out." Rorty's connoisseurs of diversity admire diversity as such: not merely the flowers but also the weeds. More precisely, his liberal utopia emancipates not only creative "genius," but also "obsession," "eccentricity," and even "perversity"; there is no distinguishing between genius and perversity. Rorty aims to "democratize" the idea of genius: the liberal political community is in the best case a world of poets and connoisseurs of poetry, so to speak, and the tolerant liberal ironist sees "every human life as a poem," and is even somehow charmed by the "private poem[s] of the pervert, the sadist, [and] the lunatic."[9]

And so, Rorty is sometimes compelled to defend certain apparently "petty" and "unheroic" human types that typically thrive in liberal communities—here, too, against MacIntyre. He argues, first, that "the prevalence of such people may be a reasonable price to pay for political freedom." More precisely, it is a reasonable price for us, since our liberal community happens to prefer freedom to heroism: there is no better reason to prefer freedom to heroism, says Rorty. In one place he even urges liberals, perhaps somewhat playfully, to confess that "democratic societies have no higher aim than what [Nietzsche] called 'the last men' "; democratic liberals do not seek "anything less banal than evening out people's chances of getting a little pleasure out of their lives." Rorty is aware, to be sure, that some human beings get "a little pleasure" from activities that are far from banal: "sexual perversion, extreme cruelty, ludicrous obsession, and manic delusion," for example. But even in such cases, Rorty appears to think that liberal communities should sanction as many of these idiosyncratic private pleasures as possible, compatible with procedural justice or freedom. At the same time, if all of this seems a bit too bleak, he sometimes suggests that we can still hope (at least) that something fine will come of letting people "try out their private visions of perfection in peace": perhaps it is not necessary after all to renounce our (private) notions of perfection in the name of liberal freedom. But what is the difference between a "private vision of perfection" and a "ludicrous obsession," for Rorty?[10]

[9]See Rorty, *Objectivity*, 203–10; and Rorty, *Contingency*, 23–43, esp. 35–38; and cf. Rorty, *Consequences of Pragmatism*, 203.

[10]Rorty, "Posties," 12; Rorty, *Contingency*, 38; see, generally, 3–43, 73–121; and Rorty, *Objectivity*, 194.

However that may be, liberals certainly should *not* respond to the charge that liberal ways of life are petty by arguing that "human beings *ought* to be ['tolerant'] liberals rather than ['crazy'] fanatics," says Rorty, since that would require us to claim that we know who counts as a decent human being and who does not—which we cannot know. Rorty's admiration for liberal diversity and his taste for liberal freedom is not the moral consequence of a philosophical "theory of human nature" that reveals how we ought to be, or how any community ought to be; that is, Rorty's defense of liberalism does not require him to deny that human beings are "historical all the way through," or that morality is in every case, including the liberal case, the creation of particular communities. Instead, his defense of liberal politics recognizes the priority of community to philosophy.[11]

And so, finally, Rorty also rejects Sandel's argument that liberal politics is defective because it must be based on a defective philosophical theory of human nature or the self—Sandel calls it the "unencumbered self." Although liberalism "may need philosophical articulation, it does not need philosophical backup," says Rorty; indeed, liberal democratic philosophers defend democratic politics best by "putting politics first and tailoring a philosophy to suit." This is presumably true as well for philosophical partisans of illiberal or antidemocratic politics: philosophers, too, are above all partisans. In addition, it happens that "a conception of the self that makes the community constitutive of the self does comport well with liberal democracy," says Rorty; and so liberal politics need not only do without the defective Kantian portrait of the self that Sandel properly rejects, it can even make use of Sandel's own communitarian account of the ("radically situated") self, if one insists that the search for philosophical justifications of liberal politics is still necessary or desirable.[12]

Rorty sometimes appears to be a liberal opponent of the new champions of the idea of community, who are mostly critics of liberalism: he is a partisan of the liberal Rawls, for example, against the communitarian Sandel. And so it is necessary, at the outset, to explain my intention to speak of Rorty as a kind of communitarian, in order to overcome the presumption that Rorty is an opponent, rather than an ally, of these theorists. This presumption is quite misleading, it seems to me, partly because

---

[11]Rorty, *Objectivity*, 175–78, 189–91 (emphasis added), 194–96; see, too, Rorty, *Essays*, 158–63.

[12]Rorty, *Objectivity*, 178–79, 189–92; see, too, Rorty, *Contingency*, 44–69.

Rorty defends a communitarian Rawls, so to speak, against the communitarian Sandel, but not only for that reason. Thus, Rorty argues that Rawls's theory of justice is "thoroughly historicist and antiuniversalist"; Rawls does not offer "a philosophical account of the human self," as Sandel supposes, so much as "a historico-sociological description of the way we live now."[13] Rorty himself, like Rawls, defends liberalism through appeals to what "we believe," rather than to what nature or God reveals. Certainly, Rorty is not an orthodox liberal; he seeks to redescribe liberalism so that it can be made to accommodate the communitarian insights of Hegel and Dewey. That is, he seeks to save liberal politics and culture from Enlightenment rationalism and liberal individualism.[14] Even Rorty's criticisms of the communitarians in defense of liberalism often reveal his own attachment to *our* community and to the *idea* of community, as I suggest above. I will argue, then, that Rorty is a "communitarian liberal," more or less: a communitarian in philosophy, and a new kind of liberal in politics.

Again and again, Rorty urges us to "identify with our own community," at least in our thoughts, and especially when we speculate or worry about what gives moral meaning and dignity to our lives. In this respect, if in no other, he is a communitarian theorist. In "Pragmatism, Relativism, and Irrationalism," for example, Rorty contrasts the pragmatist's acceptance of the necessarily contingent starting points of all thought with the Platonic (as well as Christian, and Kantian) effort to "evade" this contingency by discovering a starting point that is beyond contingency, in nature (or God, or Reason). For Rorty, thought properly begins with the recognition that "our inheritance from, and our conversation with, our fellow-humans [is] our only source of guidance": we begin where we are, as participants in a continuing dialogue among members of a particular historical community. He denounces the "hope" that possesses the Platonic philosopher and others, who seek to step outside this conversation and gain access to "the ahistorical and nonhuman nature of reality itself." The philosopher is not animated by an irresistible urge to know, or constrained above all by the necessity to follow the argument, as is generally supposed; on the contrary, he is in fact propelled by a need for a certain "metaphysical comfort," to believe

[13]Rorty, *Objectivity*, 180–81, 185–89. For a more measured analysis of Rawls's recent move toward a more communitarian understanding of the nature of moral philosophy as historically contingent, see Galston, "Moral Personality and Liberal Theory: John Rawls's 'Dewey Lectures.'"

[14]Rorty, *Contingency*, 44, 177.

that the world has a certain intelligible order, or to "find something ahistorical and necessary to cling to." But for Rorty, recognition of the authority of community is not only a philosophical necessity that thoughtful human beings must "accept"; identification with one's community is also a moral good that decent citizens come to cherish. We should "cling" to community, then, for both theoretical and moral reasons. And so, he praises the pragmatist's acceptance of contingency on the grounds that it makes possible a "renewed sense of community" and even an "identification with our community"; this identification can emerge when we see our community as "*ours* rather than *nature's*, *shaped* rather than *found*," and it is much stronger than the more modest identification with one's community that is possible for the philosopher and others who elevate objectivity over solidarity. That is, Rorty seeks to replace the philosophic quest for a metaphysical comfort (that the world should be intelligible) with a pragmatic quest for a certain moral comfort (that we should have a home here): "In the end, the pragmatists tell us, what matters is our loyalty to other human beings clinging together against the dark, not our hope of getting things right." The issue between pragmatism and Platonism, or between community and philosophy, is just a question of what we ought to "cling" to: nature, or our community. That is, it is a moral issue.[15]

Rorty makes similar arguments in defense of a pragmatic acceptance of contingency, and of the identification with one's community in thought that this pragmatism entails, in a number of other essays. Thus, in "Solidarity or Objectivity?" Rorty praises those human beings who "give sense" to their lives by "telling the story of their contribution to a community," and he argues that the "desire to escape the limitations of one's community" (the "desire for objectivity") is a foolish one, since "we have to start from where we are"—and end there, too. Here, and in "On Ethnocentrism," Rorty praises the admirable "ethnocentric" disposition to "attach a special privilege to our own community," and he blames the relativist disposition to "pretend an impossible tolerance for every other group," as well as the philosophical disposition to seek an "ahistorical standpoint from which to endorse the habits of modern democracies." In "The Priority of Democracy to Philosophy," Rorty suggests that liberals should repudiate universalistic Enlightenment rationalism, and instead found liberal

---

[15]Rorty, *Consequences*, 165–66. Cf. Rorty, *Objectivity*, 32: "[The pragmatist] wants solidarity to be our *only* comfort, and to be seen not to require metaphysical support."

politics on a "quasi-Hegelian identification with our own community, thought of as a historical product."[16]

In "Habermas and Lyotard on Postmodernity," Rorty argues that the prospects for liberal "social reform" are enhanced by "our sense of identification with our community," rather than by the misplaced aspiration to discover a transhistorical standpoint from which to submit or impose reforms. In "Method, Social Science, Social Hope," Rorty suggests that we should "get rid of traditional notions of 'objectivity,' " and so understand "the social sciences as continuous with literature—as interpreting other people to us, and thus enlarging and deepening our sense of community"; he even speaks here about "the sense of community which liberalism requires." In "Science as Solidarity," Rorty goes so far as to suggest that scientific rationality is not the search for "objective" understanding, but is rather a "model of human solidarity" and "civility"—a model of "free and open encounter" for representative political institutions in a democratic community, for example. In "Freud and Moral Reflection," he discusses the psychological benefits of a certain "sense worth having" that enables one to "identify oneself with communal movements"; this sense of identification with one's community "helps reconcile an existentialist sense of contingency and mortality with a Romantic sense of grandeur." In "Postmodernist Bourgeois Liberalism," Rorty describes "morality as the interest of a historically conditioned community," and "human dignity" as "derivative from the dignity of some specific community": "loyalty to [our society] is morality enough." In "That Old-Time Philosophy," he praises Dewey's attempt (now opposed by the "Straussians," says Rorty) "to find one's moral identity in membership in a democratic community."[17]

At the same time, Rorty suggests that identification with one's own community in thought will inevitably, or almost inevitably, give rise to an identification with one's own community in deed. Human beings who "identify" morally with some community—who understand themselves to be citizens (or whatever) above all, rather than autonomous or solitary individuals—will surely be inclined to believe that they ought to love and serve that community, as the needful and benevolent author of their hap-

---

[16]Rorty, *Objectivity*, 21–23, 29–31, 176–77, 207–8. The essays named in this and the next paragraph are collected in *Objectivity, Essays,* and *Consequences,* unless seperately cited in the notes.

[17]Rorty, *Essays*, 163, 173–76 (cf. Rorty, "Posties," 12); Rorty, *Consequences,* 203, 207; Rorty, "Science as Solidarity," 44–48; Rorty, *Objectivity,* 197–98; and Rorty, "That Old-Time Philosophy," 28.

piness and dignity. Patriotic deeds are likely to be among the ordinary political manifestations of a moral identification with one's own community in thought. So it is not surprising that Rorty's communitarian understanding of thought and morality yields an "ethnocentric" politics. For Rorty, that is, identification with one's community in thought usually yields "ethnocentrism," not "relativism"—proud loyalty, not frivolous or "sneering" indifference. The pragmatist "can only be criticized for taking his community *too* seriously," and not at all for refusing "to take the choice between communities seriously."[18]

Indeed, Rorty is arguably one of our most radical and intransigent partisans of community. Other communitarians are content to say, with Sandel, that *certain* "loyalties and convictions" acquire "moral force" *partly* because these moral commitments are essentially bound up with our various self-understandings as members of particular communities. We know ourselves not simply as lonely individuals, but also as loyal members of various communities. These belongings have a moral force that obligates us in important ways; for Sandel, such obligations go beyond, but apparently do not altogether supplant, more routine duties—including not only those that we incur through our free and rational choices as individuals, but also (what is more important) those that bind us as human beings simply.[19] But Rorty characteristically goes much further; in his response to Sandel here, he affirms that identification with one's community is the *only* warrant for one's moral judgments and moral duties: "I would argue that the moral force of such loyalties and convictions consists *wholly* in this fact, and that nothing else has *any* moral force. There is no 'ground' for such loyalties and convictions save the fact that the beliefs and desires and emotions which buttress them

---

[18]Rorty, *Objectivity*, 29–31, 203–4, 207–8; Rorty, "Science as Solidarity," 42–43; and Rorty, *Contingency*, 198. "Patriotic" is my ascription. For a classical discussion of the moral meaning of such "identification with one's own community," see Plato, *Republic*, 462a–464e, 412b–417b.

[19]Unfortunately, Sandel is not very clear on this point. In the passage that Rorty cites, Sandel says that we cannot regard ourselves as Kantians or liberals—that is, as "free and rational" agents—"without great cost to those loyalties and convictions whose moral force consists partly in the fact that living by them is inseparable from understanding ourselves as the particular people we are—as members of this family or community or nation or people, as bearers of this history, as sons and daughters of that revolution, as citizens of this republic" (Sandel, *Liberalism*, 179; cited in Rorty, *Objectivity*, 200). But Sandel does not tell us very much, here or elsewhere, about the *other* possible grounds of the moral force of our loyalties and convictions, whose existence is implied by the words "those" and "partly" in this passage. Are these "natural" obligations? And how do these other obligations relate to our communal obligations, especially when they conflict?

overlap those of lots of other members of the group with which we identify for purposes of moral and political deliberations."[20] In matters of
morality, says Rorty, we may *never* appeal to the idea of "natural duties"
or to the virtue of "humanity" (except perhaps rhetorically, among fools
or children), since these notions are based on the old-fashioned and now
discredited philosophical aspiration to see the natural human being as he
"really is," stripped of all cultural or conventional accretions. On the
contrary, since "there is nothing to people except what has been socialized into them," we are only able to justify our moral choices in the language, and according to the standards, of the community with which we
happen to identify (for whatever historical or idiosyncratic reasons). For
Rorty, a human being "really is" nothing more than what his community
has made him. It is for this reason, above all, that I speak of Rorty as a
"communitarian."[21] Rorty's praise of community is a praise of democratic community in particular. Indeed, it is "an exaltation of democracy for
its own sake"; we now discover our "moral identity in membership in a
democratic community."[22]

Perhaps none of this is incompatible with Rorty's claim that he is a
liberal in politics, if not in philosophy. Yet it is already clear that Rorty's
liberalism must be an altogether novel liberalism; he must undertake to
"redescribe" liberalism, so to speak, in order to make it harmonize with
his redescriptions of the human self, human dignity, the nature of
morality, and so on. Postmodernist bourgeois liberalism, says Rorty,
can do without the individualism and the ahistorical rationalism of so-
called philosophical liberalism: it can be ethnocentric. But philosophical (Lockean and Kantian) liberalism, precisely to the extent that it has
emancipated the rational individual from the shackles of community
and religion, is able to vindicate a pleasing intuition about the moral
autonomy of human beings, which Rorty must now reject: that individual men and women are sometimes, and surely in the best cases, the authors of their moral lives and their communities, rather than merely
texts written by those communities. But what is left of liberalism, for
Rorty, once it becomes necessary to do without this pleasing portrait of
human freedom? There is good reason, it seems to me, to be presumptively skeptical of Rorty's suggestion that he is a commonplace liberal in
politics, not only or primarily because he rejects the various philosoph-

---

[20]Rorty, *Objectivity*, 200 (emphasis in original).
[21]Rorty, *Contingency*, 177; and cf. xiii, 185, 195.
[22]Rorty, "Education," 204; and Rorty, "That Old-Time Philosophy," 28.

ical foundations of liberalism, but also because he seems to repudiate the moral core of liberalism (an aspiration to vindicate the cause of human freedom). Rorty's pragmatist liberalism turns out to be a new and very different species of liberalism, founded on a new and very different idea of freedom.[23]

II

Whether or not Rorty is properly described as a communitarian or as a liberal, it is clear that he is a "pragmatist," as he often says.[24] So it might be useful to begin again with this question: what is pragmatism?

The pragmatist, says Rorty, is characterized above all by a certain intellectual disposition: a "pragmatic" attachment to whatever "works," so to speak, together with an inclination to dismiss as fruitless and perverse the sorts of ("foundational") questions that philosophers (and others) too often raise about *why* some practices and opinions "work" and others do not. The pragmatist seeks to "liberate" us from the "neurotic" hope that philosophy can conjure up some way of " 'grounding' our culture, our moral lives, our politics, our religious beliefs, upon 'philosophical bases.' "[25] Once liberated in this way, we can begin to live our moral (and other) lives more wholeheartedly, now untroubled by the doubts that too often emerge from failed efforts to discover the "foundations" of our ways of life. Pragmatism, one might say, is the moral equivalent of the political philosophy of President George Bush, as revealed (partly) in his fondness for the popular song "Don't Worry, Be Happy"—and in his disdain for the "vision thing."

This pragmatic disposition manifests itself not only in Rorty's moral and political judgments, but also in his understanding of science and the other modes of human inquiry; that is, Rorty propounds a pragmatist interpretation of what should count as "true" or "rational" in the natural

[23]I discuss Rorty's account of freedom in "Privacy and Community." For "redescribe," see Rorty, *Contingency*, 44.

[24]In *Contingency*, Rorty seems to prefer to call himself an "ironist," not a "pragmatist" (xv; cf. 39). But in two recent essays, Rorty is still describing himself as a "pragmatist": see Rorty, *Objectivity*, 175–77; and Rorty, "Science as Solidarity," 41, where he refers to Thomas Kuhn's "pragmatist friends (such as myself)." Moreover, Rorty remains an enthusiastic "Deweyan" even in his most recent writings; see, for example, Rorty, "Education without Dogma"; and Rorty, *Contingency*, 44–69.

[25]On philosophy as a "foundational discipline," see Rorty, *Consequences*, 160–61; and Rorty, "Taking Philosophy Seriously." This quest for foundations is "neurotic," says Rorty, because it is in large measure an unhealthy response to the moral vacuum mistakenly thought to be left by modern science. For other examples of this moral argument against philosophy, see Rorty, *Consequences*, 191–93; and Rorty, *Objectivity*, 30–34.

sciences and in humane studies, as well as such an interpretation of what should count as "just" or "good" for human beings and communities.[26] Rorty is no more interested in the question "why science works" than he is in the question "why liberal culture works": "we do not itch for an explanation of the success of recent Western science any more than for the success of recent Western politics."[27] But Rorty is quite sure that both science and liberal culture somehow "work."

In politics, says Rorty, the pragmatist possesses a Deweyan taste for "experimentalism" or "social engineering": the Deweyan pragmatist is neither a conservative nor a revolutionary, but a social reformer. The pragmatist is not a conservative, because he knows that "tradition" is only the accumulation, by trial and error, of certain habits, institutions, and ideas that for some reason now suit our particular community well; but he sees no reason not to continue this experiment, in the reasonable expectation that social reform can bring into being new thoughts and practices that will perhaps "work" for us even better than our old ways.[28] But the pragmatist is also not a revolutionary, because he does not trust the abstract (universal) claims that justify revolution only by compelling citizens to judge their community according to standards that are alien to the community and must be imposed on it. So the pragmatist social reformer answers doubts about the justification of our way of life and political culture "not by Socratic requests for definitions and principles, but by Deweyan requests for concrete alternatives and programs." Rorty even describes his political project of reform as a "Deweyan attempt to make concrete concerns with the daily problems of one's community—social engineering—the substitute for traditional religion." Thus, the greatest benefactors of political communities are imaginative "poets," or perhaps "superficial dream-

---

[26]Actually, Rorty's pragmatism goes further than Kuhn's. See Rorty, "Science as Solidarity," 41–42, on Rorty's "left-wing Kuhnianism"; and cf. 47. See, too, Rorty, *Consequences*, 164.

[27]Rorty, *Contingency*, 169–75, 44–69; Rorty, "Science as Solidarity," 40–41.

[28]Rorty sometimes speaks of such pragmatic change as "progress" (e.g. Rorty, *Contingency*, 192); this is somewhat strange, since it seems to imply that we can know the transhistorical or natural end of human communities, which would enable us to distinguish between progress and decline. See, too, Rorty, *Objectivity*, 22–23. More generally, Rorty does not say much about how we can distinguish between what "works" and what does not, in the absence of natural (as opposed to merely communal) standards. He sometimes argues that "better" means nothing more than "*seems* clearly better," or that "progress" is only a "story" that communities tell about their history. See Rorty, *Consequences*, xxix, xxxvii (emphasis in original); and Rorty, *Contingency*, 55. See, too, Stephen Macedo, "Liberal Virtues, Constitutional Community," 237, n. 37.

ers," like Martin Luther King and others, who "supply local hope, not universal knowledge."[29]

In morals, the pragmatist is inclined toward a taste for idiosyncratic experimentation with one's "self," which Rorty calls "self-creation": "My emphasis on Freud's claim that we should think of ourselves as just one more among Nature's experiments, not as the culmination of Nature's design, echoes Berlin's use of J. S. Mill's phrase 'experiments in living' (as well as echoing Jefferson's and Dewey's use of the term 'experiment' to describe American democracy)." Rorty argues that the human "self" has no "core," that there is no "true self" that a human being should strive to awaken or discover; the pragmatist sees "the self as centerless, as a historical contingency all the way through." That is, the human self is merely a "network of beliefs, desires, and emotions with nothing behind it—no substrate behind the attributes."[30] This network is, in the first place, the creation of the community; Rorty argues, again, that "there is nothing to people except what has been socialized into them."[31] Yet, because "who gets to do the socializing is often a matter of who manages to kill whom first," this account of the self might seem to justify the spiritual enslavement of all human beings to their community, and even to those in the community who most effectively use force or fraud to impose their idiosyncratic ways of thinking and acting on the rest of us (perhaps the so-called "strong poets").[32]

We may escape this slavish condition, says Rorty, only if we somehow create ourselves anew, through the "continual reweaving of [this] web of beliefs and desires." But there is no "essential humanity" or "true self" that can be the object of our aspirations, or guide our quest for freedom: "there is only the shaping of an animal into a human being by the process of socialization, followed (with luck) by the self-individualization and self-creation of that human being through his or her own later revolt against that very process." Self-creation is a kind of freedom from community, but it is a freedom that is not directed by any law of nature or by reason. Moral freedom is, above all, the "recognition of contingency,"

[29]Rorty, *Contingency*, 87, 61; Rorty, *Essays*, 175–76; and Rorty, "Posties," 12. Cf. Rorty, *Objectivity*, 200–201.

[30]Rorty, *Contingency*, 45; see, generally, 23–43, 96–121; Rorty, "Education and Dogma," 198–200; and Rorty, *Objectivity*, 188–89, 199–200, 207–8.

[31]Rorty, *Contingency*, 177; see, too, Rorty, *Consequences*, 208 ("there is nothing much to 'man' except one more animal, until culture, the meshes of power, begin to shape him into something else"); and xlii ("there is nothing deep down inside us except what we have put there ourselves").

[32]Rorty, *Contingency*, 185; see 37.

says Rorty; thus, the greatest slavery consists in "obedience to permanent
nonhuman constraints," like God or nature, not in obedience to the
"conversational constraints" imposed (perhaps through force or fraud)
by our various communities. (The philosophical or religious attempt to
escape the contingency of community, says Rorty, only turns human beings into "properly programmed machines.") And so, Rorty's creative individuals accept no guidance from God or nature in their revolt against
their "socialization," but instead undertake to write their own "private
poems." These poets (and "every human life" is "a poem") pursue a
"hit-or-miss," experimental project of liberation—not one guided by the
reasonable awareness that, as Locke put it, "*where there is no Law, there
is no Freedom.*"[33] "Experimentation" with one's self is, for Rorty, the
way of life of the truly free human being, the "strong poet," who escapes
the terrible fate of those who fail to "break free from an idiosyncratic
past" and so live in "an inherited world," but without falling into the
slavish habits of those who obey imaginary masters.[34]

Finally, in science, the pragmatist adopts a new "experimental" conception of rationality and truth. Truth is "what is good in the way of belief"—whatever enables us to "cope" well with our world. Since human
beings need to cope with the world in a variety of ways, it is not surprising that we have devised (through experiment, or trial and error) a variety of ways of thinking about human beings and their place in the world
(the natural sciences, social sciences, and humanities). Each of these
modes of human inquiry employs a different method and vocabulary;
these vocabularies are not more or less "true" or "objective," but only
more or less useful in enabling human beings to cope with their world.
Thus, the social sciences enable human beings to predict and to control
human affairs, while the humanities (and the new "interpretive" social
sciences) enable human beings to give meaning to their ways of life.[35]

In the remainder of this chapter, I consider whether Rorty's pragmatism provides an adequate foundation for liberal politics and morality.

[33]Rorty, *Contingency*, 46, 38, 35; Rorty, "Education and Dogma," 200; Rorty,
Objectivity, 199–200, 208; Rorty, *Consequences*, 165–66. See also Locke, *Second Treatise*,
§57 (emphasis in original).
[34]Rorty, *Contingency*, 45, 33, 29; cf. 23–24; in another passage, which concerns not only
experimentation in politics, but also moral (and scientific) experimentation, Rorty charac-
terizes Dewey's "experimentalism" in the following way: "this move 'beyond method' gives
mankind an opportunity to grow up, to be *free* to make itself, rather than seeking direction
from some *imagined* outside source"; see Rorty, *Consequences*, 204 (emphases added). For
Rorty's most detailed account of the "self," see Rorty, *Essays*, 143–63.
[35]Rorty, *Consequences*, xvii, xxv, 191–203.

III

What is "humanity"? "Humanity" is above all the name of a "natural kind"—a species with a certain nature, all of whose members share a "central essence."[36] But it is also the name of a moral virtue or sentiment; indeed, humanity is perhaps *the* distinctive liberal virtue. What Burke said of the philosophers of the French Revolution might also be said of liberals in general: " 'The Parisian philosophers . . . explode or render odious or contemptible, that class of virtues which restrain the appetite. . . . In the place of all this, they substitute a virtue which they call humanity or benevolence.' "[37] The idea of humanity, then, has both a scientific and a moral sense, which are nicely joined at the heart of our Declaration of Independence: "all men are created equal, . . . with certain unalienable rights." In what follows, I discuss the relation between these two aspects of the liberal idea of humanity. I ask whether one can reasonably argue that "humanity" is the name of a moral virtue without also admitting that it is the name of a natural kind. Is it reasonable, for example, to speak of inalienable human rights, or even to denounce inhumane acts of cruelty, and at the same time to deny, as Rorty does, that "all men" designates an intelligible class of beings with a certain (moral) nature? I begin with the liberal view, and turn later to Rorty's contrary account.

What is this liberal virtue, "humanity"? A humane liberal is one who acts on this moral conviction: that "all men are created equal." Now, this idea of humanity has many names and takes many forms within the liberal tradition: I do not want to insist here on the name "humanity." Yet, however one names this liberal virtue or sentiment, the humane man is one who strives (for it is not always easy) to treat each of his fellow human beings, except those who somehow renounce their humanity, in a way that acknowledges the moral significance of their shared membership in the human species. For the liberal who is confronted by strange or alien human beings, recognition of their common humanity is dispositive for purposes of moral judgment, in rudimentary cases at least: that one is a human being is all we need to know, in such cases, and then the moral inquiry ends.[38]

---

[36]Cf. Rorty, *Essays*, 143–45; in this passage and others, Rorty denies that "humanity" is the name of a "natural kind," and indeed seems to deny that the world is "a world of natural kinds."

[37]Edmund Burke, "Letter to Rivarol of June 1, 1791," quoted in Strauss, *Natural Right and History*, 188; see, too, 1–8.

[38]See Lincoln's speech on the infamous Dred Scott decision (which hinges in part on the question at issue here), 26 June 1857 (in *Speeches and Writings*); here, Lincoln discusses the

The liberal humanitarian believes that what "all men" have in common is more "constitutive" of the human self, to borrow the communitarian language favored by Sandel and Rorty, than what separates some human beings from others. Certain fundamental rights and duties belong to all human beings, in the beginning, by virtue of their common human nature. Only later do some human beings acquire further rights and duties, arising from certain natural qualities or cultural inheritances that belong to some, but not to others—and even then, these secondary rights and duties cannot undermine the common duties and rights of humanity. What divides human beings—natural inequalities between wise and unwise, heroic and wretched, virtuous and wicked, as well as cultural and historical distinctions between European and African, pagan and Christian, modern and ancient—is less fundamental than what belongs to us in common. So, at any rate, says the liberal. That is the humanitarian creed: each human being, save the unnaturally defective (such as "*Lunaticks* and *Ideots*"), possesses some (natural) faculty that entitles him, if only presumptively, to the moral respect of other human beings. Human beings can, of course, act in ways that overcome this presumption—as criminals and tyrants do, according to Locke; indeed, such so-called human beings reveal that they are not really human after all, but are the moral equivalent of "Savage Beasts," or rather are themselves savage beasts.[39] Nevertheless, however liberals understand these perverse cases, a humane sense of the moral equality of human beings qua human beings is somehow at the core of all liberal teachings.

If humanity is the first of the liberal virtues, then inhumanity has pride of place among the liberal vices. Inhumanity too has many names: it is commonly called cruelty, for example. Inhumanity is surely the most distinctive and despised liberal vice. This is the vice of those who deny the fundamental moral equality of all human beings: liberals say, for example, that it is inhumane to contend that some human beings are naturally masters and others are naturally slaves, or that some cultures or peoples are civilized and others are irremediably barbaric. If nature or culture can so elevate some human beings over others, or so alienate some groups of human beings from others, that it becomes necessary (in order to make the most important moral judgments) to attend more closely to these nat-

---

meaning of the announcement in the Declaration that "all men are created equal" (which disposes of certain fundamental moral questions but not all moral questions, once one recognizes who is a man).

[39]Locke, *Second Treatise*, §§60, 11; and cf. §172.

ural hierarchies and cultural differences among human beings than to their (merely biological) common natures, then it can no longer be said that the idea of "humanity" is the fixed point on our moral compasses. In the worst case, the liberal worries, an inhumane man treats other human beings as if they were not (really) human but rather as petty as beasts—perhaps because they are thought to be wretched creatures or perhaps because they are merely alien. Such a vicious disposition, says the liberal, induces one to play the beast oneself, by indulging in inhumane acts of cruelty or cruel indifference.

Thus Montesquieu, in a humane chapter on the origins of slavery in *The Spirit of the Laws*, provides an example of the sort of inhumanity that can arise from cultural perplexities:

> I would as soon say that the right of slavery comes from the scorn that one nation conceives for another, founded on the difference in customs. Lopez de Gomara says that "the Spanish found, close to Sainte-Marie, baskets in which the inhabitants had put produce; there were crabs, snails, crickets, and grasshoppers. The victors treated this as a crime in the vanquished." The author claims that the right that made the Americans slaves of the Spanish was founded on this, not to mention the fact that they smoked tobacco and that they did not cut their beards in the Spanish fashion. Knowledge makes men gentle, and reason inclines toward humanity; only prejudices cause these to be renounced.

For the liberal Montesquieu, as Judith Shklar says, "humanity is always prior to citizenship": our duties and rights as human beings are prior to our rights and duties as members of any community. But the prejudices of communities, and especially religious communities, are often the true sources of inhumane opinions concerning natural inequalities among men, as the example of black slavery suggests, according to Montesquieu: "*It is impossible for us to assume that these people are men* because if we assumed they were men one would begin to believe that we ourselves were not Christians." Here is one further example of the inhumane prejudices fostered by religion, which Montesquieu borrows from a Jew's "very humble remonstrance to the inquisitors of Spain and Portugal": "But if you do not want to be Christians, *at least be men*; treat us as you would if, having only the feeble lights of justice that nature gives us, you had no religion to guide you and no revelation to enlighten you." The moralities or prejudices of religions and communities are properly judged, says Montesquieu, by the humane standards of "natural reason" or "philosophy," which has enlightened the minds of men, and so made them gentle.[40]

Montesquieu's great humanity is especially striking for this additional reason: he also saw clearly, and even somehow celebrated, the "infinite diversity of laws and mores" that have been instituted by "man, that flexible being." His political science, as everyone knows, recognizes the moral force of such cultural distinctions among peoples, which are associated with variations in climate and religion and commerce, among other things. But he was nevertheless repelled by the inhumanity that is excused and even fostered within this infinite variety of human communities, and is often inflicted by one community or people upon another. Montesquieu can thus perhaps offer some guidance to today's perplexed liberals. These liberals, like Rorty, often share Montesquieu's fascination with the remarkable diversity of human institutions, or cultures; and they also want to be able to say, with Montesquieu, that inhumanity or "cruelty is the worst thing we do." But today's liberals have in many cases lost their faith in (universal) reason and therefore in the idea of (common) humanity; some even worry that "liberalism is . . . just one more example of cultural bias."[41]

Montesquieu's liberal political science, on the contrary, somehow combines a reliance on universal or "human reason"—which teaches each human being what "his own nature" is—with a recognition of the constitutive force of particular (religious and other) educations—which are even able to deprive a human being of "his sense of [his own nature]." It is true that this political science largely eschews the juridical deduction of (universal) human rights that is favored by some other liberal rationalists. But Montesquieu does not renounce the universal idea of rights primarily in order to protect the putative charms of the many so-called civilizations of the world from the homogenizing and leveling effects of Enlightenment rationalism: an honest survey of the nations of the world

[40]Montesquieu, *Spirit*, 15.3 (footnote omitted from quoted passage); 15.5 (emphasis added; also, see the context); 15.7 (but see the context, esp. the immediate sequel to the passage quoted); and 25.13 (emphasis added; see the context). Cf. 15.4. For Shklar's remark, see her *Montesquieu*, 74. On Montesquieu's humanity, see, too: *Spirit*, 10.2–4, on certain humane limits on the rights of war and conquest; 4.6–8, a somewhat ironic account of the inhumanity or "ferocity" of certain "singular" institutions of the classical republics of virtue, including the institution of slavery. I should also mention, in this context, Montesquieu's humane analysis of the criminal law (6, 12). For Montesquieu's most sustained account of religion, see 24–25; cf. 12.4; but there are many other relevant passages on the prejudices fostered by religion, including some of those cited above.

[41]Montesquieu, *Spirit*, Preface; Rorty, *Objectivity*, 203; Rorty, *Contingency*, xv.

reveals more brutality than charm; *The Spirit of the Laws* is less a joyful celebration of human cultural creativity than it is a melancholy commentary on man's remarkably creative inhumanity to man. And so, Montesquieu is always guided by the same fundamental aim, an aim that is given by natural reason: to vindicate the human capacity for a reasonable or moderate politics, which provides for our "liberty" or our "security" so far as that is possible in particular circumstances, against the various and sometimes even enchanting "prejudices" that blind us to our true nature and needs, and thereby emancipate inhumane passions.[42]

Montesquieu says, to repeat, "Knowledge makes men gentle, and reason inclines toward humanity." Liberal reason teaches humanity, because it reveals the common human needs and aspirations that stand at the foundations of all human communities, to which human beings are so often blinded by religion, or by community. That is, classical liberal philosophy teaches that we are all somehow brothers under the skin, so to speak, and this awareness deprives human beings of one powerful motive for hatred and cruelty.[43]

In the same humane spirit, Locke, too, "impartially survey[s] the Nations of the World." He, too, sees the extraordinary diversity of human institutions, but rather few pleasing spectacles and many "Sacred" follies and brutalities. And so, this impartial but humane observer has "but little Reverence for the Practices which are in use and credit amongst Men." Like Montesquieu, Locke argues that the cure of these ills, which have their origins in the "Custom" and "Authority" of communities, can be found only by attending to the guidance of "calm

---

[42]See Montesquieu, *Spirit*, Preface (on Montesquieu's intention in this book); 1.3 (on "human reason" and its relation to particular laws, which "should be only the particular cases to which human reason is applied"). On the "natural laws" and the natural needs of human beings, see 1.1–3. On the "moderate" politics of liberty, which is properly understood as the "tranquillity of spirit which comes from the opinion each one has of his security," see 11.1–6; cf. 12.1–2. For evidence that Montesquieu sometimes celebrates diversity, see 19.27, 11.6, 4.2, 2.4. In addition to the several passages cited in a previous note on Montesquieu's hatred of inhumanity, see, too: 3.8–10; 4.3; 5.11–18; 6.9, 13 (on the horrors of despotic government, which is a recurring theme); and 16.6, 8–10, 14 (on certain barbaric sexual practices). Further, consider Montesquieu's discussions of the beneficial effects of commerce, which to some extent undermines diversity, esp. in 20.1–3.

[43]Montesquieu, *Spirit*, Preface, 15.3. On Montesquieu's humanity, and how Montesquieu reconciles this (universal) humanity with awareness of the great diversity of (particular) human institutions, a diversity that reflects the "flexible" nature of the human soul, see Pangle, *Montesquieu's Philosophy*, 5–9, 28–29, 42–46, 203–10, and esp. 170–72 ("in order to benefit humanity one must never permit the sense of humanity to blur one's clarity of vision," 172; see the context, on Montesquieu's humane, but not unreasonably sentimental, treatment of various institutions of slavery). See, too, 200–248, on the effects of commerce.

reason," the natural capacity that restrains cruel passions. But reason must be protected from the various conceits of "fancy and passion"; these corruptions of human judgment are then too frequently established in diverse human institutions by custom, religion, authority, and the rest. Like Montesquieu, Locke fears that "fancy" or "imagination" (what Rorty might call "creativity") more often inspires cruelty and barbarism than civilization or humanity. Thus, after referring to one especially inhumane practice, Locke writes: "Thus far can the busie mind of Man carry him to a Brutality below the level of Beasts, when he quits his reason, which places him almost equal to Angels. Nor can it be otherwise in a Creature, whose thoughts are more than the Sands, and wider than the Ocean, where fancy and passion must needs run him into strange courses, if reason, which is his only Star and compass, be not that he steers by." For Locke as for Montesquieu, human beings avoid brutality worse than that of the beasts only if they learn to be reasonable: reason makes men gentle.[44]

It is surely possible to admit that natural and even cultural distinctions within the class of human beings are decisive for many (and some of the most important) moral judgments, while nevertheless affirming that the moral differences between the class of human beings as a whole and, say, the class of beings that includes only the other animals, are decisive for some rather rudimentary moral judgments. In such a case, even a moral philosopher who rejects the liberal idea of humanity (in the strong sense that affirms the presumptive moral equality of human beings simply) might defend a lesser virtue of humanity that insists on the propriety of treating all human beings with greater respect than is due to the other animals, if not with the presumption of moral equality that liberals demand. Such a view would still imply that humanity is the name of a "natural kind," a natural moral (not merely biological) class; but our common human nature would, on this account, be of less moral significance than liberals typically say. Strictly speaking, then, the idea of humanity is compatible with a less egalitarian view of human nature than that proffered by liberals: it is possible to be a more or less conservative humanitarian. That is, to anticipate a later argument: just as there is a way to recognize the moral importance of (unequal) virtue even in an egalitarian ethics that is based on a liberal idea of humanity, so there is a way to recognize the moral impor-

---

[44]Locke, *First Treatise*, §58; see the whole context. For "calm reason," see Locke, *Second Treatise*, §8. Cf. Aristotle, *Politics*, 1253a30–40.

tance of (equal) humanity even in an inegalitarian ethics that is based on a conservative idea of virtue. The liberal and conservative humanitarians differ only on this issue: how far can our moral concerns be resolved simply by reference to our common humanity? What is much more problematic, as I will argue, is the communitarian attempt to find a place for the virtue of humanity in an ethics that denies that humanity is in any sense (except perhaps a simply biological sense) the name of a natural kind.

What is this natural kind, "humanity"? For the liberal, to repeat, some aspect of our common humanity or human nature (here "humanity" has a scientific sense, and designates a species with a certain nature) justifies treating other human beings in a "humane" way, or with humanity (here "humanity" designates a moral virtue, although it is variously named). But what is the mysterious element or faculty of human beings that earns such humane treatment? Liberals disagree; and so, to repeat, liberal "humanity" has many names and takes many forms. Here, I will discuss Locke's defense of humanity most fully; I will refer above all to those (surprisingly frequent) passages where Locke insists on the moral significance of the natural distinction between the human species (as a whole) and the other species of animals, a distinction which is the ground of the humane virtues.

Why should human beings acknowledge a fundamental moral distinction between all human beings and beasts, but not between some human beings and others? To speak plainly, why are we permitted to use the other animals for "Meat and Drink," but not to enslave our fellow human beings, or even to use them, borrowing an expression from one of Locke's sources, as " 'Roasters' "?[45]

Locke, in the *Second Treatise*, traces the natural equality and freedom of human beings to our common humanity: "there being nothing more evident, than that Creatures of the same species and rank promiscuously born to all the same advantages of Nature, and the use of the same faculties, should also be equal one amongst another without Subordination or Subjection." Human beings are equal, then, in this sense: no human beings possess any special faculty or virtue that justifies any claim to rule over other members of the human species; there are no masters or slaves by nature, but only free individuals. Locke next describes the (limited)

---

[45]On the right to use animals for food, see Locke, *Second Treatise*, §§25–26, 30, 37–38; cf. Locke, *First Treatise*, §§38–39, 86–87. On cannibalism, see *First Treatise*, §§57–58, where Locke actually speaks not only of cannibalism in general but even of a particularly inhumane practice of it.

moral duty of human beings in the state of nature in a way that similarly recognizes the moral importance of our common humanity, as beings "furnished with like Faculties, sharing all in one Community of Nature": "Every one as he is *bound to preserve himself*, and not to quit his Station wilfully; so by the like reason when his own Preservation comes not in competition, ought he, as much as he can, *to preserve the rest of Mankind.*" To be sure, this "ought" is soon revealed to be a "Right," rather than a duty: there is no natural duty to sacrifice oneself to the interests of mankind. But even in the state of nature, where the threats to one's own security are everywhere evident, human beings are enjoined by the law of nature not to "declare War against all Mankind," through violence. That is, says Locke, they are enjoined to act like human beings, who are able to make reason, not force, their "rule of right."[46] But *why* should human beings make reason, not force, their rule of right, and so obey the law of nature? To be ruled by a law of nature, says Locke, is not "confinement," but "freedom":

> For *Law*, in its true Notion, is not so much the Limitation as *the direction of a free and intelligent Agent* to his proper Interest, and prescribes no farther than is for the general Good of those under that Law. Could they be happier without it, the *Law*, as an useless thing would of it self vanish; and that ill deserves the Name of Confinement which hedges us in only from Bogs and Precipices. So that, however it may be mistaken, *the end of Law* is not to abolish or restrain, but *to preserve and enlarge Freedom*: For in all the states of created beings capable of Laws, *where there is no Law, there is no Freedom.*

If human beings are obligated under the law of nature to respect their fellow human beings, to acknowledge their natural equality, and to preserve their innocent fellows when their own preservation is not at risk, then it must be reasonable for a "free and intelligent agent" who seeks his own "proper Interest" to make these choices.[47] But why is this "humanity" a reasonable liberal virtue, or a part of the law of nature?

Locke soon reveals what elements ("like faculties") of our common human natures justify treating fellow human beings with greater solicitude than we show beasts—as when we reason with our companions rather than wound or tame them. Human beings, unlike beasts (and

---

[46]Locke, *Second Treatise*, §§4, 6, 8, 11, 172. See, too, Locke, *First Treatise*, §§21–31.
[47]Locke, *Second Treatise*, §57 (emphases in original).

with the important exception of those human beings who are somehow akin to beasts), are capable of understanding the law of nature, which is a law of reason. And so, they can be made to understand the propriety and even the wisdom of vindicating that law, when it is possible to do so, by exercising the "right . . . to preserve Mankind in general"— that is, by punishing or executing those human beings who are like "Savage Beasts," and who have by violence "trespass[ed] against the whole species" and "declared War against all Mankind." (It is of course likely that many human beings in the state of nature may be little more than such beasts, insofar as they are not "Studier[s]" of the law of nature, and so do not know that their own "proper Interest" dictates moderation and the quest for peaceful accommodation; that is, many "human beings" in the state of nature may not be fully human, and may not have earned the respect of the reasonable persons who know the law of nature.)[48]

For Locke, it is the human capacity for reasonable freedom—the ability of human beings to live according to the law of nature, which is a law of reason—that distinguishes us from the beasts. A fellow human being, but not a beast, is potentially reasonable, and so potentially a trustworthy companion, at least "when his own Preservation comes not into competition." Human beings, but not "Lyons" and "Tygers," can sometimes be persuaded that peace is a common good, and that moderation and respect for rights (among other things) are the means to peace. It is therefore reasonable to respect one's fellow human beings, and not merely to fear them. It is reasonable to remain alert, not only to protect oneself from enemies, but also to make friends with those reasonable companions who are able to see the advantages of efforts to work out a common way of life that might temper our common fears and suspicions. It is, of course, not reasonable to seek such accommodations with lions and tigers. This is obvious, but not trivial. The fundamental ground, says Locke, for the respect that is due to other human beings under the law of nature, but not to beasts, is this common faculty—reason—that makes possible true freedom. "For who could be free, when every other Man's Humour might domineer over him?"[49] That is, the fundamental ground of "respect," and of the moral distinction between human beings and beasts, is *not* that man is made in the image of God, or that the "good will" is the only respectable faculty of rational beings, or that the human

[48]Locke, *Second Treatise*, §§4, 6, 8, 11, 12.
[49]Locke, *Second Treatise*, §57, 6.

species somehow possesses an intrinsic dignity that sets it apart from other natural beings.[50]

And so, the law of nature directs reasonable human beings to seek alliances for peace with their fellow human beings, and thus to cultivate the humane virtues—at least until one's fellows somehow betray one's trust. It is necessary, so to speak, to "trust, but verify." All human beings, save the mentally incompetent and (perhaps) the utterly wicked, are capable of behaving reasonably, on Locke's view; in addition, every human being is proud, and so thinks that he is capable of this reasonable self-government.[51]

But there are, to be sure, some human beings who renounce their humanity by behaving like beasts: above all, criminals and tyrants. These human beings should be treated like the beasts they imitate. Thus, Locke explains the right to punish criminals (even with death) in the following way: the criminal, "who having renounced Reason, the common Rule and Measure, God hath given to Mankind, hath by the unjust Violence and Slaughter he hath committed upon one, declared War against all Mankind, and therefore may be destroyed as a *Lyon* or a *Tyger*, one of those wild Savage Beasts, with whom Men can have no Society nor Security." "And one may destroy a Man who makes War upon him, . . . for the same Reason, that he may kill a *Wolf* or a *Lyon*; because such Men are not under the ties of the Common Law of Reason, have no other Rule, but that of Force and Violence, and so may be treated as Beasts of Prey, those dangerous and noxious Creatures, that will be sure to destroy him, whenever he falls into their Power."[52] Locke condemns despotical power in similar language:

> For having quitted *Reason*, which God hath given to be the Rule betwixt Man and Man, and *the common bond whereby humane kind is united into one fellowship and societie*; and having renounced the way of peace, which that teaches, and made use of the Force of War to compasse his unjust ends

[50]It is sometimes said that the moral distinction between human beings and animals depends on such claims about the intrinsic "dignity" of the human species. See, for example, Taylor, "Atomism," 191–94. This is clearly wrong. Those who are able to obey the injunction, "*Be reasonable*," surely merit respect as much as, and perhaps more than, those whose dignity consists in their possession of a Kantian "good will."

[51]On the mentally incompetent, see Locke, *Second Treatise*, §60. Also, Locke would perhaps not concede the distinction between wickedness and folly that is implied in the text. On natural "pride," see Hobbes, *Leviathan*, ch. 15; and Tarcov, *Locke's Education*, 171 and context.

[52]Locke, *Second Treatise*, §§11, 16 (emphases in original).

upon an other, where he has no right, *and so revolting from his own kind to that of Beasts* by making Force which is theirs, to be his rule of right, he renders himself liable to be destroied by the injur'd person and the rest of mankind, that will joyn with him in the execution of Justice, as any other wild beast, or noxious brute with whom Mankind can have neither Society nor Security.[53]

The human species is a respectable species, for this reason: human beings are able to live together with "Society" and "Security"—making reason, not force, their rule of right. Every human being (more or less, and potentially) possesses the faculties that make the species respectable. Our capacity for reasonable freedom under a law of nature distinguishes humanity from the beasts in a more fundamental way than any excellence or virtue of particular human beings distinguishes them from their fellow humans.[54]

IV

"Humanity" is not the name of a "natural kind," says Rorty, for there is not "something within each of us—our essential humanity—which resonates to the presence of this same thing in other human beings": the human self is a human creation, and the specific contours of the self are "a matter of sheer contingent fact—as contingent as a comet or a virus."[55] It follows that there are no universal human virtues, but only the particular virtues that are practiced by the progeny of specific com-

---

[53]Locke, *Second Treatise*, §172 (emphases added); cf. §176.
[54]Cf. Rorty, *Objectivity*, 201–2.
[55]Rorty, *Contingency*, 189, 183; see, too, xiii, 185. Rorty repeats this argument on a number of occasions in this book. Here are a few typical passages: "There are no problems which bind the generations together into a single natural kind called 'humanity' " (20). "We can keep the notion of 'morality' just insofar as we can cease to think of morality as the voice of the divine part of ourselves and instead think of it as the voice of ourselves as members of a community, speakers of a common language. . . . The importance of this shift is that it makes it impossible to ask the question 'Is ours a moral society?' It makes it impossible to think that there is something which stands to my community as my community stands to me, some larger community called 'humanity' which has an intrinsic nature" (59–60). "For Freud himself eschewed the very idea of a paradigm human being. He does not see humanity as a natural kind with an intrinsic nature" (35). See, too, Rorty, *Essays*, 143–45, 155–57 (where Rorty rejects the "Aristotelian" claim that "man is a natural kind" on the grounds that we have no "central essence"—rather, human beings are machines, and so "it is up to us to invent a use for ourselves"); and Rorty, *Objectivity*, 197 (where Rorty suggests that " 'humanity' is a biological rather than a moral notion," and denies that there is any natural "supercommunity" that makes possible an appeal beyond existing communities— no "humanity as such").

munities; for Rorty, " 'one of us human beings' " cannot have the same moral "force" as " 'our sort of people,' " among other (frequently ugly) invocations of camaraderie. The idea of a universal humane morality would make sense, on Rorty's view, "only if 'humanity' had a nature over and above the various forms of life which history has thrown up so far"; but it does not, and so morality is in fact "the voice of a contingent human artifact, a community which has grown up subject to the vicissitudes of time and chance." Thus, an immoral deed is simply the "sort of thing *we* don't do"; but "other families, tribes, cultures, or historical epochs" might approve the very same deeds, which would then be called moral actions, or virtues. Indeed, it is now "impossible for us to retain the notion that some actions and attitudes are naturally 'inhuman' ": Rorty goes so far as to refer here to "the audiences in the Coliseum" and "the guards at Auschwitz."[56] Thus, if we deny that humanity is the name of a natural kind, we must also repudiate any appeal to our common human natures, or to our "essential humanity," as a ground of principles of right conduct.

And yet, cruelty is surely the worst thing "we" can do, says Rorty; and the great achievement of liberal politics has been its "progress . . . in the direction of greater human solidarity." We liberals have learned to enlarge our community, or to "try to extend our sense of 'we' to people whom we have previously thought of as 'they.' " Our humanity, so to speak, is our greatest virtue: we no longer make invidious distinctions among human beings that justify cruelty. But why do liberals pride themselves on treating all human beings as if they were among "us," if "us" has greater moral force than "human being"? How can a postmodern liberal be a partisan of the solidarity of mankind? Rorty insists that his "position is *not* incompatible with urging that we try to extend our sense of 'we' "; rather, "my position entails that feelings of solidarity are necessarily a matter of which similarities and dissimilarities *strike us as salient*, and that such salience is a function of a historically contingent final vocabulary." But this is an extraordinary notion for a liberal, since many human beings often insist on the "salience" of certain kinds of differences that liberals strive to ignore: race, religion, sex. It is a historical accident, Rorty concedes, that our community today does not recognize the salience of such facts about human beings. But perhaps this liberal

---

[56]Rorty, *Contingency*, 59–60, 189–90. Here is the sequel to the passage quoted in the text, 189: "For, this insistence [on contingency] implies that what counts as being a decent human being is relative to historical circumstance, a matter of transient consensus about what attitudes are normal and what practices are just or unjust."

virtue is not an accident; perhaps it is the result of a liberal argument about justice and humanity that Rorty would have us repudiate.[57]

In a passage on race relations in America, Rorty argues that his denial of the idea of "humanity" is not only compatible with the "generous" treatment of American blacks, but makes such generosity more intelligible than the alternative, universalistic account of morality:

> Consider, as a final example, the attitude of contemporary American liberals to the unending hopelessness and misery of the lives of the young blacks in American cities. Do we say that these people must be helped because they are our fellow human beings? We may, but it is much more persuasive, morally as well as politically, to describe them as our fellow *Americans*—to insist that it is outrageous that an *American* should live without hope. The point of these examples is that our sense of solidarity is strongest when those with whom solidarity is expressed are thought of as "one of us," where "us" means something smaller and more local than the human race. That is why "because she is a human being" is a weak, unconvincing explanation of a generous action.[58]

It is surely true that certain feelings of "solidarity" are strongest when they are directed toward fellow members of our own communities. Solidarity is especially powerful among family and friends, but it is even present in communities as large as New York City, says Rorty, or America itself.[59] But it is also much easier to deny that a human being is "one of us" (on the grounds of some dissimilarity that might strike some of us as "salient") than it is to deny that a human being is a human being. And so, the idea of solidarity, at least when separated from the idea of humanity, is a recipe for collective selfishness and prejudice. After all, the sentimental attachment to "our" community is strongest where the members of the community are familiar, even intimates—in small, *homogeneous* communities, where there are no "moral strangers." The liberal idea of "humanity," in other words, only provides a floor to our moral

---

[57]Rorty, *Contingency*, 192 (emphasis added). Rorty's confidence that we Americans have indeed overcome such prejudices is itself remarkable, especially since he here tries to abolish the notion that they are prejudices.

[58]Rorty, *Contingency*, 191.

[59]As Rorty says: "We may feel that there is something morally dubious about a greater concern for a fellow *New Yorker* than for someone facing an equally hopeless and barren life in the slums of Manila or Dakar" (*Contingency*, 191, emphasis in original). Rorty goes on to deny that there is anything morally dubious about this. Cf. Plato, *Republic*, 331e–335e; and Rorty, *Contingency*, xv.

world, not a ceiling. Liberals may have deeper sentimental and moral attachments to members of their own communities (families, sects, parties), but they have some more-than-minimal obligations to all those who are fellow members of the human species, on the liberal view.

The most formidable opponents of slavery and advocates of civil rights in America have generally held a more complicated position than the one that Rorty here describes. Abraham Lincoln, Frederick Douglass, and Martin Luther King often referred to the Declaration of Independence and to the Constitution, the founding American documents, as well as to the Bible; they thereby demanded that their fellow citizens practice what they preach, and so appealed to them in some measure as Americans and not simply as human beings. But they referred to the Declaration not only as our founding document, but also because it embodies an honorable claim about humanity, and implies a moral aspiration: "all men are created equal." Would that appeal have been as effective if the document had been more parochial: "all Englishmen are created equal" (as Lincoln suggested to Douglas)? Thus, King: "One day the South will know that when these disinherited children of God sat down at lunch counters, they were in reality standing up for what is best in the American dream and for the most sacred values in our Judaeo-Christian heritage, thereby bringing our nation back to those great wells of democracy which were dug deep by the founding fathers in their formulation of the Constitution and the Declaration of Independence." And Douglass, in a Fourth of July oration: "I will, in the name of humanity which is outraged, . . . in the name of the constitution and the Bible, which are disregarded and trampled upon, dare to call in question and to denounce, with all the emphasis I can command, everything that serves to perpetuate slavery—the great sin and shame of America."[60] The idea of "human rights" is a strong bulwark against those who would define what it means to be among "us Americans" in a narrow way—since to be an American somehow includes holding the view that "all men are created equal," and not just Americans.

Liberals, of course, admit that there is a difference between the moral obligations that are owed to the rest of "us" in the community and those that are owed to "humanity." This difference is partly (at least) captured by the liberal idea of consent. The liberal emphasizes not only that universal

[60]On Frederick Douglass and Martin Luther King, Jr., see the remarkable essay by Herbert J. Storing, "The Case against Civil Disobedience." See, too, Lincoln, *Speeches and Writings*, 303–4, 352–65; and the speeches by Douglass and King, in Storing, *What Country Have I? Political Writings by Black Americans*, esp. 28–38, 129–30.

human or natural rights are the ground of moral obligations, but also that the idea of reasonable "consent" is a ground of moral obligations. We liberals are free to choose our companions in the community, and we may make such choices for reasons that are private, idiosyncratic, or perverse. In establishing a community, we may choose to make demands on each other that go some way beyond the strict demands of the law of nature, as long as they do not contravene those demands. We consent to be Americans, and to decide who else can become an American; and we decide what privileges and responsibilities belong to an American but not to every human being. We may, from time to time, make this choice in a somewhat foolish manner; that does not violate the law of nature. We may deny citizenship, or fellowship, to other human beings; what we may not deny is the *humanity* of those others whom we do not, for whatever reason, permit to become members of our community. We may not neglect the law of nature, which requires justice toward humanity, simply because we also have obligations and attachments to our friends and neighbors that extend beyond this natural justice. We may not say that those other human beings are not really human beings, and we may not deny them their natural rights even as we deny them (as we may) the civil rights that Americans enjoy. A visitor to our country who is not a citizen may not be permitted to vote, but he may not be enslaved. The liberal American would perhaps be willing to fight in a war to preserve our American way of life, and even to die for our families and fellow countrymen; but liberals are under no obligation to concern themselves with the preservation of the ways of life of those who are not members of our community.[61]

And so, the reasonable liberal understands that human beings are not simply individuals; we are also members of communities, with obligations and attachments to our fellows in those communities that extend beyond the requirements of the law of nature. But this liberal account of the moral meaning of community is not the same as the communitarian view. First, the liberal preserves certain duties to humanity; second, the liberal demands that moral obligations within the community measure up to reasonable standards. Duties to one's fellow citizens may not violate the law of nature. It does no moral good to abolish the floor of our moral world (our "humanity") simply because we fear that some foolish individualists may mistake the floor for the ceiling.

[61]For a humane discussion of the problem of the relation between humane duties and community morality, see Walzer, *Spheres*, esp. 31–63. Indeed, Walzer's account is in certain respects too humane, it seems to me; Walzer sometimes emphasizes duties to humanity at the expense of the duties and rights of consenting liberal individuals.

5

Barber's
Democratic Community

For us, here and now, political community must be a community that enlightened men and women would choose even were they free of the blinding moral authority of tradition (or religion, or ideology). Michael Walzer captures well the spirit of liberalism when he writes that liberal citizens today are "rationalists of everyday life" who have by now "learned to think of themselves as individuals": "it has been the great triumph of liberal theorists and politicians to undermine every sort of political divinity, to shatter all the forms of ritual obfuscation, and to turn the mysterious oath into a rational contract."[1] Our innocence was long ago lost, and now individualism and rationalism are second nature to us. As Locke says, there came a time, after "vain Ambition, and *amor sceleratus habendi*, evil Concupiscence, had corrupted Mens minds into a Mistake of true Power and Honour," when "Men found it necessary to examine more carefully *the Original* and Rights of *Government*": and so human beings began to learn to think of themselves as individuals and became "Studier[s]" of the "Law of Reason." Community comes naturally to human beings, but we must from time to time learn the hard way to guard against abuse of authority even in the hands of those gentle masters who are guided by "Affection and Love." (Locke's portrait of preliberal communities founded on trust is a credible and sobering reminder of the reasons for rationalism and individualism in politics.)[2] The skeptical, vig-

---

[1] Cf. Walzer, *Radical Principles*, 13–15, 24–26. And see Walzer, *Spheres*, 64–65: "We are rationalists of everyday life; we come together, we sign the social contract or reiterate the signing of it, in order to provide for our needs. And we value the contract insofar as those needs are met."

[2] Locke, *Second Treatise*, §§111, 12, 57, 107; and see, generally, §§74–76, 105–12.

ilant liberal politics of consent and rights is by now an old habit, and it is
impossible to imagine a return to the innocence ("trust") of traditional
community.

And yet, we long for community; indeed, among critics of liberalism
we hear again of the possibility of a community founded on "affection"
or even "love," but now somehow chastened by liberal memories of trust
betrayed.[3] Even liberals, today, can hardly deny, as Tarcov puts it, that "a
cold constitutionalism of rights is continually driven to borrow human
warmth from kinder sentiments."[4] Perhaps our liberal individualism is,
in the end, too cold and calculating to sustain the human intimacy that
human beings desire; perhaps the liberal pleasures are too base and fleet-
ing to provide the happiness that even liberals pursue; perhaps the liberal
morality of peace through rights is not sufficiently noble or benevolent to
satisfy our more honorable aspirations. Above all, liberal individualism
destroys citizenship and undermines civic virtue; it is incapable of providing an adequate foundation for a truly democratic community of free
and equal citizens. As we have wholeheartedly embraced private life, we
have also neglected to cultivate the virtues and other habits of citizenship
that even a liberal community must sometimes summon. Thus, we now
find ourselves disempowered in face of the various impersonal modes of
authority that are present in a modern bureaucratic state with a capitalist economy. What is more, we have lost the capacity to endure even the
most modest forms of self-restraint or public-spiritedness, much less old-
fashioned republican virtue. This combination of slavishness and selfishness gives rise to a contemptible mode of liberal politics. We are the
(happy) slaves of paternalistic elites who purchase public passivity and
conformity by base appeals to selfishness: "bread and circuses," but now
administered in an efficient and rational manner by hidden authorities
(owing to these qualities of the bureaucratic state and capitalist economy). This is far from the liberal imagination of autonomous individuals
capable of reasonable self-government. Only the revival of truly democratic citizenship, which teaches human beings to consider the common
good and not only their private rights and interests, can generate the civic
virtues and political judgment that might enable modern men and
women to take control of their common life once again, and to throw off
their new masters. Beyond all this, it is no longer evident that our de-

---

[3]For "Affection and Love" in communitarian politics, see Barber, *Conquest*, 147–51; and
Barber, *Strong Democracy*, 186–90.

[4]Tarcov, "American Constitutionalism," 121; and Tarcov, "A 'Non-Lockean' Locke,"
138.

cayed liberalism has the capacity to inspire an "honorable determination" to vindicate the cause of human freedom, or to call forth a willingness on our part, as citizens, to "mutually pledge to each other our Lives, our Fortunes and our sacred Honor" in its defense: for that pledge is surely more-than-rational and can be made only by those who do not think of themselves only as individuals.[5]

Here is the question that must be confronted by those who hope to build community in the modern world, "after virtue": is it possible to revive moral community and democratic citizenship without altogether repudiating liberal rationalism and individualism, since these qualities of the liberal soul are inescapable and even somehow admirable?[6] In this chapter and the next, I consider the prospects for democratic citizenship and moral community in a liberal world of rationalists who have learned to think of themselves as individuals. In this chapter, I discuss Benjamin Barber's defense of "strong democracy." Barber is a leading republican theorist, a partisan of participatory democracy who nevertheless appreciates the achievements of liberalism, and who therefore hopes to discover a mode of democratic politics and democratic citizenship that "can build community as well as maintain rights" and so make room for "patriotism as well as . . . individuality."[7] Then, in the next chapter, I consider the case of patriotism directly: is patriotism a virtue? For patriotism, love of the republic and the homeland, is the first virtue of any truly communitarian politics, as Montesquieu argues.[8] The ambivalence of communitarian theorists regarding the idea of patriotism reflects a certain ambivalence regarding liberal individualism generally. Here, above all, individual prerogatives and communal responsibilities collide. The chapter on patriotism concludes with a discussion of Walzer's account of civic virtue, citizenship, and patriotism. Michael Walzer is a leading social democratic theorist, a partisan of egalitarian democracy who seeks a revival of community but, like Barber, appreciates the achievements of liberalism: "We [socialists] seek communities, then, of a certain sort, not of any sort. . . . Only a democratic and egalitarian community can accommodate *liberated* men and women."[9] By reflecting on these accounts of de-

---

[5]*Federalist* #39: 240.

[6]See Barber's criticism of MacIntyre's *After Virtue*, which appears in *Conquest*, 177–92 (esp. 177–79, 188–92): "virtue's ancient vices . . . make some of us glad, for all the perils of modernity, that we live in its lengthening shadow rather than under the parching sun of ancient Athens" (192).

[7]Barber, *Strong Democracy*, 177.

[8]Montesquieu, *Spirit*, Preface, 5.2–3.

[9]Walzer, *Radical Principles*, 13 (emphasis added).

mocratic citizenship, we can see the limits of communitarian politics in the modern world, where the idea of virtue has been conquered by the idea of liberty.

A digression on terms. In this chapter, I call "republican" any polity that is wholly or substantially popular, where the people undertakes to rule itself; as Publius says, "we may define a republic to be, or at least may bestow that name on, a government which derives all its powers directly or indirectly from the great body of the people." This choice of terminology is of course somewhat arbitrary, but it provides a useful analytical framework for present purposes. There are surely other ways of defining "republican" politics, and I make no claim here that any particular way is essentially more reasonable than the others. Thus, for some purposes it might be useful to conceive of republican politics in opposition to democratic politics, as Publius does on one occasion when he distinguishes between "pure democracy" and "a republic, by which I mean a government in which the scheme of representation takes place."[10] So, too, for other purposes it might be useful to conceive of republican politics in opposition to liberal politics, where liberal politics is founded on commerce and enlightened self-interest and republican politics is founded on virtue and a love of the common good. Such a conception of republicanism is employed, for example, in the influential work of J. G. A. Pocock and in the work of certain communitarian theorists. I employ the distinction between liberals and republicans throughout the rest of this book, with one amendment (inclusion of a third party, the democrats). But here I choose the more generic usage, following Montesquieu and Publius, because it seems to me that this usage helps to raise the problem of self-government to prominence, and that is my principal concern here. Because republicanism thus understood has both democratic and liberal variants, I will distinguish between democratic republicanism and liberal republicanism in the pages that follow.[11]

[10]*Federalist* #39: 240–41; *Federalist* #10: 81; cf. #63: 387 and #49: 313–14. (On the usage of the *Federalist*, see, too, #9: 72–73, where the distinction between democracy and republic seems to be replaced by the distinction between old and new republics; and #37: 226–27, #57: 350–53, #14: 100–101. Publius's usage is more or less consistently the same as the usage I adopt here.)

[11]Pocock, *Machiavellian Moment*; Pocock, *Virtue, Commerce, and History*; Pangle, *Spirit*; and Sandel, "The Procedural Republic and the Unencumbered Self," 81–96. For my own usage elsewhere in this book, see above, Chapter 3, §§II & III, and below, Chapter 6, §§II & III. To be clear: the republicans of previous chapters (esp. ch. 3) are here democratic republicans; the liberals of previous chapters are here liberal republicans; and the democrats of previous chapters reappear below, pp. 119–35.

I

Here is the paradox of republican politics: in a republican polity, says Montesquieu, "the people are, in certain respects, the monarch; in other respects, they are the subjects." Where "*the people as a body . . . have sovereign power,*" they must somehow both rule and be ruled: the problem of republican politics is the problem of self-government.[12]

Because human beings are not angels, government is required. Where there is no government, order and prosperity will surely be threatened by general lawlessness. Hobbes' classic statement: "In such condition, there is no place for Industry; because the fruit thereof is uncertain: and consequently no Culture of the Earth; no Navigation, nor use of the commodities that may be imported by Sea; no commodious Building; no Instruments of moving, and removing such things as require much force; no Knowledge of the face of the Earth; no account of Time; no Arts; no Letters; no Society; and which is worst of all, continuall feare, and danger of violent death; And the life of man, solitary, poore, nasty, brutish, and short."[13] Beyond all this, and of particular concern to republicans, equality and liberty are vulnerable too where the immoderate and partisan appetites of human beings, which sometimes carry us toward dominion and license, are not somehow governed. Indeed, there is no cure for lawlessness in a republican polity, says Montesquieu: "in a popular government when the laws have ceased to be executed, as this can come only from the corruption of the republic, the state is already lost"; such lawlessness ("the spirit of extreme equality") leads "to the despotism of one alone."[14] So republican polities, no less than other forms, require government: rulers who can when necessary correct the dangerous passions and foolish judgments of the ruled. Government, even republican government, is fundamentally an order constituted and maintained by law and by force, thereby confining the freedom of citizens or subjects.

Republican polities, where the people are sovereign and "all power should be derived from the people," differ from monarchies, tyrannies, and aristocracies in a decisive respect. "Here, in strictness, the people

---

[12]I cite here Montesquieu's definition of a *democratic* republic, *Spirit*, 2.1–2.2 (emphasis in original), and exclude from consideration the "less perfect" aristocratic form (as he also does, more or less; see 2.3, end, and 2–8 generally).

[13]See *Federalist* #51: 322; Hobbes, *Leviathan*, ch. 13; see, too, Locke, *Second Treatise*, §123; Adam Smith, *An Inquiry into the Nature and Causes of the Wealth of Nations*, V.i.b.

[14]Montesquieu, *Spirit*, 3.3, 8.2; see, too, Aristotle, *Politics*, 1290a30–1292a38, 1318b5–1319b33; and Thucydides, *The Peloponnesian War*, 3.70–84, esp. 3.80–82.

surrender nothing."[15] In the other forms of government, one part of the community rules over the rest of the community; and this rule is sustained by force or the threat of force, often (but certainly not always) mitigated by the rule of law and various other moderating measures designed to make such rule tolerable for the subjects. (It is only barely imaginable that such rule might be sustained by persuasion alone, without fear of force, not only because of the folly or pride of the people but above all because of the almost inevitable arrogance of the rulers.[16]) As for monarchy and despotism, here is Montesquieu: "the force of the laws in the one and the prince's ever-raised arm in the other can rule or contain the whole." So too in the case of aristocracy: the "sovereign power is in the hands of a certain number of persons. They make the laws and see to their execution, and the rest of the people mean at best no more to these persons than the subjects in a monarchy mean to the monarch."[17]

But in a republican polity, it must be possible to supply the defect of force and fear in order that the people may rule themselves. Certainly, other forms of government have their own troubles: above all, the necessity to guard against abuse of power by those who rule. Indeed, these problems seem to me, what I take to be the traditional view of the matter, insoluble. Government (the rule of one part of the community over the other parts) will always, or almost always, decay into a kind of tyranny. The only reasonable alternative to self-government (the rule of the people over itself) is balanced government or the mixed regime (the more or less stable division of rule among the parts of the community), which has its own specific weakness: "tumult."[18] But the peculiarly republican problem is the problem of self-government.

So republican polities are most likely to be threatened by laxity and corruption, while other forms are most likely to be threatened by arrogance and oppression. On this fundamental threat to republican polities, Montesquieu writes: "As far as the sky is from the earth, so far is the true spirit of equality from the spirit of extreme equality. The former consists neither in making everyone command nor in making no one command, but in obeying and commanding one's equals. It seeks not to have no master but to have only one's equals for masters."[19] Republican *govern-*

---

[15]*Federalist* #37: 227, #84: 513.

[16]See, for example, Montesquieu's attack on aristocracy, *Spirit*, 2.3, 3.4. And see Aristotle, *Politics*, 1281a25–30, 1287a28–1287b5, 1295b1–1296a12.

[17]Montesquieu, *Spirit*, 2.3, 3.3.

[18]See Machiavelli, *Discourses*, I.4–6.

[19]Montesquieu, *Spirit*, 8.3.

ment requires "obeying and commanding one's equals," or "ruling and being ruled in turn" (as Aristotle says); but republican *subjects* are tempted to seek escape from rule altogether, "to have no master," not even a master who exercises "the power they [the people themselves] entrust." At the end of this road, says Montesquieu, is tyranny born of corruption and demagoguery, where the people lose their equality, their liberties, and "even the advantages of their corruption."[20]

For this reason, republican polities depend, more than other forms, on the character of their citizens. The prudent republican citizen must learn to recognize the ordinary vices of peoples, or of a particular people; anticipating the appearance of these vices in times of crisis, the prudent citizen acts in calmer times to guard against them by various means—education, laws, institutions, constitutions. The *Federalist* is just such an undertaking: an attempt to put in place "republican remed[ies] for the diseases most incident to republican government." Perhaps the people are fickle, as Montesquieu suggests: "The people always act too much or too little. Sometimes with a hundred thousand arms they upset everything; sometimes with a hundred thousand feet they move only like insects." Then a prudent republican must somehow guard against his own (future) inconstancy, and that of his fellow citizens, for example (as Publius says) by establishing institutions that will "blend stability with liberty," ensuring that the "cool and deliberate sense of the community" will prevail in the end and that the foolish or fanatical whims of the people can be thwarted. Or perhaps the people possess a "natural ability to perceive merit" in their governors but are less able to govern themselves directly, as Montesquieu also argues: "Just as most citizens, who are competent enough to elect, are not competent enough to be elected, so the people, who are sufficiently capable to call others to account for their management, are not suited to manage by themselves." In that case, self-government requires a moderate people that will authorize "*the total exclusion of the people in their collective capacity*" from government, according to Publius: indeed, that exclusion is evidently *the* ground of the superiority of (modern) representative self-government to (ancient) participatory self-government.[21]

[20]Aristotle, *Politics*, 1317b1 (and see 1292a5–40, 1319b1–32, 1320a5–35); and Montesquieu, *Spirit*, 8.2–8.3 (and see, 3.2, 5.3–5).

[21]*Federalist* #10: 81–84, #63: 384–87 (emphasis in original); and Montesquieu, *Spirit*, 2.2. See, too, *Federalist* #9: 71–73, #14: 100, #57: 350–53. Among the "infirmities incident to collective meetings of the people": "Ignorance will be the dupe of cunning, and passion the slave of sophistry and declamation" (#58: 360). And see Aristotle, *Politics*, 1318b5–40.

Or consider certain popular vices that spring from passion rather than judgment. If the people, "whose nature is to act from passion," are often aroused by zeal to form what Publius calls a majority "faction," "united and actuated by some common impulse of passion, or of interest, adverse to the rights of other citizens," then some cure will be needed for the natural intolerance and even fanaticism, perhaps especially religious fanaticism, that would otherwise trouble the republican polity. Here, Publius's *liberal* republican solution ("extend the sphere") differs from the *democratic* republican solution described by Montesquieu ("the full power of education" put to the task of inspiring "virtue" or "love of equality").[22] And then there is the classic popular vice: it may be that the people will from time to time be vulnerable to the enterprising ambition of a demagogue, who might successfully flatter the people and so encourage their corruption and even venality on the way to undermining the republic itself. Thus, as Publius remarks, "Men of factious tempers, of local prejudices, or of sinister designs, may, by intrigue, by corruption, or by other means, first obtain the suffrages, and then betray the interests of the people." Here too, a republican remedy ("refine and enlarge the public views" by various means) is required for a republican disease. And so on through the list of the ordinary popular vices.[23]

What is required is a miracle, or two. In a republic, to repeat, the people are both monarch and subject, ruler and ruled. So the people, who are naturally somewhat foolish and fickle, at least in public affairs, must restrain themselves from acting on intemperate or whimsical opinions, for no one else will stop them. They must arrange the republic so that the "cool and deliberate sense of the community" might prevail over their own worse judgment. And the people, who are naturally somewhat fac-

---

[22]*Federalist* #10: 77–84; and Montesquieu, *Spirit*, 2.2, 4.5. Montesquieu says that "*virtue* in a republic is love of the homeland, that is, love of equality" (Author's Preface; and see 5.3). I should reiterate that Montesquieu is not a partisan of the democratic republicanism that he describes so powerfully in Bks. 3–8: see Pangle, *Montesquieu's Philosophy*, 48–160. In #10, Publius adds, "So strong is this propensity of mankind to fall into mutual animosities that where no substantial occasion presents itself the most frivolous and fanciful distinctions have been sufficient to kindle their unfriendly passions and excite their most violent conflicts."

[23]*Federalist* #10: 82. See, too, Montesquieu, *Spirit*, 2.2, 3.3, 8.2–4; cf. 5.6; and see Aristotle, *Politics*, passages cited in n. 14. Cf. *Federalist* #48: 309, #70: 423. One further vice worth mentioning: perhaps "living in a disorderly way is more pleasant to the many than living with moderation," as Aristotle suggests (*Politics*, 1319b31–32). Irving Kristol offers this nice definition of self-government: "the willingness of people to permit their baser selves to be directed by their better selves" (Kristol, *On the Democratic Idea*, 6; see 1–21).

tious and fanatical, must also restrain themselves from indulging zealous and intolerant fevers: again, no one else will stop them; if the people cannot find a way to calm themselves, they will not be calmed. What is required for self-government, in short, is a people of a certain quality: moderate, responsible, capable of self-restraint, aware of their own ordinary vices. Thus, Publius writes:

> As there is a degree of depravity in mankind which requires a certain degree of circumspection and distrust, so there are other qualities in human nature which justify a certain portion of esteem and confidence. Republican government presupposes the existence of these qualities in a higher degree than any other form. Were the pictures which have been drawn by the political jealousy of some among us faithful likenesses of the human character, the inference would be that there is not sufficient virtue among men for self-government; and that nothing less than the chains of despotism can restrain them from destroying and devouring one another.

Indeed, even if the solutions to the problems of self-government are institutional (representation, extend the sphere, separation of powers, and the rest), and so do not depend directly on the moral education of the people, the sober and cautious judgment that enables a people to abide, and perhaps even to embrace, these self-imposed restraints on self-government, itself "presupposes" a kind of virtue.[24]

So much on the problem of republican self-government. What are the solutions? Broadly speaking, one might say that partisans of republicanism (at least since Locke) have employed two strategies in seeking republican cures for republican ills. The *liberal* republican strategy is, roughly, enlightenment: Tocqueville's "self-interest properly understood" plus Publius's new "science of politics" (separation of powers, representation, and the rest). The *democratic* republican strategy is, roughly, the inculcation of "virtue": censorious moral education plus "love of the republic" (patriotism, love of equality).[25] Much of the drama of modern political theory consists in quarrels and rapprochements between these branches of the republican tradition. The liberal republicans have won most of the victories, but remain troubled by a

[24]*Federalist* #63: 384, #55: 346. Cf.· Aristotle, *Politics*, 1281a40–1281b22, 1295a25–1295b35, 1318b10–1319a5.

[25]Tocqueville, *Democracy in America*, II.ii.8; *Federalist* #9: 72; Montesquieu, *Spirit*, 4.5, 5.2–6, 7.2; and Rousseau, *Social Contract*, 2.7, 4.7. See, too, on enlightened self-interest, Locke, *Second Treatise*, §57.

certain doubt: perhaps we need virtue too, if only as the "seedbed" of our vaunted enlightenment.[26]

Here is a sketch of the liberal republican strategy. The liberal republican hopes that enlightened self-interest can somehow be made to do the work that is elsewhere done by fear or virtue, curing the natural disease of immoderate and lawless passions.[27] Certain private habits of self-restraint and certain public habits of civility are reasonable, or so it appears to the liberal, if only because they are conducive to civil peace and a measure of good fellowship. Perhaps there is no natural disharmony between public and private good. To be sure, enlightened self-interest cannot inspire splendid self-sacrifice: but who needs it? Better to remind human beings of the utility of the modest virtues: it is often prudent to be good. Liberal republicanism aims to *tame* the souls of human beings, by various means—e.g. commerce ("everywhere there is commerce, there are gentle mores") and enlightenment ("knowledge makes men gentle, and reason inclines toward humanity"). These kinder, gentler liberal virtues are far from the unnatural, harsh and even savage (*sauvage*) virtues of the democratic republican, about whom more presently.[28] Think of the liberal soul so richly described in Franklin's *Autobiography*.

But no one really supposes that such enlightened self-interest is a sufficient foundation for popular government, so the argument continues. The liberal republican next relies on another triumph of enlightenment rationalism, the new "science of politics"—by which, says Publius, "the excellencies of republican government may be retained and its imperfections lessened or avoided." Among these modern improvements in the science of politics: separation of powers, bicameralism, an independent judiciary, representation, the extended sphere. These institutions are principally designed to put some distance between the people and the government (or between the people qua subjects and the peo-

---

[26]See, for example, Glendon, *Rights Talk*. Perhaps, as Kristol suggests, we have not sufficiently noticed that liberal society has long been "living off the accumulated moral capital of traditional religion and traditional moral philosophy" (*Two Cheers*, 65–66): in my terms, that the strategy of liberal republicanism relies on moral "capital" accumulated during a prior history of something akin to democratic republicanism, which it depletes.

[27]On this natural disease, see Hobbes, *Leviathan*, ch. 17, beginning: "For the Lawes of Nature (as *Justice, Equity, Modesty, Mercy*, and (in summe) *doing to others, as wee would be done to*,) of themselves, without the terrour of some Power, to cause them to be observed, are contrary to our naturall Passions, that carry us to Partiality, Pride, Revenge, and the like."

[28]Montesquieu, *Spirit*, 20.1, 15.3, 4.8. These "gentle mores" can perhaps be traced to Hobbes's virtue of "compleasance" ("*That every man strive to accommodate himselfe to the rest*"), *Leviathan*, ch. 15, emphasis in original.

ple qua monarch), so that even when popular judgment and passion prove to be immune, for a time, to the doctrine of self-interest properly understood, the people can yet do no harm and in time the "cool and deliberate sense of the community" will prevail. In these ways, the liberal republican aims to cure the ordinary republican diseases, or to treat their symptoms.[29]

Democratic republicans are perhaps more troubled than their liberal cousins by the natural lawlessness of human beings. Is it not a great folly, asks Rousseau, to suppose that reason can itself sustain the social virtues? "For all their morality, men would never have been anything but monsters if Nature had not given them pity in support of reason."[30] A much stronger remedy is required than self-interest properly understood: call it "virtue." Here is a sketch of that democratic republican doctrine. Virtue is patriotism, a "love of the republic" that requires, says Montesquieu, "a continuous preference of the public interest over one's own" and even "a renunciation of oneself, which is always a very painful thing."[31] So virtue is not natural: it will be necessary, as Rousseau says, to "change human nature," to transform "each individual, who by himself is a perfect and solitary whole, into a part of a larger whole from which this individual receives, in a sense, his life and his being." Where virtue reigns, "each citizen is nothing, and can do nothing, except with all the others."[32] It is no wonder that the inculcation of republican virtue requires, as Montesquieu says, the "full power of education." Such virtue "is singularly connected with democracies" (hence, *democratic* republicanism), and so with "love of equality" and "love of frugality," because where there is luxury there is inequality, where there is inequality there is arrogance and envy, and these are the origins of faction. So the democratic republican embraces an egalitarian, participatory politics that is almost the opposite of liberal republican politics. (Rousseau goes so far as to insist that representation is a kind of slavery.) With respect to private affairs, the preservation of virtue ("a continuous preference of the public interest") requires a censorious public moralism, vigilance against the return of immoderate private passions and venal private interests. Finally, virtue is not a kind of knowledge but a feeling, and so it is not dependent on any science of politics or even prudent judgment ("the lowest man in the state, like the

---

[29]*Federalist #9*: 72–73.
[30]Rousseau, *Second Discourse*, 161.
[31]Montesquieu, *Spirit*, 4.5.
[32]Rousseau, *Social Contract*, 2.7.

first, can have this feeling").[33] Not enlightenment, but a restoration of that "sublime science of simple souls," which is virtue, is required.[34] The aim of the democratic republican is not to tame the passions, but to transform human beings into citizens: not "gentle mores" but severe virtues. Such virtue, were it achieved, would doubtless be a remedy for the diseases most incident to republican government—or, at least, for those diseases arising from corrupt private passions and interests.

Certainly there are today very few partisans of either democratic or liberal republicanism in their pristine forms. Contemporary republican theory is marked by an uneasy tension between these two competing impulses, toward enlightenment and toward virtue. Since I have frequently cited the *Federalist* here, let me add that Publius's argument seems to me to contain a judicious blending of the two strategies, though it is tolerably clear that the liberal republicanism predominates, mixed with certain leavening democratic ingredients. Publius might agree with the sober Montesquieu: "Who would think it! Even virtue has need of limits." And yet, Publius was also prepared to admit that sober reason sometimes seeks the aid of intoxicating virtue.[35]

II

Benjamin Barber is a partisan of a new idea of participatory ("strong") democracy: this is the new republican faith of critics of liberal republicanism today. Here, I begin with what is for Barber "the first and most significant" aspect of strong democratic politics: "strong democratic talk." For Barber, the measure of a republican polity is not the quality of

---

[33]Montesquieu, *Spirit*, 4.8, 5.2–4; see, too, 5.19. And see Rousseau, *Social Contract*, 3.15, 4.7. Besides, knowledge does not make men gentle; on the contrary, says Rousseau, "it is Philosophy that isolates him; it is by means of Philosophy that he secretly says at the sight of a suffering man, perish if you wish, I am safe" (*Second Discourse*, 162). And commerce, which does soften human souls, is yet a threat to republican morals: Montesquieu, *Spirit*, 7.1–2; and Rousseau, *First Discourse*, 16–17. On the severity of virtue, Montesquieu goes so far as to compare the citizen to a monk, whose love is as great as his affliction is great (*Spirit*, 5.2). Unlike Rousseau, Montesquieu is not, to repeat, a partisan of the democratic republicanism that he describes in these passages.

[34]Rousseau, *First Discourse*, 27.

[35]Montesquieu, *Spirit*, 11.4. For this sentiment in the *Federalist*, see #10: 78. On the *Federalist*, see David F. Epstein, *The Political Theory of "The Federalist"*; Pangle, *Spirit*; and cf. Garry Wills, *Explaining America: The Federalist*. For the reasons outlined in the text, the republican idea of "virtue" is somewhat ambiguous, ranging in meaning from the self-sacrificing virtue praised by Rousseau and Montesquieu, to the more moderate yet still more-than-rational idea of civic virtue as the condition of Enlightenment liberal politics (now favored by neoconservatives), to the strictly rational sort of virtue as self-interest properly understood that was invented by Hobbes (*Leviathan*, ch. 15) and praised by Tocqueville.

the speeches of its "first citizens," but the quality of the "talk" of its ordinary citizens. Strong leaders make lazy and incompetent citizens, says
Barber; but we need strong citizens. Participatory politics (above all,
strong democratic talk) enables citizens of republican communities to do
without imposing leaders. Thus, today's republican theorists, including
Barber, are typically fans of popular modes of political speech: not the
rousing or enlightening speeches of statesmen, but the prosaic talk of citizens at town meetings and elsewhere. Indeed, what distinguishes many
contemporary republican theorists from earlier republican theorists (including, say, Rousseau and Publius) is an enthusiasm for "unmediated"
self-government ("democracy"): "We suffer, in the face of our era's manifold crises, not from too much but from too little democracy." As
Walzer, another leading republican theorist, says in a review of Barber's
The Conquest of Politics: "It is his commitment to a democratic radicalism that has made Barber one of the leading—he is also one of the most
intelligent—representatives of contemporary republican political theory." Barber, I would say, is the founder of a new species of democratic
republicanism: he is above all a critic of liberal republicanism, like
Rousseau; unlike Rousseau, I will argue, his republicanism is not a republicanism of *virtue*, but a republicanism of *warmth*.[36]

Once again, a digression on terms. For the sake of clarity, and in order
to accommodate the introduction of this new species of democratic republicanism into the argument, I propose to refer, hereafter, to the three
parties as follows: liberal republicans (Publius) as *liberals*; old-fashioned
democratic republicans (Rousseau) as *republicans*; newfangled democratic republicans (Barber) as *democrats*. But I continue to regard each doctrine as a species of the republicanism described earlier.[37]

Barber's participatory republicanism has both a political and a philosophical aspect. "Political theory and the politics of democracy share a
profound and provoking kinship," according to Barber. "Both are rooted
in the quest for a language that must be common and conversational." In
two recent books, Barber has examined the kinship between conversational democratic politics and conversational political theory from both
sides. In *Strong Democracy*, he describes certain supposed pathologies of
our liberal political practice, including above all our incapacity for "genuine" self-government, which can be traced to an excess of liberalism: its

---

[36]Barber, "Neither Leaders nor Followers: Citizenship Under Strong Democracy,"
117–21, 128–32; Barber, *Strong Democracy*, xi, 117–18, 173, 261; and Walzer, "Flight
from Philosophy."
[37]See above, p. 110.

hedonistic moral psychology, its "pervasive privatization of the *res publica*," its reductionist conception of political reason, among other vices. In contrast, a strong democratic politics, says Barber, is "capable of transforming dependent private individuals into free citizens and partial and private interests into public goods"—above all by means of strong democratic talk. "At the heart of strong democracy is talk," says Barber, for it is by means of talk that solitary individuals learn the art of "public seeing" and so become citizens who "distinguish the requirements of 'we' styles of thinking from those of 'me' styles of thinking": "talk is . . . a force with which we can create a community."[38] And in *The Conquest of Politics*, Barber decries the conquest of democratic politics by (foundationalist) liberal philosophy, which supplants the "real talk" and political judgment of citizens by granting authority—beyond its proper domain—to the hypothetical talk and philosophical certainty of philosophers and their ministers (especially, as Walzer emphasizes, judges). "The primary political target of foundationalism is democracy itself," argues Barber, since the claim of democrats to rule themselves rests on a suspicion about the limits of philosophy: that "public opinion agreed upon overrules private 'truth' disputed"; that "politics is what men do when metaphysics fails." Beyond this, philosophy "tends to suffuse the *vita activa* of politics with an untoward and enervating torpor," relieving citizens of the duty to judge for themselves and enabling them to retire to their private worlds. Once more, democratic talk—perhaps facilitated by philosophical "conversationalists"—is the cure for liberal ills: talk draws alienated or lazy individuals out of their private worlds, enabling them to participate in the civic task of "public thinking."[39] Here, I begin with the political aspect of democratic talk.

What is "strong democracy"? Barber aims his fire at liberalism, in defense of democracy: "an excess of liberalism has undone democratic institutions." Above all, liberalism has destroyed citizenship by emancipating "man's lower nature"—even the "solitary Hobbesian predator" in each of us. Politics is thus reduced to "bargaining . . . in a world of base competition." So the task of strong democracy is to "transform [interest-motivated individuals] into citizens capable of reassessing themselves and their interests in terms of newly invented communal norms and newly imagined public goods." But why is a transformation required? Why not rather ap-

---

[38]Barber, *Conquest*, 21, 210; Barber, *Strong Democracy*, xiv, 151, 170–73, 198; and see also xi–xiv, 133–37.

[39]Barber, *Conquest*, 7, 15, 209, 11, 153, 200; cf. Barber, *Strong Democracy*, 129–30, 135–36; and Walzer, "Flight from Philosophy."

peal to "man's 'higher nature' " against his lower nature—thus elevating human beings, so to speak, rather than transforming them? Barber's answer reveals a certain agreement with his liberal enemies: "democratic politics makes possible cooperation and an approximation of concord where they *do not exist by nature.*" Indeed, Barber argues, "the stress on transformation is at the heart of the strong democratic conception of politics. Every politics confronts the competition of private interests and the conflict that competition engenders." Concord is *not* natural, so "strong democracy *transforms conflict.* It turns dissensus into an occasion for mutualism." Perhaps there is no " 'higher nature,' " no natural love of virtue or community (hence, the inverted commas); human beings *are* selfish predators, if not by nature then at least wherever there is no strong democratic politics. Citizens must be *"created"* by a "politics of transformation." Besides, any regard for a putatively 'higher' nature leads quickly to the "dangers of totalism."[40]

With Rousseau, then, Barber argues that republican politics requires "*transforming* each individual, who by himself is a perfect and solitary whole, into part of a larger whole from which this individual receives, in a sense, his life and his being." The various liberal attempts to tame the predatory or at any rate selfish souls of human beings have failed (on this point, too, Barber's reasons resemble Rousseau's), and so a more radical cure is required. Since human beings possess "malleable natures," politics can achieve empathy, mutualism, even affection—where these do not exist by nature. And yet, Barber does not embrace the severe republicanism of virtue that is praised by Rousseau. He is hostile to "unitary" forms of democracy, for good but recognizably liberal reasons: above all, these can be "perilous to freedom." That is, to come to the present point, Barber aims to achieve a democratic republicanism of common purposes, but he repudiates virtue and the harsh accoutrements of virtue (the necessary conditions, Rousseau supposed, of any such republicanism); or, again, he repudiates the liberal republicanism of self-interested bargaining, but aims to preserve pluralism and diversity, the various liberal freedoms, even (in a sense) the liberal respect for individuals.[41] Barber confronts the dilemma of self-government—how to tame or transform the naturally recalcitrant passions so that the people might govern themselves—but he hopes to avoid the supposed excesses of the old solutions.

[40]Barber, *Strong Democracy*, xi, 118–19 (emphasis added), 136, 173–74, 151 (emphasis in original); and see 128, 153, 213–16; and Barber, *Conquest*, 209.

[41]Rousseau, *Social Contract*, 2.7 (emphasis added); Barber, *Strong Democracy*, 117–118, 148–50, 184–90. Cf. Strauss, "On the Intention of Rousseau."

But how is this radical transformation of human nature to be achieved, as in Barber's gentler democratic republicanism, by means of democratic talk, and no more?

Barber has remarkably high hopes that the promotion of strong democratic talk can have valuable civic consequences. In the concluding, programmatic chapter of *Strong Democracy*, he outlines a number of reforms designed to "institutionalize strong democratic talk." Most important, strong democracy demands "institutions that will involve individuals at both the neighborhood and the national level in common talk." To begin, a "national system of *neighborhood assemblies* in every rural, suburban, and urban district in America" must be established. These assemblies would "meet often, perhaps weekly" (Saturday afternoons and Wednesday evenings, Barber suggests); owing to prevailing civic incompetence, they would not (at first) be legislative bodies, but would simply provide a public space for citizen talk—"an open and ongoing forum for the discussion of a flexible and citizen-generated agenda." In time, a competent citizenry might even exercise certain political powers in assembly. Yet local participation can sometimes "divide and parochialize," so it is also necessary to provide forums, such as electronic town meetings, "in which participation is direct yet communication is regional or even national." Barber even suggests that interactive television technologies might be "put to serious civic use": what works for "home shopping," says Barber, can work for "multichoice polling and voting" as well.[42]

As Barber acknowledges, there are serious "Madisonian" objections to these proposals. Beyond the danger already noted of neighborhood parochialism, Barber also recognizes the various dangers of direct democracy that led Publius and other liberals to embrace representation as a way to escape the excesses of an untutored and "tumultuous populace": "plebiscitary tyranny," a tendency to "fall prey to peer pressure, eloquence, social conformity," "popular prejudice," "elite manipulation." Indeed, these dangers are even more pressing in the case of large-scale electronic town meetings, because, as Barber recognizes, the various technologies that might make possible a national system of participation can be used in "manipulative and destructive ways." But Barber dismisses most such complaints as "Luddite," for reasons that are not always convincing. Thus, he argues that because our communities are "no longer seared by Puritan zest," "uniformitarian coerciveness" is no longer a

---

[42]Barber, *Strong Democracy*, 261, 267–78.

threat—as if no comparable fervor were imaginable today. In any case, in the wake of the Perot phenomenon it may now be more difficult to suppose that such popular vices are altogether a thing of the past. (Indeed, Barber's own ambivalence toward liberalism, and especially his love of freedom and diversity, does lead him to worry a bit that in strong democracy, "conservatism" will too often win.)[43] But these sobering liberal doubts regarding participatory democracy are well known, and they are not my principal concern here.

What is the purpose of all this talk? Good democratic talk transforms human beings into citizens, says Barber, by promoting civility, mutualism, empathy, affection, even patriotism. Such talk enables citizens to "invent alternative futures, create mutual purposes, and construct competing visions of community." "Think of . . . two college freshmen talking over a first cup of coffee: there are no debates, no arguments, no challenges. . . . There is only a 'getting to know you' and thereby 'getting to know *us*'—exploring the common context, traits, circumstances, or passions that make of two separate identities one single *we*."[44] Above all, strong democrats do not "imprison speech in reason." Rather, they learn to appreciate the *affective* and *creative* powers of talk: such talk breeds empathy, and empathy makes possible an "*artificial*" friendship that is superior to the natural kind ("for the attachments we feel toward natural kith and kin can be constricting and parochializing": again, democratic citizenship is not natural). Strong democratic talk teaches individuals to undertake an "imaginative effort" to "reformulate their interests, purposes, norms, and plans in a mutualistic language of public goods"—and so to learn the art of "public seeing." Throughout *Strong Democracy*, Barber displays a remarkable optimism about the "transformative" power of democratic talk: "the affective power of talk is, then, the power to stretch the human imagination so that the *I* of private self-interest can be reconceptualized and reconstituted as a *we* that makes possible civility and common political action."[45]

Barber frequently describes political talk in strangely antipolitical terms ("think of two college freshmen"). If liberals sometimes look only

[43]Barber, *Strong Democracy*, 268–84; and see 158–61, 309.

[44]Barber, *Strong Democracy*, 182–84, 176–77. Or again: "Voting suggests a group of men in a cafeteria bargaining about what they can buy as a group that will suit their individual tastes. Strong democratic politics suggests a group of men in a cafeteria contriving new menus, inventing new recipes, and experimenting with new diets in the effort to create a public taste that they can all share" (136–37).

[45]Barber, *Strong Democracy*, 176, 188–90, 170–71; and see Barber, *Conquest*, 210.

at the most vulgar forms of political speech, and so seem to "make our words the slaves of our interests," Barber often does not seem to be looking at politics at all. Like other communitarian theorists, Barber hopes that it will be possible to transform the language of politics into something akin to the language of love ("make of two separate identities one single *we*"). Thus, in Barber's dialogic response to Ackerman, the character "Barber" says: "the power of political talk lies in its creativity, its variety, its openness and flexibility, its inventiveness, its capacity for discovery, its subtlety and complexity, its potential for empathetic and affective expression." This speech occurs immediately after a dialogue that is said to show that "speech is affective as well as cognitive in *politically relevant ways.*" What is this example of "politically relevant" affective speech? Romeo and Juliet are discussing a political problem: how "to put an end to Montagu versus Capulet." At first, they try "neutral dialogue"; but they soon recognize that no mere "bargain" can settle the controversy. But then:

> ROMEO: Then bargains be damned, my sweet, and in honor to unreason let us marry forthwith; and *that* precious bargain shall supersede every other our careless families have made and broken. . . .
>
> JULIET: Dare we, dearest? Could we truly marry though but moments ago we were locked in the confines of heartless neutral dialogue? That loveless discourse of the lonely and the vain?

A little later:

> JULIET: Why, then, Capulet and Montagu shall become one, and all conflict will subside. Where there is a community of love, there is no enmity. Where purposes are bound together by trust and by mutuality, there are no private interests. Oh unreasonable Romeo, kiss me!

This is not the only place where Barber suggests that democratic citizenship is a species of love.[46]

Here is Barber's utopian dream: to create citizens who will be inspired by political love or *"artificial"* friendship to embrace the democratic community of common seers wholeheartedly—and all of this principally by means of talk, "the first and most significant" aspect of strong demo-

---

[46]Barber, *Conquest*, 147–51 (emphasis added); cf. 51–53, 198; and cf. Rorty, *Objectivity*, 205–7.

cratic politics. But Barber nowhere offers friends of republicanism good reasons to suppose that democratic talk can be as "mutualistic" as the talk of lovers, or even as warm as the talk of two college freshmen who are becoming friends. There is no natural inclination toward political community that is akin to the natural inclination toward community that consumes lovers (or that more gently binds families, or friends)—as Barber admits: the "attachments we feel toward *natural* kith and kin . . . can exclude and subvert rather than nourish citizenship"; *political* "concord" does not "exist by nature." From the point of view of old-fashioned republicans, Barber is unreasonably hopeful regarding the power of mundane talk to tame the human soul. Thus, Barber's republican hero Rousseau describes what is involved in giving human beings a second nature, and the lesson is chastening: "He must, in short, take away man's own forces in order to give him forces that are foreign to him and that he cannot make use of without the help of others. The more these natural forces are dead and destroyed, and the acquired ones great and lasting, the more the institution as well is solid and perfect."[47]

Certain forms of republican speech can doubtless contribute to this transformation, as I have already argued. But such a transformation of natural individuals into republican citizens can hardly be achieved by means of *democratic* talk, without aid of inspiriting speeches of statesmen and much more besides. Indeed, Rousseau's legislator must make use of extraordinary "mystifications": "Since the legislator is . . . unable to use either force or reasoning, he must necessarily have recourse to another order of authority, which can win over without violence and persuade without convincing. This is what has always forced the fathers of nations to have recourse to the intervention of heaven and to attribute their own wisdom to the Gods." Beyond this, talk alone is not enough to change human nature, says Rousseau; various modes of censorious public moralism—perhaps including establishment of a religion, surely including sumptuary laws and other illiberal measures—must be employed by the republican legislator. All of this is too harsh for Barber, who wants the warmth (mutualism, affection, patriotism) of republican community, but without the severity and austerity of republican virtue; or again, Barber aims to preserve the "gentle mores" and broad freedoms of liberal polities while somehow exciting republican sentiments. (Compare Rousseau's republican radicalism to Barber's most specific example of the

---

[47]Barber, *Strong Democracy*, 173, 189 (emphasis of "natural" added), 119; and Rousseau, *Social Contract*, 2.7.

power of democratic talk "to nurture empathetic forms of reasoning": feedback polls at video town meeting debates regarding abortion, which present a "varied and searching set of choices," not only extremist voices, and thereby encourage "public seeing.")[48]

So much for republican objections to the idea of democratic talk. From the point of view of the liberal as well, Barber's account of political talk is incredibly thin, divorced from the reality of politics. He is a critic of liberal talk: liberal styles of thinking are, of course, "me" styles. Liberal talk is often "a form of aggression," little more than "animal expletives meant to signify bargaining positions in a world of base competition," according to Barber: "the war of all against all carried on by other means." For such liberals, talk is principally useful because it helps us to be selfish in a civil way, to reason with one another about our private interests in peace; it surely cannot transform naturally solitary and querulous individuals ("avaricious but prudent beasts") into citizens who have learned the art of "public seeing." Even the more high-minded (Kantian) liberal talk, which is disciplined by philosophy to recognize the constraints of neutrality, reasonableness, and equal respect, is politically impoverishing, says Barber, because it too denigrates the affective uses of speech, which can create citizens and communities. Liberal philosophy sanctions both selfish and disinterested talk, but it cannot recognize mutualist common talk. But both forms of liberal talk, it seems to me, reflect an underlying realism that is absent from Barber's more hopeful vision of a political community founded on little more than a new way of talking. In this respect, at least, Hobbesian liberal talk is more like the "real talk" to which Barber sometimes appeals in chastising the "hypothetical talk" of Kantian liberals (Ackerman's "neutral conversation," Rawls's "original position") than is his democratic talk; indeed, it is precisely because "real talk" so often seems to be talk about power and interest, even when it is disguised as talk about distributive justice or patriotism or piety, that Kantian liberal theorists seek to escape it in the name of fairness or neutrality.[49]

Barber displays remarkably little interest in the manifold partisan uses of the human faculty of speech: for example, the *angry* speech of partisans. When Aristotle, the first republican theorist of speech, makes his democrat and even his aristocrat speak, they soon curse. It is not only or

---

[48]Rousseau, *Social Contract*, 2.7; see, too, 4.7–8; and Barber, *Strong Democracy*, 286–89.

[49]Barber, *Strong Democracy*, 174–76; and Barber, *Conquest*, 54–151, esp. 132–36.

even primarily interests (justified in speeches that consist only of "animal expletives," according to Barber) that engender partisan conflict among human beings in political communities. Rather, it is precisely the more human kinds of speech that are most dangerous (as well as most ennobling), according to Aristotle. It is not bestial "voice," but human speech, that "serves to reveal the advantageous and the harmful, and hence also the just and the unjust"; it is speech that makes it possible for human beings to quarrel about justice, and to do so in the angry tones of moral indignation. The curses of Aristotle's partisans reflect the natural intractability of partisan "perceptions" and partisan opinions about justice; the natural articulation of the political world into parties is the consequence of the cultivation of the human faculty of speech, through which human beings constitute and express these diverse perceptions and opinions. Indeed, it seems to me that liberals properly cultivate the conciliatory language of liberal bargaining, which is self-interested and even bestial, in part because they hope to tame the angry republican language of partisan indignation, which is the more moral and human language of civil strife. Thus, liberal civility rests in part on respectful silences regarding contentious religious and moral opinions that might otherwise disturb civil peace: constitutional gag rules. For Barber, talk is the medium of bestial liberal negotiation or humane republican community; but the rich tradition of republican political thought and practice reveals many other, more ambiguous forms of republican speech.[50]

We also know that there are indeed statesmen and demagogues who seem to "make the Gods speak," and (more generally) that these speeches are often as important in republican politics as the debates of legislators or the chatter of democrats at town meetings. And yet, how can the republican people, who are themselves commonly imprudent and animated by passions that delude them, recognize those who will govern them well? As a result of this worry, republican political philosophers often raise the question whether it is possible to educate or otherwise constitute a people that will be able to distinguish between the demagogue who flatters them and the statesman who seeks to govern them. Even republican statesmen who are not mere demagogues must often persuade the people by appeal to their passions, since popular reason is often defective. Perhaps it is not always possible to tell the people the truth; at any rate, it is seldom necessary and rarely sufficient for a republican statesman to tell the truth. When a republican statesman finds that

[50] Aristotle, *Politics*, 1281a15–23, 1281b15–20, 1253a1–20.

it is necessary to alert a quiescent people that danger approaches, or to sustain a troubled people in time of hardship, or to calm an angry people when they are tempted to great injustice or imprudence on that account, and so on through the list of natural popular vices, it will often be necessary for the statesman to use the tools of the demagogue. Thus, it has long been recognized by sober partisans of republican government that the most fundamental problem that confronts such communities is the problem of the demagogue, or of populist speech: one can hardly rely upon the ambitious few to lead the people toward their proper interest, since ambition is notoriously flexible.[51] (Consider Thucydides' account of the debate between Cleon and Diodotus before the Athenian people; and see Orwin's "Democracy and Distrust," on this debate.[52]) If this is so, then republican theorists must ask how it is possible to constitute a people that can tell the difference between the "best citizens," who enable the people to rule themselves well, and the demagogues, who flatter the people and thereby lead them to succumb to foolish or wicked temptations. If we cannot do without "first citizens," then it is necessary to ensure that they will be as respectable as possible. But that is a problem that does not trouble Barber, or so it seems.

III

Liberal philosophy is perhaps the principal cause of our civic incompetence today, according to Barber, and so I turn now to the philosophic aspect of Barber's praise of democratic talk. In "substituting reason for common sense," foundationalist liberal philosophers have "declared the sense of commoners to be nonsense." And we have too often submitted to their authority: the authoritarian philosophers of liberal democracy have stolen politics from its citizens. Philosophy privileges the voices of

---

[51]Consider Lincoln's Lyceum speech, when he spoke as a young man about love of glory: "whether at the expense of emancipating slaves, or enslaving freemen." Or consider this (unguarded) account of a master of the art of republican oratory, this "key to the hearts of men": "A meeting of grave citizens, protected by all the cynicism of these prosaic days, is unable to resist its influence. From unresponsive silence they advance to grudging approval and thence to complete agreement with the speaker. The cheers become louder and more frequent; the enthusiasm momentarily increases; until they are convulsed by emotions they are unable to control and shaken by passions of which they have resigned the direction." "Indeed," Churchill continues, "the orator is the embodiment of the passions of the multitude," whose achievement (but it is also a frightful power) is founded on an ability to "allay the commonplace influences and critical faculties of his audience" (Churchill, 817–21; cf. Walzer, *Radical Principles*, 26, 44–45, 55–57, 67–71).

[52]Thucydides, *Peloponnesian War*, 3.36–49; Orwin, "Democracy and Distrust."

the most reasonable; but a truly democratic politics takes as its standard "common willing, not private reasoning," and so it cannot admit the authority of philosophy, says Barber.[53] Indeed, Barber is not alone. It is now quite fashionable to argue that "democratic" political philosophy recognizes no authority beyond (more or less constrained) "conversation." Conversation, it is said, respects democratic equality in a way that philosophy, which seems to imply the superior moral authority of those who are reasonable, does not: "So it is with democratic talk, where no voice is privileged, no position advantaged, no authority other than the process itself acknowledged."[54] And yet, if there is no reasonable means of grounding political beliefs on some foundation that transcends human choice or will, as many political theorists now argue, then it will surely be necessary for democrats to learn as well how to constrain such choice democratically even as they emancipate it from the constraints of the philosophers—or strength of will may supplant reason as a formidable antidemocratic claim to rule. The "democratic" mode of choosing, then, is through conversation or "dialogue," which equally evades the two authoritarian threats (or "monologues"): the authority of the reasonable philosopher and the authority of the willful master.[55]

[53]Barber, *Conquest*, 193, 13. Liberal philosophy is defective in other ways, according to Barber. Liberal philosophers cannot abide the contingency or messiness of political life, and so they seek to guide politics by abstract rules, neglecting the historical and other contexts that limit what is possible or desirable (*Conquest*, 115–16, 165). Liberal philosophers are content with a skepticism that yields inaction, but politics always demands action (*Conquest*, 10–12, 206–8). Liberal philosophy seeks to reduce the political to its prepolitical or natural elements, but politics resists such reductionism (*Conquest*, 99–102). And more.

[54]Barber, *Strong Democracy*, 183. See, too, Rorty, *Objectivity*, 175–96; Walzer, "Philosophy and Democracy"; and Bruce Ackerman, *Social Justice in the Liberal State.*

[55]For example, Ackerman, a liberal theorist who is also a partisan of "conversation," makes a similar argument about the connection between political talk and philosophical conversation—except that in Ackerman's case, the escape from (foundationalist) philosophy to conversation is in the service of liberal toleration, not republican "public seeing" or citizenship. In *Social Justice in the Liberal State*, he argues: "There is a perfect parallelism, then, between the role of political conversation *within* a liberal state, and the role of philosophical conversation *in defense of* a liberal state. Political talk within a liberal state is a device for organizing people who are otherwise free to follow very different paths to the good. Philosophical conversation in defense of a liberal state is a device for persuading people who are otherwise free to pursue very different paths to understanding. The task of *political* conversation is to make it possible for each citizen to defend his power without declaring himself intrinsically superior to any other citizen. The task of *philosophical* conversation is to make it possible for a person to reason his way to Neutrality without declaring that the path he has chosen is intrinsically better than any other route to liberalism." (Ackerman 1980, 359; see, too, Ackerman, "Why Dialogue?") Both Ackerman and Barber seem to believe that nonconversational foundationalist philosophy is a threat to democratic politics, for something like the same reason: the philosopher who claims to know true principles of

Thus, Barber's program for "strong democracy" gives rise to a new way of understanding political knowledge. "Politics in the participatory mode is the art of public seeing and of political judgment—of envisioning a common world." So Barber's political and philosophical arguments come together in an account of political judgment, his conversational alternative to traditional foundational reasoning about politics. For Barber, politics is an epistemologically autonomous world: "philosophy cannot legislate the meaning of the critical concepts entwined in our common life; rather, the politics definitive of our common life establishes the meaning of the critical normative ideas on which our mutuality hinges." To repeat, this democratic claim rests on a suspicion about the limits of philosophy: that "politics is what men do when metaphysics fails." Political judgment is sovereign "under conditions of epistemological uncertainty," but the opinions of political philosophers (as opposed to scientists, say) are almost always "contentious private opinion[s]." So political theorists and democratic citizens should conceive of "politics *as* epistemology," as the source of its own norms: here "there are no standards independent of . . . the sovereign citizenry." "Political judgment is the multitude deliberating, the multitude in action"; it is simply "common civic activity," the capacity to assume "the mantle of citizenship," by which "the I becomes a We," and then to undertake the task of envisioning and willing a common future.[56]

Political judgment can only emerge, then, where there is strong democratic citizenship: "Democracy turns out to be uniquely supportive of political judgment, because it maximizes interaction." But not any democracy. "Wise" political judgment requires no special cognitive powers, but it does require "dynamic, ongoing, common deliberation and action" among individuals who have been "transformed by social interaction into citizens." Thus, Barber would perhaps be prepared to admit that in our own weak liberal democracy the idea of political judgment would "leave the forging of political wisdom not to a ship of state but to a ship of fools," or to admit that such political judgment would be indistinguishable from "mob rule" or "mass prejudice." However that may be, "when politics in the *participatory* mode becomes the source of political knowledge—when such knowledge is severed from formal philosophy and becomes its own epistemology—then knowledge itself is redefined in terms of the chief

political right will too often also claim a political authority that properly belongs only to democratic (or liberal) citizens. They disagree about whether liberal tolerance or republican participation provides the greater security against these tyrants.

[56]Barber, *Conquest*, 105, 209–10, 14–17, 199–201; and see 116; Barber, *Strong Democracy*, 166, 201; and see 197.

virtues of democratic politics." In strong democratic politics, "there are no 'true' or 'false' answers," but only "alternative visions that compete for communal acceptance." For Barber, then, political judgment is *the* faculty of democratic imagination: it is a creative or poetic faculty, not a speculative or reasonable one; it belongs (in principle) equally to all citizens in common, and it is not the private possession of any authority. That is, there is no test of such knowledge beyond the communal will itself: political judgments are "produced by an ongoing process of democratic talk, deliberation, judgment, and action, and *they are legitimized solely by that process.*"[57]

Richard Rorty is another leading partisan of democratic community and democratic conversation, another voice against philosophy. For Rorty, thought properly begins with recognition that "our inheritance from, and our conversation with, our fellow-humans [is] our only source of guidance." So he denounces the "hope" that possesses philosophers, who seek a certain "metaphysical comfort": to find "something ahistorical and necessary to cling to." Rorty's praise of community is, of course, praise of democratic community in particular, even "an exaltation of democracy for its own sake." In the absence of philosophical foundations, democracy must be understood in a new way: "Instead of justifying democratic freedoms by reference to an account of human nature and the nature of reason," we should now embrace these freedoms as the "starting point—something we need not look behind," says Rorty; democracy is nothing more than the regime where citizens are prepared to "call 'true' whatever belief results from a free and open encounter of opinions, without asking whether this result agrees with something beyond that encounter." So there is nothing behind liberal democratic freedoms: there is only the democratic conversation. In the face of reasonable doubts regarding the ordinary vices of democracy of the sort expressed by liberal democrats, including Publius—that is, that democrats too often agree to "call 'true' " opinions that are silly or wicked—Rorty can offer only "utopian hope," indeed "criterionless hope": "Hope—the ability to believe that the future will be unspecifiably different from, and unspecifiably freer than, the past." Here is the democratic faith: "In the end, . . . what matters is our loyalty to other human beings clinging together against the dark, not our hope of getting things right."[58] Thus, the choice

---

[57]Barber, *Conquest,* 200, 204, 209–10; and Barber, *Strong Democracy,* 167–70 (emphasis added); cf. 127.

[58]Rorty, *Consequences,* 165–66; and Rorty, "Education," 200–204; see, too, Rorty, *Contingency,* 52, 84; cf. 48.

between democratic conversation and solitary philosophy is at bottom a moral choice: Rorty would replace the philosophic quest for metaphysical comfort ("something necessary and ahistorical to cling to") with a communal quest for moral comfort ("clinging together against the dark"). Again, he seeks to replace the "hope" of philosophers with the "hope" of democratic citizens.[59]

"Clinging together against the dark": the democratic humanism of Barber and Rorty is often expressed in tones of barely concealed despair, as if we must now live in the face of a nihilism from which there is no real escape. For this reason, too, Barber's democratic republicanism is a republicanism of *warmth*: warmth to comfort human beings against the "inconsolable coldness of modernity." Or again: "human freedom will be found not in caverns of private solitude but in the noisy assemblies where women and men meet daily as citizens and discover in each other's talk the consolation of a common humanity."[60] But if the desperation is well founded, then it is hard to credit the happy face of Barber's "strong democracy" or Rorty's "postmodern liberal ironism." What good reason is there to suppose that the hugs of our neighbors can deliver us from metaphysical despair, even if it were possible to achieve the strong democratic citizenship praised by Barber?[61]

Moreover, it is not obvious that "conversation" is a truly democratic account of moral reasoning in the face of the death of God, or that it can enable the democrat to evade one or another sort of tyranny: a victory over philosophy may simply deliver the democratic community into the hands of other sorts of masters. Conversation may not be democratic, since unconstrained conversation invites the rule not indeed of the wise,

[59]The notion that (democratic) conversation can offer a moral comfort that is not available to philosophers and other solitaries is also present in Ackerman's work. Consider the following remarkable passage in his *Social Justice in the Liberal State* (a passage that is explicitly offered as a kind of response to Nietzschean doubts about liberalism; this is the "highway to liberalism" that bypasses the death of God): "The hard truth is this: There is no moral meaning hidden in the bowels of the universe. All there is is you and I struggling in a world that neither we, nor any other thing, created. Yet there is not need to be overwhelmed by the void. We may create our own meanings, you and I; however transient or superficial, these are the only meanings we will ever know. And the first meaningful reality we must create—one presupposed by all other acts of meaningful conversation—is the idea that you and I are persons capable of giving meanings to the world. Yet this is just the achievement of a Neutral conversation" (368).

[60]Barber, *Conquest*, 179; and Barber, *Strong Democracy*, 311. Cf. Wolff, *Poverty*, on Durkheim: "The only hope is for men to huddle together and collectively create the warm world of meaning and coherence which impersonal nature cannot offer" (144).

[61]For a more thorough discussion of this issue, see my "Postmodern Liberalism and the Politics of Liberal Education."

but of the clever: certain kinds of sophists who are eager to deceive and to defraud the people. Even Barber acknowledges that it is necessary to protect the people from their temptation to be misled by flatterers: consider the comic figure of the "facilitator."[62] (This is the problem of the demagogue, to which I have already alluded.) Further, it is hard to see how such conversations can be constrained to respect equality without admitting appeals to universal reason of the sort that the idea of "conversation" is meant to prohibit. Besides, we can only *hope* that such a conversation will be a friendly one; we have no good reason to think that it will be so. A true conversation depends on the availability of a common language, but if nature provides no such common language, so that every language is in some measure a private language ("every human life is a poem"), then conversation cannot consist of the more or less peaceful appeal to common meanings. It will often consist of the willful (and potentially warlike) effort to bring about the "coincidence of a private obsession with a public need," as Rorty says, or to secure the community's endorsement of one's private language. What is the point of a conversation where there are no good reasons? As Rorty admits, where we "call 'true' whatever belief results from a free and open encounter of opinions, without asking whether this result agrees with something beyond that encounter," there is "no neat way to draw the line between persuasion and force." Then there are the "messier cases: brainwashing, media hype, and what the Marxists call 'false consciousness.' "[63] The democratic conversation can surely be made to serve the enemies of democracy and liberty.

Who gets to join the democratic conversation? It appears that no one is invited to this meeting of *moral strangers* (for there are no *citizens* until they are created by the conversation itself) except professors and kindred spirits: those who are committed to the moral value of speech as a mode of conflict resolution. Those who prefer force and fraud to speech are excluded. From the point of view of these thugs, who might even find the way of life of intellectuals to be cowardly or frivolous or self-indulgent, such conversationalists are only the weaklings who perversely think that their specific advantage (in talk) has a special dignity. That is, partisans of the idea of democratic talk have not yet answered the question that stands at the very beginning of the tradition of political philosophy, on the first

---

[62]Barber, *Strong Democracy*, 271–72, 310; and Barber, "Neither Leaders nor Followers," 125–30.

[63]Rorty, *Contingency*, 35–37, 48; and Rorty, "Education," 200.

page of the *Republic*, where Polemarchus asks Socrates: "What if we won't listen?" If reason has no claim to rule, then the taste for democratic conversation is just the peculiar will to power of those who are too cowardly to be really corrupt and too weak to be really violent. As a result, a whole range of important kinds of human beings will not participate in any such meeting of moral strangers. Tyrants and potential tyrants (as well as petty imitators) will not attend: Glaucon, not to mention more formidable foes of democracy, gets no satisfaction here. Fanatics and prophets who claim to speak with God will surely have no inclination to respect the rules of democratic conversation. Even ordinary folks who are happy enough with prevailing dogmas will stay home: to recall Oscar Wilde's famous remark, socialism takes too many evenings. And more. Many human beings, among these some of the most interesting and dangerous, will not pay the price of admission to this meeting—a concession that the peaceful resolution of conflict through conversation is more to be desired than other goods, whether moral goods or goods of other kinds.

Here is an ordinary vice of republicans (and others), as Aristotle says: to suppose that "words alone would suffice to make us good."[64] In this chapter, I have argued that responsible partisans of republican politics have good reasons to be troubled by the recent revival of the idea of democratic talk or conversation, most fully advanced in the work of Benjamin Barber but present in one form or another in the work of many other democratic theorists today. Above all, contemporary democratic theorists do not face up to the fundamental problem of republican government, with which this essay begins: how is honorable self-government possible, if such government requires the people to master their own ordinary vices? The new democratic theorists are, in brief, unreasonably hopeful regarding the roots of democratic citizenship; and this hopefulness is revealed in a failure to recognize the limits of democratic talk.

Certainly there are reasons for concern, even despair, regarding democratic possibilities today: as Barber and other democratic theorists contend, the people are now alienated and corrupt, no longer able to enjoy the rights and responsibilities of citizenship. Whether these and other republican diseases are somehow natural, so that any republican polity must seek their cures (as Barber suggests in agreement with the traditional views), or are rather the product of an enervating politics, it is tolerably clear that liberal republican regimes are today in need of measures to arouse citizenship.

[64]Aristotle, *Nicomachean Ethics*, 1179b4.

But democratic talk is no cure for our ills. Against the classical liberal and democratic traditions of republican thought, contemporary theorists fail to recognize the limits of talk or speech. Certainly, democratic talk can help to sustain a republican politics, as any reader of Tocqueville on the "spirit of liberty" and the New England town meeting must be aware. But it is as clear today as ever—after all, we live in a time of populist talk radio and Perot-style town meetings—that untutored ("unmediated") talk is often dogmatic, self-indulgent, and provincial, and that it mostly nourishes the ordinary vices (passions and follies) of the people. What is required is a people of a certain quality, whose common talk can (as Barber hopes) reinforce and sustain habits of good citizenship over time (not even this is reliable, as Lincoln suggested in his Lyceum speech). But there is no reason to suppose that talk itself can be the foundation of good citizenship, because untutored talk cannot ennoble or enlighten human beings, thus transforming them into virtuous (democratic republican) citizens or reasonable and moderate (liberal republican) citizens. Rather, such talk ordinarily exacerbates prevailing popular vices. Finally, the emerging faith in democratic talk or conversation for its own sake suggests, as I have argued, that contemporary democratic theorists have established a new aim of democratic citizenship, and so of democratic talk: such talk is "therapeutic," not a means to enlighten or ennoble a people that hopes to become capable of self-government, but a source of moral comfort or warmth in the face of "the inconsolable coldness of modernity." As a result, our democratic theorists are often tempted to indulge the very habits of complacency and self-pity that are among the principal roots of our particular vices.

6

Liberalism
and the Idea of Patriotism

Human beings belong in communities: is there not something perverse, even inhuman, about the solitary individual who lives beside but not quite among his neighbors, rubbing up against them from time to time for purely private purposes without ever embracing any of them wholeheartedly, without ever discovering that there are joys known only to those who submerge their private selves in some community and who thereby cease to be individuals but become lovers or friends or patriots—or whatever? Even the solitary Socrates was perhaps not quite human: for he was, it seems, unable to distinguish between a "friend" and a "good man," and so he lived his life, so to speak, beyond friendship.[1] We certainly admire, or praise, those human beings who love others before themselves, who nobly sacrifice themselves (but not really, since there is no longer a private self to be sacrificed) in devotion to, or despair of, some common good: Romeo and Juliet, Achilles, the nameless Spartans at Thermopylae, among other dead heroes.[2] Perhaps we even admire the patriot, who loves the republic before himself, above the lover or the friend. For the cause seems more noble, more enduring, more just.

So patriotism is a kind of love: but everyone knows that love is blind and that love is foolish. Thus, the lover is known to bestow virtues where they do not exist, and to be blind to vices that are plain enough; and the lover is often prepared to render awesome and horrible service to his beloved, risking everything, sometimes to no good end. For these reasons, says Pangle, "patriotism, like every other form of loyalty or allegiance,

---

[1]Plato, *Republic*, 334c–335a.
[2]*Iliad* 18:80–82: Patroclus was as dear to Achilles as life itself.

must be judged by the intrinsic worth of that to which we give allegiance." For now, then, set aside the question of self-interest: " 'Why should I be the fuel rather than warmed by the fire?' " Consider here the question of the justice of patriotism.[3] In the *Republic*, Polemarchus offers the patriot's definition of justice: "Justice is doing good to friends and harm to enemies." But Socrates soon compels Polemarchus to see a problem that confronts every patriot who is not altogether blind to the difference between what is one's own and what is good: is it then just "to help the bad and harm the good"? Surely not. But then, are we not obliged to repudiate the charms of patriotism in favor of a more humane (but also more sterile) morality, perhaps a liberal morality? Or is a humane patriotism, uniting reasonable pride in the virtues of our own community with service to humanity, somehow possible?

In a fine essay on the idea of patriotism—*Is Patriotism a Virtue?*— Alasdair MacIntyre shows how nearly, and in what way, the problem of patriotism is at the heart of contemporary debates between liberals and communitarians. MacIntyre emphasizes the "essential and ineliminable" particularity of patriotism: the primary object of our regard is the community and not the ideals it champions. If that is so, says MacIntyre, then the liberal must admit that patriotism is incompatible with morality, or that patriotism is a vice, because the essence of morality (according to the liberal) is to judge impersonally, and so to refuse allegiance to any particular community, wherever that loyalty is at odds with liberal neutrality and impartiality. (His focus on Kantian liberalism blinds MacIntyre to a certain Lockean aspect of liberal patriotism: gratitude to the community for relieving individuals of the hardships of the state of nature, perhaps joined to reasonable pride in that achievement. Set that aside, though it is not a small matter.)

But there is an alternative view of morality, a communitarian view according to which "it is an *essential* characteristic of the morality which each of us acquires that it is learned from, in and through the way of life of some particular community." Not only our understanding of moral rules, but also the justification of these in terms of particular goods, is given to us by our communities; if this is the nature of morality, then "deprived of the life of that community, *I* would have no reason to be moral." And so, there is no good reason to oppose morality to patriotism, in the manner of Socrates or the humane liberal, for "loyalty to that community . . . is, on this view a prerequisite for

---

[3]Pangle, "Patriotism, American Style," 30.

morality." Perhaps Polemarchus was right all along. Here is the end of the argument: "For while the liberal moralist was able to conclude that patriotism is a permanent source of moral danger because of the way it places our ties to our nation beyond rational criticism, the moralist who defends patriotism is able to conclude that liberal morality is a permanent source of moral danger because of the way it renders our social and moral ties too open to dissolution by rational criticism. And each party is in fact in the right against the other." The dispute between liberals and communitarians, then, concerns not only the morality of patriotism but also the origins, or status, of morality itself. For the liberal, "detachment" from the community is the "necessary condition of moral freedom"; but the communitarian "must exempt at least some fundamental structures of [the] community's life from criticism." So the case for patriotism is essentially illiberal, on MacIntyre's account: as "patriotism has to be a loyalty that is in some respects unconditional, so in just those respects rational criticism is ruled out." But this a liberal cannot abide.[4]

Here is the challenge for liberals: can patriotism ever be reasonable, or liberal? Such a liberal patriotism would be no more or less than reasonable pride in one's own community, thus taming the unconditional patriotism of communitarians while inspiriting the rational moralism of liberals. Or must human beings face the unhappy choice put to us by MacIntyre: between sterile liberal moralism and fanatical communitarian patriotism?[5] These are the questions I address in this chapter.

I

Patriotism is somehow natural. The sentiment of patriotism, in its primary and original expression, is simply the love of one's home, of the "ways that nurture us" and that to some extent constitute us, or provide us with our 'second nature.' Tocqueville speaks of an "instinctive love" of country: this natural patriotism springs from the ease of a life ordered by agreeable habits, from fond memories of persons and places and events, and from gratitude for the benefactions of one's ancestors and fellow citizens; above all, it is associated with the quiet contentment that comes from knowing that one always has a fit "place" in the world, a haven that offers refuge from human enemies as well as moral

[4]MacIntyre, *Is Patriotism a Virtue?* 5–13 (emphasis added), 18.
[5]For the unhappiness of the choice, see MacIntyre, *Is Patriotism a Virtue?* 15–17.

doubts. It is natural, so to speak, to feel at home in a familiar physical and moral environment, provided that the conventions of one's particular home are not too perverse, that one's 'second nature' does not too greatly constrain or distort one's primary human nature. The importance of this patriotic attachment can be seen by observing the "melancholy figure of the lone wanderer, or of the Stoic whose 'my home is everywhere' meant he had a home nowhere."[6] But such patriotism is perhaps not altogether natural: it is somehow natural because human beings always seek refuge in communities, which shield us from a natural world that provides little moral comfort or even physical security; but it is not simply natural because these homes, which constitute our second natures, are always more or less in tension with the natural passions that urge us to seek, as Glaucon says, "what any nature naturally pursues as good."[7] Even the liberal, who knows that natural freedom is intolerable, must confront this dilemma. Thus, the moral experience of community is always ambiguous: community brings moral comfort as well as physical security, but it also constrains natural appetites and confines natural freedom. Not only patriotism, but also the chafing for liberation, is somehow natural.

Tocqueville also suggests that this instinctive patriotism is too often weak. He argues that it can sometimes be "exalted by religious zeal," and thus made to "work wonders"; for this reason, among others, such patriotism is most at home, according to Tocqueville, in communities that maintain respect for ancestors, and for "an ancient order of things." (This use of religion as an aid to patriotism is already a step away from the second nature of instinctive patriotism toward the less natural "republican" patriotism, which I discuss below.) Instinctive love of one's community and attachment to traditional ways are no doubt easily transformed by poets or priests or partisans into a more-than-instinctive belief that these traditions were established by gods; but then, such patriotism and morality will be found vulnerable wherever it becomes possible or necessary to doubt the authority of the gods (or their present interpreters), since that is now said to be its foundation. Exalted republican patriotism is perhaps stronger but certainly more dubious than instinctive patriotism, because the authority of the gods is more compelling (when acknowledged) but also more easily undermined than the fond

---

[6]Tocqueville, *Democracy in America*, I.ii.6 (in the section on "Public Spirit in the United States"); John Schaar, "The Case for Patriotism," 63; and see, generally, 62–68. See, too, MacIntyre, *After Virtue*, 32; and Walzer, *Interpretation*, 14–16.
[7]Plato, *Republic*, 359c.

memories of benefactors and the other comforts of home that inspire grateful instinctive patriots.[8]

Not only pious or republican patriotism, but even natural or instinctive patriotism, is surely questionable, for thoughtful citizens. Love of one's country, like other kinds of love, is vulnerable to at least two objections: that it is blind and that it is foolish. The natural patriot, because his patriotism is instinctive and not the product of a moral or philosophical education, has few resources that might enable him to respond to those more thoughtful citizens who begin to wonder whether patriotism is good, or whether patriotism here and now is good. Thus, for example: awareness of other communities and other ways of life might give rise to doubts about whether this particular community is truly worthy of patriotic love or devotion, whether its ways *are* the best ways. Indeed, human beings may be so constituted that they cannot, in the end, be content to love their country simply because it is their country; certainly, citizens routinely affirm that they love their country not only because it is their own, but also because it is good.[9] No doubt, they are often wrong.

And yet, there is something honorable about this aspect of traditional conservatism: it implies that there is some authority or horizon beyond the community itself, in the light of which one must distinguish between the best ways and the inferior ways. Such conservatism affirms the possibility and even the necessity (as many communitarians do not) of a certain kind of philosophical radicalism. So far as traditional conservatism admits this distinction between "the good" and "one's own," it is marked by a kind of dignity or even courage. Consider the courage of Polemarchus, who cannot abide the political consequence of his conservatism, that he must harm good men who happen to be his enemies, and who is therefore willing to undertake a journey with Socrates toward a more reasonable (if still not wholly satisfactory) conservatism. Polemarchus is reduced to the silly (but somehow honorable) expedient of splitting the difference (" 'the man who seems to be, and is, good, is a friend,' he said, 'while the man who seems good and is not, seems to be but is not a friend' "). Here is Rorty's response to Socrates' inquiry: "This question strikes liberal ironists as just as hopeless as . . . the question 'When may one favor members of one's family, or one's community, over other, randomly chosen, human beings?' Anybody who thinks that there are well-grounded theoretical an-

[8]Tocqueville, *Democracy in America*, I.ii.6; and cf. Strauss, *Natural Right*, 83–84. See this chapter ("The Origin of the Idea of Natural Right") of Strauss more generally, esp. 81–89. On "gratitude" and patriotism, see, too, MacIntyre, *Is Patriotism a Virtue?* 4–5.
[9]See Strauss, *Natural Right*, 83–87.

swers to this sort of question . . . is still, in his heart, a theologian or a metaphysician."[10] Anyway, instinctive love is surely not an adequate ground for the honorable patriotism even of a Polemarchus, for love is blind; thoughtful patriots are not blind, but can give reasons. And if good reasons are not available, then the instinctive or natural patriotism of citizens will, once doubt is possible, be undermined by thoughtful critics.

Certainly, less thoughtful patriots will often offer false and even ridiculous reasons for their patriotism. And yet, it is as much a mistake to forget the moral reasons of honorable patriots as it is to forget the "ineliminable particularity" of their patriotic attachments. MacIntyre, for example, emphasizes the constitutive moral force of community in his account of patriotism; in so doing, he sharply distinguishes patriotism from the love of one's country as "*the* champion of some great moral ideal," which is not patriotism because "it is the ideal and not the nation which is the primary object of their regard." Such a love implies that it is possible to judge one's own community according to standards that are not constituted by one's community. It is obvious that some citizens are more easily satisfied on this point than are others; nevertheless, the desire to praise the human virtues that have a home in one's own community seems to be as ineliminable as the desire simply to praise one's own community—for some human beings at least. As soon as we say, "This is good" (rather than merely, "This is mine"), we reveal this hope and thereby open a certain inquiry: "Is ours a moral society?"[11] And there can be no doubt that some human beings, and among these some patriots, will find this question inescapable: as Lincoln does, at a fitting moment, in his remarkable Second Inaugural.[12] Perhaps one could never truly be a patriot in an alien land (although it is surely possible to "adopt" a country); but, as MacIntyre acknowledges, it is also hard to imagine a patriot who would frankly confess that his country is no good.

MacIntyre's emphasis on the essential particularity of patriotism leads him, however, to neglect the other side of patriotism: the aspirations of honorable or thoughtful patriots to measure their community by some

[10]Plato, *Republic*, 334d–335a; Rorty, *Contingency*, xv. The question that is similarly set aside by Rorty is "Why not be cruel?"

[11]MacIntyre, *Is Patriotism a Virtue?* 3–5; cf. 8–11. Recall Rorty on this point: it is "impossible to ask the question 'Is ours a moral society?' " for there is no "larger community called 'humanity' which has an intrinsic nature" and which "stands to my community as my community stands to me" (Rorty, *Contingency*, 59–60). For a somewhat similar criticism of MacIntyre's essay, see Stephen Nathanson, "In Defense of 'Moderate Patriotism.' "

[12]Thus: "He gives to both North and South, this terrible war, as the woe due to those by whom the offense came." And see the powerful sequel ("Yet, if God wills that it continue. . . .").

moral standard beyond the community. Such patriots claim to love not only this particular country but also that moral good, which this community happens to sustain. Here is Lincoln's praise of Henry Clay's admirable patriotism: "He loved his country partly because it was his own country, but mostly because it was a free country; and he burned with a zeal for its advancement, prosperity, and glory, because he saw in such, the advancement, prosperity, and glory, of human liberty, human right, and human nature. He desired the prosperity of his countrymen partly because they were his countrymen, but chiefly to show to the world that freemen could be prosperous." That is our moral experience of patriotism: an honorable ambivalence, enabling the patriot to know both the duties arising from citizenship and the duties arising from our essential humanity.[13]

So some patriots, at least, are thoughtful citizens; because they hope that it will be possible to reconcile their love of a particular community and their devotion to a moral ideal, they are driven to raise doubts about how far this particular community can be said to be truly good; they may even at some point be compelled to make a choice between these competing claims on their allegiance. That is, for some human beings at least, patriotism itself inspires a turn to (universal) moral philosophy: the thoughtful citizen is compelled by his predicament to move from blind loyalty to philosophy, for it would be unreasonable to affirm that one's own community is a good community without knowledge of what constitutes a good community. To abandon the question, by forgetting the dilemma that thoughtful patriots must face, and even somehow want to face, is to deny, I think, an inescapable aspect of our moral experience of patriotism. It is not only honorable to ask such questions about the justice of patriotism; it is also natural, at least for certain kinds of human beings, as is revealed in the evidently "ineliminable" propensity of patriots to say of their own community that it is a good or even the best community. But communitarian theorists such as Rorty and MacIntyre cannot do justice to this aspect of our moral experience.[14]

---

[13]Lincoln, "Eulogy on Henry Clay," 6 July 1852, in *Speeches and Writings*, 270; and see, too, 315. One might say that it is the "mostly" or "chiefly" in this remark that MacIntyre finds inexplicable. MacIntyre does not, of course, deny that a patriot might *also* love his country as "*the* champion of some great moral ideal"; but that a patriot might place duties to humanity before duties to community is not possible, on MacIntyre's account. Yet it seems to me that this patriotism is no less real, and vastly more honorable, for being conditional (and for refusing to "exempt" even "the nation conceived *as a project*" from rational criticism). *Is Patriotism a Virtue?* 3–4, 13. See also nn. 54–55 below.

[14]See Rorty, *Contingency*, 44–69, 189–98; *Objectivity*, 175–96, 203–10; and MacIntyre, *Is Patriotism a Virtue?* esp. 3–5; but cf. 13–15. Cf. Pangle, "Patriotism, American Style," 31.

Natural patriotism is vulnerable for another reason. Perhaps the critics of patriotism will argue that love of one's country is foolish, that the sacrifices of private welfare that this love requires are too great: above all, that it can never be reasonable to risk death for one's country. Again, the natural patriot, who loves his country but cannot say why, is terribly vulnerable. His affection for the country is too dependent on the benefactions of his fellows, on his continued ease of life in a happy home, on fond memories that can quickly be clouded by an unhappy present: natural patriotism is too easy. In a time of crisis, when the community requires more than it can for a time repay, he will be unable easily to resist the temptation, into which some sophist will doubtless lead him, to deny in his heart that the good of the individual is intimately linked to the good of the community.[15] And he will then be compelled to make an unhappy choice.

I turn, in the sections that follow, to two possible responses to these arguments about the limits of natural patriotism: republican patriotism and liberal patriotism. These modifications of our natural instincts are the products of two very different sorts of answers to the questions posed by thoughtful citizens and demoralizing sophists. Both the republican and the liberal can argue that patriotism is good or right for human beings, perhaps even that patriotism is a virtue, and not merely a sentiment. In the next section of this chapter, I consider republican patriotism; and, in the following section, liberal patriotism. Then, I turn to the particular case of American patriotism. Finally, I discuss Michael Walzer's account of patriotism, which is neither republican nor liberal patriotism, but an uncertain combination of the two.[16]

II

Republican patriotism is the noble disposition of the citizen who loves his country not for his own sake but for the sake of his country.[17] This brand of patriotism is so far from being natural or instinctive that legislators must "change human nature" in order to inculcate it, according to the greatest modern partisan of republican citizenship, Rousseau.[18] But

[15]Cf. Tocqueville, *Democracy in America*, I.ii.6.
[16]Walzer, *Radical Principles*, especially "Dissatisfaction in the Welfare State" (23–53) and "Civility and Civic Virtue in America" (54–72); and Walzer, *Obligations*, especially "The Obligation to Die for the State" (77–98).
[17]Montesquieu, *Spirit*, 3.6, 4.5, 5.2–3.
[18]See *Emile*, 39–40: "Natural man is entirely for himself. . . . Good social institutions are those that best know how to denature man, to take his absolute existence from him in order to give him a relative one and transport the *I* into the common unity, with the result that each individual believes himself no longer one but a part of the unity and no longer feels except within the whole."

once this transformation from human beings to citizens has been achieved, the community will boast loyal servants who are prodigies of virtue: republican patriotism is (almost) inhuman, but it is also a powerful motive for selfless actions and beliefs. Such citizens happily sacrifice their private interests for the good of the community; or, rather, they do not understand wholehearted devotion to the community to be a sacrifice. In *Emile*, Rousseau offers several examples of republican citizens who "loved the country exclusive of [themselves]," including this notable one: "A Spartan woman had five sons in the army and was awaiting news of the battle. A Helot arrives; trembling, she asks him for news. 'Your five sons were killed.' 'Base slave, did I ask you that?' 'We won the victory.' The mother runs to the temple and gives thanks to the gods. This is the female citizen." It is not surprising, then, that Walzer turns to Rousseau, in "The Obligation to Die for the State," for an argument that citizens can be obligated, and will even sometimes be willing, to die for their country.[19]

Montesquieu teaches that "virtue in a republic is love of the homeland": republican virtue is patriotism. Moreover, the virtue that animates or inspires republican citizens is a passion or "modification of the soul": "it is a feeling and not a result of knowledge." As Tocqueville says, such patriotism "does not reason, but believes, feels, acts." Further, republican patriotism requires an unnatural, and perhaps unreasonable, renunciation of one's private happiness. The republican citizen must "identify" passionately (rather than reasonably) with his community; he must affirm in his heart, so to speak, that what is good for the community is in every case also good for him. But republican patriotism, on Montesquieu's account, is a terrible burden. "Political virtue is a renunciation of oneself, which is always a very painful thing"; this love of one's country requires "a continuous preference of the public interest over one's own." Indeed, republican patriotism is manifestly unnatural; Montesquieu even compares the devotion of republicans to the public good to the devotion of monks to their order: "what remains . . . is the passion for the very rule that afflicts them."[20]

As this example suggests, human passions are remarkably "flexible," because they are greatly under the sway of human opinions, which can be taught. Education, which has produced among human beings an ex-

---

[19]Rousseau, *Emile*, 39–40; and see *Social Contract*, 1.8, 2.7; and Walzer, *Obligations*, 77–98, esp. 90–94. See, too, my "Privacy and Community."

[20]Montesquieu, *Spirit*, Foreword, 5.2, 3.3, 4.5; Tocqueville, *Democracy in America*, I.ii.6.

traordinary array of bizarre opinions, can make us "unaware" of our selves and can cause one to lose even the feeling of his own nature, says Montesquieu. Virtue is the origin and end of republican politics (and it can only be achieved by means of the "full power of education"), but it is certainly not the most fundamental or natural end of politics. That natural end is "political liberty" or the "tranquillity of spirit which comes from the opinion each one has of his security." For Montesquieu, "peace" is the "first natural law," and "the preservation of his being" is the first concern of every human being; the restoration of peace and security, which is destroyed with the emergence of human beings into society, is properly the fundamental object of every political community. In the end, Montesquieu praises most highly those "moderate" political communities that preserve liberty and security: republics "are not free states by their nature."[21] Moreover, it appears that republican patriotism arises only under severe conditions that are, happily, not our conditions: a small territory and population, a simple economy that depends on slaves to secure leisure for the citizens, equality of poverty, and perhaps a political religion, among others. It is also clear that republican patriotism requires a high degree of cultural, ethnic, and religious homogeneity, since such fundamental divisions among the people would surely undermine the necessary unity of the republican community.[22]

And yet, even partisans of patriotism who are not republicans are frequently driven to acknowledge, in grudging or qualified ways, their adherence to the idea of republican patriotism, however arduous that way of life appears. This is true for the following reason, among others: patriotism is put to the test, perhaps above all, when the community asks its citizens to risk death, in war; but if this is the highest test of patriotism, then the republican citizen is surely the truest patriot. Every patriotic citizen or statesman knows that the political community he loves sometimes requires citizens who are prepared to die in its defense; every patriot therefore admires the awesome self-sacrifice exhibited, most often, only by republican patriots. Even liberal patriots, then, when they have occasion to fear for the future of their country, must admit that republican

---

[21]Montesquieu, *Spirit*, Preface, 11.6, 1.2–3, 11.4; and see 11.5; on moderate government, see 2.2, 3.3–4, 3.7, 4.2, 5.8, 11.1–6, 12.1–13; and cf. 11.11–18.
[22]Montesquieu, *Spirit*, 8.16, 4.8, 5.3–7. For a description of the gentler liberal alternative, see esp. 19.27; see, too, 11.6. On Montesquieu, and on the differences between liberal and republican politics more generally, see Pangle, *Montesquieu's Philosophy*, esp. 48–160; on Rousseau and Montesquieu, see Strauss, "On the Intention of Rousseau," 458–60. See, too, Walzer, "Pluralism in Political Perspective," 16–17.

citizenship is a useful and noble thing. And even liberal statesmen sometimes resort to inspiriting republican encomiums to virtue: how else might republican statesmen inspire and justify the voluntary sacrifices that free communities evidently require, but by offering a cause worth dying for ("dedicated to the proposition that all men are created equal"), or the promise of enduring glory ("it can never forget what they did here"), or some other inducement to abandon our natural privacy and self-concern?[23]

Walzer considers the idea of republican citizenship in an essay on "The Obligation to Die for the State," in which he compares Hobbes's liberalism and Rousseau's republicanism.[24] The liberal argues that a good community is a community that provides for the security and welfare of its individual citizens; Walzer largely agrees that this liberal teaching is true, if only a partial truth.[25] But the republican replies that a good community is, rather, one that is "worth dying for," just as a human being might say that his best friend or most beloved is not the one who most serves his interests, but the one who inspires a willingness to renounce everything for the other's good. But what kind of community is "worth dying for"? When is it reasonable to risk one's life for the sake of the community?

Such a community can come into being, argues Walzer (in agreement with Rousseau), only on the basis of a "moral transformation" of natural human beings. The human being becomes a citizen when he renounces his natural life, his petty concern for preservation and even happiness, and receives from the community "a second life, a moral life." This moral life is no longer really the life of an individual at all: for the citizen, the "common life" of the republic is "the totality of their present existence." Such citizens will "rush" to the defense of their community, and die willingly, because "so long as the state survives, something of the citizen lives on, even after the natural man is dead"; the death of the com-

[23]And cf. Thucydides, *Peloponnesian War*, 2.35–46. Many of Lincoln's speeches are masterpieces of republican rhetoric: marrying rousing appeals for republican virtue to enlightening, but evidently more fundamental, expositions of republican principles—designed to educate the public mind. Thus, it is worth noting that most of Lincoln's own war speeches, including at times of great crisis, are prosaic liberal speeches, so to speak, containing only a few inspiriting republican moments. Consider an extraordinary Fourth of July speech: the July 4, 1861, Message to Congress. And compare the First Inaugural to the Second Inaugural, all in *Speeches and Writings*.

[24]Walzer, *Obligations*, 77–98. In what follows, I discuss the argument of 90–98, which is largely an interpretation of Rousseau. I do not focus here on Walzer's main concern, which is the problem of political obligation.

[25]See, for example, Walzer, *Spheres*, 64–83; and Walzer, *Radical Principles*, 25–37.

munity would be "literally a fate worse than death." But the liberal citizen can imagine such devotion only with difficulty.

Walzer immediately retracts the suggestion that citizens seek to "live on" through their community, or that republican virtue aims at some kind of immortality for the individual citizen. Further, he denies that the "dream of glory and eternal renown" is the source of republican virtue: the republican cares about his country's immortality, not his own. Now this implies an even greater renunciation of nature than is required by the attempt to overcome the petty concerns of self-preservation; on this view, the republican citizen transcends *any* concern with his own good, however that good is̄ understood. But it seems to me that the earlier formulation, which emphasizes "living on," is psychologically more adequate (not necessarily as an account of the self-understanding of citizens, but as an account of their true motives). If that is true, then the republican cannot quite escape the question of the reasonableness of the life of the citizen, and of this quest for immortality, because he cannot deny that all human beings by nature somehow seek their own good.[26]

Walzer seems to admire the republican vision, but he also doubts whether such citizenship is really possible, or whether it is possible in the absence of propaganda: great lies, however noble. Even for Rousseau, Walzer says, "the transformation of natural man into citizen is never complete": the natural man is always at war with the citizen in the souls of even the most virtuous republican patriot. Certainly, the natural man will win that battle in the souls of most human beings most of the time. Every actual political community will include "political strangers" among its members, men and women who do not fully share in the common life of the political community. Even a so-called republican political community, then, cannot rely on all its citizens to "rush to its defense": there will always be "traitors" who will not fight or who must be compelled to fight. Few communities can, without exaggeration, be called republics, because few so-called citizens are republican patriots. That such political "strangers" exist, and that they must be punished, is evidence that the republican "moral transformation" has not occurred in their cases. Such persons cannot be expected to behave like citizens, since they are not citizens, according to Walzer. One might say that republican and liberal communities differ only in degree, not in quality: republican communities need compulsion too, for virtue is weak.[27]

[26]Walzer, *Obligations*, 90–93; and cf. 79.
[27]Walzer, *Obligations*, 92–98. This argument reveals that Walzer does not share Barber's great hopefulness regarding the "transformative" potential of democratic or republican politics.

But in a republican community, where the citizen assumes no obligations on the basis of liberal consent, the compulsion when required is
surely unjust. The transformation from natural man to citizen is most
nearly achieved, Walzer seems to suspect, by means of various "na-
tionalistic or ideological mystifications that lead men to believe they
are living in a community when in fact they are not." Republican patriotism can usually be achieved only by illicit means. But when the
community asks its citizens to risk death for the sake of the community, it implies that "they have chosen or will choose, and also that
they *can* choose, to live like citizens"; that is, it implies not only that
the "moral transformation" has occurred, but also that this transformation was somehow the consequence of a free choice, or many free
choices, by an individual. For Walzer, the obligations of citizenship,
even republican citizenship, can arise only from the "consent" of individual human beings. Walzer is, in this sense, an individualist: his
community would arise from the reasonable choices of free individuals.[28] But this consent is not real, nor is the common life, when it is
made possible by lies. And it is hard to imagine how it can be secured
without lies. Thus, it is worth recalling that Rousseau's legislator
makes use of enormous "mystifications":

> Wise men who want to use their own language, rather than that of the com-
> mon people, cannot be understood by the people. . . . In order for an emerg-
> ing people to appreciate the healthy maxims of politics, . . . the effect would
> have to become the cause; the social spirit, which should be the result of the
> institution, would have to preside over the founding of the institution itself;
> and men would have to be prior to laws what they ought to become by
> means of laws. Since the legislator is therefore unable to use either force or
> reasoning, he must necessarily have recourse to another order of authority,
> which can win over without violence and persuade without convincing.
> This is what has always forced the fathers of nations to have recourse to the
> intervention of heaven and to attribute their own wisdom to the Gods.

[28]Walzer, *Obligations*, 93–98. *Obligations* is a collection of "essays in consent theory"
(ix). It is somewhat hard to reconcile this aspect of Walzer's politics, which is pervasive, with
his occasional intimations that human beings are, to borrow Sandel's language, "constituted" by their communities in ways that they can "neither summon nor command" (see
Sandel, *Liberalism*, 179; cf. Walzer, *Interpretation*, 22–23; and see, too, *Spheres*, 3–10). It
is possible that this problem points toward an evolution in Walzer's thought, in a somewhat
more communitarian direction. Cf. Galston, "Community, Democracy, Philosophy: The
Political Thought of Michael Walzer," 120–21.

In the sequel, Rousseau argues that we have little reason to fear charlatans, because only "wisdom" can found enduring communities in this way: "it is not every man who can make the Gods speak."[29] But this assurance would presumably not satisfy Walzer, or any liberal rationalist. The communitarian Walzer is evidently not a republican: republican politics and patriotism do not suit a community of "rationalists of everyday life," who have "learned to think of themselves as individuals."

III

Liberal patriotism is rational patriotism. Tocqueville writes, even as he expresses regrets about the decline of instinctive patriotism, that: "There is also another sort of patriotism more rational than that; less generous, perhaps less ardent, but more creative and more lasting, it is engendered by enlightenment, grows by the aid of laws and the exercise of rights, and in the end becomes, in a sense, mingled with personal interest. A man . . . takes an interest in his country's prosperity, first as a thing useful to him and then as something he has created." And yet, the idea of patriotism will always be a problem for liberal citizens and statesmen. As John Schaar says, "as enlightenment advances, patriotism recedes." A patriotism that is founded on enlightened self-interest is surely more vulnerable than the self-forgetting patriotism that animates republicans. Beyond that, as Tocqueville says, when "enlightenment has remained incomplete," when human beings somehow "escape from prejudices without recognizing the rule of reason," or when they renounce the rule of reason in the grip of despair or misology, they are then likely to "retreat into a narrow and unenlightened egoism."[30] (Here is another answer to Rorty's hopeful project, joined in some measure by Barber, of building "solidarity" without and even against "enlightenment": the ordinary psychological consequence of the failure of reason is vulgar egoism rather than "clinging together against the dark," at least in the absence of robust republican virtue.)[31]

Liberal patriotism is also vulnerable to attack on other grounds as well: the claim of the community to contribute to the welfare of its citizens may be false, and it may be known to be false by its enlightened citizens, who will not long remain patriots. But this is obviously a less troubling difficulty; it might even be said that one of the advantages of

[29]Rousseau, *Social Contract*, 2.7.
[30]Tocqueville, *Democracy in America*, I.ii.6; and Schaar, "The Case for Patriotism," 59.
[31]See Rorty, *Contingency*, 44–95.

liberal politics is the fact that such failures cannot as easily be obscured by appeals to putatively nobler sentiments. And as I have already noted, that natural patriotism may be threatened by arguments founded on reasonable claims about justice, to which the liberal rationalist is also especially vulnerable.

So the great task of liberal statesmanship is to keep constantly before the eyes of liberal citizens the intimate connection between their private welfare and the public welfare. The thoughtful liberal citizen is certain that there is such a connection, because he knows that it is only the liberal political community that stands between our present security and prosperity and the miserable insecurity of our natural condition.[32] But human beings, especially happy ones, easily forget their benefactors. Thus, liberal citizens often forget their debts to the community, and neglect the appropriate expressions of gratitude. The liberal community must therefore remind them, from time to time, that the security and prosperity that liberal citizens enjoy are not gifts of a bountiful nature, or just rewards for their private virtues, but the precarious possession of a community of terribly vulnerable individuals.

But this is a hard message to convey. Precisely the achievements of liberal political communities make the harsh conditions of the state of nature, and the unhappy civil discords so prevalent in other times and places, seem remote and even irrelevant. A peculiar kind of citizen education seems to be required: not moral education, but rather the historical and philosophical education that makes distant dangers seem familiar. That is, liberal politics requires enlightened citizens. The liberal patriot knows that peace and liberty are historically precarious possessions, and that prudent citizens must be constantly vigilant in their defense against zealous partisans and sectarians at home and illiberal enemies abroad. Liberal patriotism, then, is above all the enlightened awareness that private happiness depends upon the preservation of a certain kind of political community, of moderate men and women who respect rights and privacy, who refrain from moral partisanship, and who

---

[32]To be sure, because this "connection" is not quite "identity," there will inevitably be temptations: from time to time, the great private benefits that might come from imposing a small public harm may be irresistible. Put another way, the liberal laws of nature ("seek peace," "compleasance") are laws of reason—or, rather, merely maxims of prudence: there will occasionally be exceptions. In response to this concern, the liberal community can do little more than teach human beings to calculate well, which they will not be disposed to do where they are judges in their own case. Or, perhaps, here is a place for little liberal lies, an order of magnitude more humane than the big republican lies. Thus, the liberal will call maxims of prudence by a more imposing name: laws of reason or even laws of nature.

are willing to defend the community against its enemies. But it is not obvious that comfortable liberal men and women can be made to feel the prudent fears that might sustain this liberal moderation and courage. (If liberal citizens are not tempted by an "unenlightened egoism," which undermines courage, they may succumb to the temptations of a republican politics of the common good, which undermines moderation.) Thus, the various modes of political self-restraint, or virtue, that liberal politics requires are undermined in the absence, or apparent absence, of the motive for that self-restraint: the danger of civil war.

Perhaps there is another way of ensuring that liberal patriotism can endure. Tocqueville suggests: "the most powerful way, and perhaps the only remaining way, in which to interest men in their country's fate is to make them take a share in its government." Indeed, *Democracy in America* is in part an account of the various modes of civic participation that contribute to the "enlightenment" of popular understandings of the relation between private welfare and the public good. Perhaps the most important arena for this civic participation is the local community. In America, says Tocqueville, "the instinct of country can hardly exist," but "each man is as interested in the affairs of his township . . . and of the whole state as he is in his own affairs."[33] Township and state, but not country, invite participation and citizenship. In another place, Tocqueville argues that "the Union is a vast body and somewhat vague as the object of patriotism"; patriotism, if it is "nothing but an extension of individual egoism," will be expressed primarily in attachment to local communities. Tocqueville also suggests here that some elements of "instinctive patriotism" survive at the local level. But attachment to the national republic will be of a different sort, as Schaar argues: "The republic for [most Americans] is a vague and distant thing, absent from their hearts, lost to their eyes. . . . Our great patriotic holidays, now administratively arranged to provide long weekends, are less occasions for shared remembrance and renewal of the political covenant than boosts to the consumer economy."[34]

For a liberal, the nature of the citizen's attachment to community is properly or reasonably determined by the nature of the activities of that community. Thus, we love the nation above all because it provides secu-

[33]Tocqueville, *Democracy in America*, I.ii.6.
[34]Tocqueville, *Democracy in America*, I.ii.10 (367); and Schaar, "The Case for Patriotism," 60. See, too, the chapters in *Democracy in America* on the New England township (I.ii.5, esp. 62–70). And see below, Chapter 6, §V, on Walzer's account of national citizenship; and above, Chapter 5, §II, on Barber's more hopeful vision.

rity against foreign enemies; this love is greatest when the threats to our security are most palpable, and naturally falls into desuetude in the meantime. But for Tocqueville's Americans, at least, attachment to the local community could be more intimate, for two reasons. First, the local community "preserves liberty, regulates rights, guarantees property, and makes the life and whole future of each citizen safe." That is, "Americans therefore have much more to expect and to fear" from local communities; "in view of the natural inclinations of the human heart, [they] are bound to feel a more lively attachment" to these communities than to the nation.[35] Second, local communities teach citizens the "spirit of liberty," which is surely an agreeable sentiment: this experience of self-government makes manifest to citizens the common elements in our private concerns, and thus the utility of common deliberation about the common good; moreover, it is surely pleasing to contemplate the community "as something [one] has created," and for which citizens have a strong sentimental affection, just as parents love their children, and authors love their writings. If "patriotism is a sort of religion strengthened by practical service," then this reasonable sentiment will naturally attach human beings to the primary arena of public service, the local community. Nathan Tarcov argues, in the spirit of Tocqueville: "Yet our federal system has perhaps best provided for a sense of community on the local level. Precisely our respect for rights provides freedom to form congenial voluntary associations that nurture a more solid and less dangerous sense of fraternity than any modern mass state, however organized or animated, can offer." Tocqueville also emphasizes the importance of voluntary association in promoting a more enlightened self-interest. For Tocqueville, then, attachment to the national government is properly rather sober and even calculating; attachment to local communities can comprise more warmth and sentiment. This division of affections is altogether reasonable, on the liberal view: the nation can make us secure, but we can only make ourselves happy someplace nearer to home.[36]

The *Federalist* often makes a similar argument regarding the continuing attachment of the people to the states, but in a more grudging or defensive tone. Indeed, the *Federalist* seems to look hopefully toward a future when the people would "become more partial to the federal than

[35]Tocqueville, *Democracy in America*, I.ii.10 (364–67).
[36]Tocqueville, *Democracy in America*, I.ii.5 (63, 69); cf. I.ii.10 (366–67); and see II.ii.5–7; see also Tarcov, "American Constitutionalism," 120. And see the "Essays of Brutus" in Storing, ed., *The Anti-Federalist: Writings by the Opponents of the Constitution*, esp. 145–47 (in Essay VII).

to the State governments"; these liberals were more concerned about what the people had "to fear" from their local communities than what they had "to expect" from them. This alternative liberal view, then, rejects participation as a solution to the problem of liberal patriotism. The authors of the *Federalist* fear the prospect of local tyrannies more than the prospect of a decline in local participation, and therewith of popular concern for the public good. But prudent liberals admit that one must pay a price for the "*total exclusion of the people in their collective capacity*" from government, which the *Federalist* recommends: a decline in the reasonable sentiment of liberal patriotism that comes from participation. One of the central dilemmas of liberal politics is this: liberal communities require patriotic citizens; but liberal patriotism seems to depend in some measure on participation, which may permit the emancipation of popular passions that are threats to liberal freedoms. The task of liberal statesmanship is to encourage the reasonable sentiment of liberal patriotism, without at the same time liberating unreasonable and intolerant (partisan or sectarian) popular passions. It is not an easy task.[37]

Tocqueville was perhaps too confident that the local community would remain the primary focus of the citizen's attention, or that the national political community would be too "feeble" ever to dominate the political thoughts of most citizens.[38] Today, many of the tasks that once belonged to local communities are the responsibility, at least in part, of the national government. Still, there can be little doubt that participation in politics contributes to sentimental and rational attachment to one's community; perhaps liberals sometimes neglect, or understate, the importance of this civic activity for citizens and patriots.[39] Participation surely draws human beings away from their private concerns, and enables them to think about the common good, by revealing the utility of common action in the pursuit of private welfare. Perhaps liberals, confronted by the problem of the weakness of liberal citizenship and patriotism, should somehow revive Tocqueville's liberal idea of participation.

Unfortunately, the problem of participation in a liberal world can no longer be solved in Tocqueville's manner, because it is now more difficult to imagine that local participation can be a source of citizenship. The de-

---

[37]See *Federalist* #46: 294–95; see, too, #49, #50, #55. The last quoted passage is from #63: 387 (emphasis in original).
[38]Tocqueville, *Democracy in America*, I.ii.10 (368).
[39]But the rise of the nation has certainly been a fortunate development, and not only for the reasons suggested by the *Federalist*. Cf. Sandel, "The Procedural Republic," 91–95, on the ambiguous legacy of the rise of the nation.

mand for greater participation today often seems either frivolous or dangerous. When advocates of participation call for a revival of local politics ("the new federalism"), their proposals seem slight, at least where the aim of such proposals is the renewal of democratic citizenship (as opposed, say, to administrative convenience). Few people seriously propose that local communities can now be entrusted, safely or efficiently, with the great tasks that might promote citizenship; economic policies, as well as defense and foreign policies, are now inescapably national concerns, for apparently good reasons. How is "local community control" of the workplaces in a community possible in a national and even international economy, unless at enormous cost to local economies? But it follows that local politics is now rather boring, and so less likely to inspire citizenship or patriotism; here is a citizenship for the kids, so to speak, whose parents are otherwise occupied with more important matters—in Washington. Even Barber, as we have seen, recognizes these, among other, limits of local participation.[40] Still, if the advocates of participatory democracy call for a participatory national politics, complete with national referenda and national town meetings, their proposals seem dangerous, for they are likely to arouse sentiments that might properly attach people to smaller communities, but that would easily be manipulated in destructive ways in mass society.

Finally, the hardest question for defenders of liberal patriotism is whether the liberal community can, both justly and successfully, ask its citizens to risk death for their country. Indeed, Walzer suggests that "the great advantage of liberal society may simply be this: that no one can be asked to die for public reasons or on behalf of the state."[41] If the purpose of the political community is to provide for the preservation of the lives of its individual members, then "a man who dies for the state defeats his only purpose in forming the state."[42] But risking death is not the same as

---

[40]It is possible that local citizenship might be founded on such concerns as education, morality, and even religion. But that solution might appear to emancipate a cultural conservatism that is a threat to liberal freedoms. Still, it would be hard to deny that greater accommodation of local community in such matters would contribute at the margins to a renewed sense of civic responsibility, as many theorists now argue. See Sandel, "Democrats and Community"; Etzioni, *The Spirit of Community*; and many other political communitarians, including those associated with the journal *Responsive Community*. So I do not deny that such policies often have merit; I argue only that there are few grounds for optimism that they will yield significantly stronger citizenship.

[41]Walzer, *Obligations*, 89. Walzer characteristically suggests, in this context, that liberal human beings may nevertheless "incur ultimate obligations" for "ethical (not political)" reasons, as in the case of love and friendship.

[42]Walzer, *Obligations*, 82; and cf. 92.

dying. A liberal, perhaps even a vulgar liberal who cares only about preservation, could consistently maintain that prudent human beings should risk death in war, where the survival of the community is at risk: for if the community were lost, then so, too, would be the security of its individual members. Perhaps it would be more precise to say that prudent human beings will agree, when they join the community, that the community should, in time of crisis, have the right to compel them to risk death, in war. This is the source of the rightful authority of the state to compel reluctant citizens to fight: they have consented to fight when called upon as a condition of their membership in the community. In sober moments, human beings can know what they might forget in dangerous or quiet times, that the community cannot survive without this power.[43] For less vulgar liberals, the argument is easier: if our pursuits of happiness, and not merely our security, depend upon the establishment of a community that secures our rights, provides the conditions for our possible prosperity, and protects a private realm within which still greater goods are available, then any prudent pursuit of happiness surely requires a willingness to defend such a community when it is threatened.[44] Some citizens might, of course, be too frightened or too complacent to make this calculation correctly; in that case, the liberal state must arrange to make it easier, by offering to punish recalcitrant citizens.

Perhaps this is not an adequate answer. But, then, how decisive is this objection to liberal patriotism? It surely suggests that the liberal political community can never be a nation of soldiers. But liberals do not want to be soldiers. Indeed, those who are too eager to risk death are dangerous men in liberal communities, for their speeches and actions might put the lives of other, more prudent, human beings at risk. Perhaps the security of the liberal state can be made to rest on the sober judgment of citizens and statesmen about more or less distant threats, rather than on vigorous republican patriotism, or the eagerness of citizens to defend the community against more immediate threats. Certainly, the citizens of a well-ordered liberal community will not be inclined to engage in unnecessary wars, but will, as Tarcov puts it, hope "to avoid even having to defend themselves."[45] It is true that liberal citizens too often fail to admit real dangers; it is nevertheless worth remembering that this is only the natural

---

[43]Locke argues that one who consents to membership in such a community "is perpetually and indispensably obliged to be and remain unalterably a Subject to it": *Second Treatise*, §§121–22; and see §§95–99.

[44]See Tarcov, "American Constitutionalism," 122–23.

[45]Tarcov, "American Constitutionalism," 123.

consequence of a liberal virtue. Thus, says Michael Walzer: "The citizen-soldier defends his hearth and home, and he also defends the political community within which the enjoyment of hearth and home is made possible. His fervor is heightened when that community is in danger. . . . Once the peril abates, the fervor declines."[46]

IV

American patriotism is a species of liberal or rational patriotism. In America, "where the inhabitants arrived but yesterday in the land they occupy, whither they brought with them neither customs nor memories," instinctive or natural patriotism was always frail; it has in recent times been further weakened by growing doubts about the prudence and the justice of American patriotism. Those primary natural attachments to one's country (to the land and familiar places, to ancestors and fellow citizens, to the habits of a settled life) were, from the beginning, less important to Americans. America is a nation of immigrants, restless individuals who voluntarily departed old homes in order to fashion new homes: "they were not only uprooted; they had uprooted themselves."[47] They left behind the communities (the places, the ancestors, the fellows, the habits) that had nurtured them.

In the beginning, these immigrants freely established new communities, some of them based, as Tocqueville says, on a remarkable combination of the spirit of religion and the spirit of freedom. In time, continued immigration produced a community of exceptional diversity, so that it has come to be necessary and somehow possible, in America, to constitute one people on the basis of shared political citizenship alone, rather than common history and culture.[48] But this means that American patriotism has been, in general, deprived of the support of cultural, religious, and ethnic community. American patriotism, says Walzer, if it is to exist at all, must "make a religion out of citizenship." But Walzer is finally somewhat pessimistic about the possibility of a patriotism based solely on citizenship, without ethnic or cultural foundations. This is above all because he suspects that it is "ethnic identification" more than a politics of "justice to individuals" that "gives meaning to the lives" of human be-

---

[46]Walzer, *Radical Principles*, 57–59.
[47]Tocqueville, *Democracy in America*, I.ii.6; and Walzer, "Pluralism," 9.
[48]Tocqueville, *Democracy in America*, I.i.2 (47). This chapter, "Concerning Their Point of Departure and Its Importance for the Future of the Anglo-Americans," 31–47, is an important account of the character of the American people at the beginning, before the full emergence of our liberalism.

ings; a world, like the liberal world, that separates politics and ethnic (or other) communities is "still an experiment" that offers "no guarantees of meaning." Walzer nevertheless wants to defend this separation of politics and ethnicity, at least in some measure—another instance of the subtlety and ambivalence of Walzer's attitude toward liberalism, and hence toward community.[49]

At the outset, John Jay could still appeal to a common heritage as the source of the "unity" of the American "people": "a people descended from the same ancestors, speaking the same language, professing the same religion"; but, in the same breath, Jay also speaks of the "attachment" of Americans "to the same principles of government" and of their "joint counsels, arms, and efforts, fighting side by side throughout a long and bloody war" for "liberty and independence," as sources of unity. Even at the beginning, the American people was constituted not just by common traditions but also by common choices (opinions, deeds). Jay's remarks should in any case be set aside Hamilton's challenge: "It seems to have been reserved to the people of this country . . . to decide the important question, whether societies of men are really capable or not of establishing good government from reflection and choice, or whether they are forever destined to depend for their political constitutions on accident and force."[50]

Nor have the instinctive roots of patriotism been replaced by new sentimental ties. Here is John Schaar: "we are a nation on the go, always moving, and always with somewhere left to move to."[51] Our physical and spiritual mobility has something to do with our individualism. Each of us is encouraged, by an authoritative founding document if not by our parents, to undertake private "pursuits of happiness"; the community (the culture, the tradition) offers no authoritative guidance when we embark on this journey, so it is perhaps not surprising that these restless quests often lead us far from our homes, even in spirit. Certainly, Americans feel no piety toward their parents (even when they feel affection), much less toward more distant ancestors. Nor are there any sacred places, for Americans, because we have no common gods; the effort to fill the "naked public square" with sectarian religious symbols, or to conduct the public business according to this or that orthodoxy, still provokes justified hostility. Sentiment, religion, culture, and tradition are weak foundations for contemporary American patriotism.

[49]Walzer, "Pluralism," 6–11 ("make a religion out of citizenship," 8), 28; see, too, 16–17.
[50]*Federalist* #2: 38; cf. the discussions of this passage in Tarcov, "American Constitutionalism," 111; in Walzer, "Pluralism," 1–2, 7. See, too, *Federalist* #1: 33.
[51]Schaar, "The Case for Patriotism," 65; cf. Tarcov, "American Constitutionalism," 105–6.

But, then, what is American patriotism? It is, to begin, surely not re-publican patriotism. As Walzer says: "the American republic is very dif-ferent from that described, for example, by Montesquieu and Rousseau. It lacks the intense political fellowship, the commitment to public affairs, that they thought necessary." Our purposes in life are generally private purposes; our loyalty to the political community rests on the conviction that it serves us well, that it provides the most important conditions—peace and prosperity and a moderate politics based on respect for rights—for success or contentment in our private pursuits. American pa-triotism is a patriotism that asks first: What has it done for me lately? That is, American patriotism is liberal patriotism.[52]

And yet, it would surely be misleading to suggest that American patri-otism is *only* liberal patriotism. I have already discussed one of the moral dimensions of American patriotism, namely, the "spirit of liberty" that arises from the experience of self-government that was perhaps once pos-sible in the local community. But our patriotism also has other important moral dimensions, to which I now turn.

It is sometimes said, more or less rightly, that America makes relatively modest moral demands on its citizens. Americans are not like the repub-lican patriots described by Montesquieu; indeed, if such a citizen were somehow to secure political power today, we might properly fear for the security of our liberties. Nevertheless, Americans have often promulgated rather high moral standards for their community, and have thus indi-rectly imposed moral responsibilities on themselves. The Declaration of Independence announces to "mankind" the principles of justice (not the maxims of prudence) that guide us, by which we judge ourselves and are willing to be judged by others. Indeed, the occasion of that Declaration made it necessary to remind citizens not only of "the Right of the People to alter or to abolish" an unjust government, but also of their "duty" to do so, and then to "institute new Government." Our love of country is, in principle at least, so far from being either a merely selfish or a blind devotion, that we openly proclaim our right and duty to repudiate a

---

[52]Walzer, "Pluralism," 16; and see Walzer, *Radical Principles*, 25. There are some, includ-ing Walzer, who suggest that this emphasis on privacy in American life is less thoroughgoing than it might seem: "The emotional life of U.S. citizens is lived mostly in private—which is not to say in solitude, but in groups considerably smaller than the community of all citizens. Americans are communal in their private affairs, individualist in their politics." This is a somewhat hopeful view, shared by some liberals, but it is problematic, as Walzer himself shows with respect to the case of ethnic communities: individualism often undermines these subpolitical communities, too. See Walzer, "Pluralism," 17; cf. 25–28; see, too, Walzer, "The Obligation to Disobey," in *Obligations*, 3–23.

community that fails to satisfy our fundamental moral aspirations, as well as our intention to exercise that right.

But what are these moral aspirations? American citizens are united, or made a people, by a shared devotion to certain political ideas, by a common love of liberty, equality, and self-government, rather than by any of the more ordinary sources of political unity. Thus, Americans fought a revolution to vindicate their declaration that just governments are instituted by consent and secure the rights to "Life, Liberty and the pursuit of Happiness"; indeed, our nation is "dedicated to the proposition that all men are created equal," a dedication that was "tested" by a "great civil war"; perhaps above all, Americans share "that honorable determination which animates every votary of freedom to rest all our political experiments on the capacity of mankind for self-government."[53] As their speeches and deeds show, the noblest American citizens and statesmen have been partisans of the cause of free government: government that secures private liberties through the exercise by the people of political liberty. These are the moral and political ideas that provide both the object of our aspirations and a reproach to our imperfections.

American patriotism is therefore not quite liberal patriotism. Our love of country is not only the product of prudent fears of harsh nature and malevolent human beings, or of an enlightened awareness that common deliberation and action is sometimes useful in the pursuit of private goods. Rather, the language of American patriotism is the moral language of justice and self-government. At our noblest, as Lincoln said of Clay, we love our country not simply for our own good, nor for the good of the country itself, but rather because we are the servants of a political idea that finds a home here. But American patriotism is also not republican patriotism, for devotion to an idea is not the same as devotion to a community. We do not love our country because it is the "totality of our existence" or because it constitutes us as moral beings.[54] Americans claim to be free individuals: we are the authors of the community, and of our principles of justice; the community is not our author, or the author of our moral aspirations.

American patriotism is thus far from the patriotism described by MacIntyre. MacIntyre, to repeat, emphasizes the constitutive power of community, and he is therefore compelled to deny that patriotism is the

---

[53]*Federalist* #39: 240.
[54]See MacIntyre, *Is Patriotism a Virtue?* 3–4, 8–11; Walzer, *Interpretation*, 21; Sandel, *Liberalism*, 149–50, 179; and cf. Schaar, "The Case for Patriotism," 69.

love of one's country primarily as *"the* champion of some great moral idea," rather than for its own sake. Though an American patriot might well admit that there are other reasons for his patriotism, he will often enough insist as well that *this* reason is a necessary condition of his patriotism, that he would cease to be a patriot if the community no longer aspired to embody this ideal. As Lincoln says, in a letter to a friend, "When it comes to this I should prefer emigrating to some country where they make no pretense of loving liberty—to Russia, for instance, where despotism can be taken pure, and without the base alloy of hypocracy [*sic*]." It is true, as MacIntyre says, that it follows that "anyone at all" could be an American patriot, on this view of patriotism, because the principles are said to be universal, not particular; it is also true that "it is the ideal and not the nation which is the primary object of their regard."[55]

We have, of course, not always lived up to our moral claims; indeed, we have sometimes failed in terrible and shameful ways. This can be a special burden for a nation that understands itself in the way that I have described, for it rightly undermines the patriotism of honest citizens. But even where our principles are not honored in our practices, they stand as a reproach to decent citizens, and sometimes make it possible for our victims and their patriotic friends to challenge the rest of the community to practice what it preaches.[56] It is also possible, of course, that our moral aspirations will give rise, in Thomas Pangle's words, to "impossibly pure and trans-political" standards that "no civil society has met or ever will meet." Thus, the American patriot must judge his community not only honestly, but also reasonably. Still, the temptation to judge too harshly is only the consequence of an American virtue.[57]

There is a second moral dimension of American patriotism, though it is perhaps but a second aspect of the same moral life. The principles of the American community are universal principles; but the community that made, and makes, a home for these principles in the world is a particular community that was constituted, nurtured, and defended by the common deliberations and actions of a particular people. Thus, as Tarcov argues, the American people is constituted not just by common adherence to a political creed, but also and perhaps above all by "the acts

---

[55]MacIntyre, *Is Patriotism a Virtue?* 3–4, where he also refers to the American example; and Lincoln, *Speeches and Writings*, 336.

[56]Consider, for example, two speeches of Douglass, "The Meaning of July Fourth for the Negro," 5 July 1852, and "Oration in Memory of Abraham Lincoln," 14 April 1876.

[57]Pangle, "Patriotism, American Style," 32.

of naturally free individuals, in particular the expenditure of the life, labor, and property that by nature belong to each of them." Nor was it only the founding generation that dedicated their "blood, toil, and treasure" to the perpetuation of our political institutions, as the example of Lincoln and his fellow citizens sufficiently demonstrates.[58] That is, it is the cause of free government itself that provides Americans with "the noblest rationale for active citizenship."[59] American patriotism is ennobled not only by our shared principles of justice and love of liberty, but also by our common actions and sacrifices, and by our common deliberations. In our best moments, we have experienced a common life, fit for free and equal citizens and founded on a common devotion to the ideas of liberty, equality, and self-government. Such a common life, when it exists, can provide a powerful support for American patriotism.

This is a national common life. It demands certain virtues, but they are not primarily the private virtues of liberal men and women in society, or the virtues of liberal citizens as they participate in local political communities. The American patriot must, of course, be prepared to defend the community that embodies our political ideas against its enemies, and the enemies of those ideas. But courage is not the first virtue of the American patriot. Defense of the idea of free government requires more than the reluctant and sober readiness to fight wars and even civil wars when necessary.[60] What is more important, for partisans of free government, is the cultivation of a kind of political prudence, a common understanding of the various forms of political moderation that make free government possible. And this requires political education: common reflections about the ideas of liberty, equality, and self-government, and common activities that solicit memories of our specific

---

[58]Tarcov, "American Constitutionalism," 106; see the context (106–8) for a discussion of Jefferson and Washington on this point. Also, recall the Jay passage discussed above: not only shared "principles of government," but also "joint counsels, arms, and efforts" unite the American people; cf. *Federalist* #14: 104. Finally, see the last words of the Declaration of Independence. For the next sentence ("blood, toil, and treasure"), see Tarcov, "American Constitutionalism," 108.

[59]Schaar, "The Case for Patriotism," 77; cf. 71–72.

[60]In any case, liberal patriotism, even in its American version, does not justify the effort to bring free government to other peoples by way of war. It is true that American statesmen have often spoken as if it had been "reserved to the people of this country" to demonstrate the possibility of free government. But we have generally "believed that American patriotism is the most effective form of philanthropy, that making a success of our own political experiment is the greatest service we can perform for humanity." See *Federalist* #1: 33; and Tarcov, "American Constitutionalism," 109 (see the context for a discussion of Clay on this point).

virtues (and vices) as a people. Insofar as there is any tendency for free peoples to forget, in happy times, the public conditions of their private prosperity and security, such a common life is needed, precisely in order to sustain the community that is the home for our various forms of private happiness. And perhaps the common deliberations of citizens can also inspire a reasonable pride in the community, augmenting the reasonable liberal attachment to a good community by promoting a proud attachment to our own community.[61] Still, this is a rather modest common life, except in grave times, and it is unlikely to satisfy the hopes of the partisans of community.

V

Michael Walzer is both a critic and a partisan of patriotism: today, says Walzer, "many of us are patriotic, if we are, for wrong or inadequate reasons." This is the predictable consequence of liberalism, according to Walzer. Liberal patriotism is "an enlightened love of ourselves, which teaches us to love the government which protects us . . . the society which works for our happiness." As Tocqueville says of the American patriot, "he works for the good of the state, not only from duty or from pride, but, I dare almost say, from greed."[62] Indeed, one of the most important achievements of liberal politics was the destruction of traditional notions of patriotic communion, which were based on various sorts of "political divinity"; liberal politics turned "the mysterious oath into a rational contract." But liberalism, even, or especially, when it is successful, is a "hard politics" that provides "few emotional rewards": the liberal community is "not a home for its citizens," but "lacks warmth and intimacy." Thus, it is perhaps not surprising that liberal politics gives rise to "dangerous desires" for "political community, passionate affirmation, explicit patriotism." Walzer is, for good liberal reasons, often frightened by the prospect of any effort to satisfy these desires. He imagines a "charismatic leader," a demagogue, who takes advantage of some crisis to "build social cohesion and political enthusiasm from above, through the use of state power," and with an appeal to the various prejudices of the people, as well as their natural, but illiberal, longing for solidarity and warmth. Thus, says Walzer, the politician who suggests that "citizens

---

[61]See Tocqueville, *Democracy in America*, I.ii.6, an amusing passage on the "irritable" patriotism of Americans, which springs from their "vanity" about a community that is the product of their common "work." Such vanity can obviously be dangerous, as well.

[62]Walzer, *Radical Principles*, 26; in the second passage, Walzer is quoting Baron d'Holbach, *La Politique Naturelle*; Tocqueville, *Democracy in America*, I.ii.6.

should do more for the state than the state does for them is a dangerous man."[63]

The liberal state is more or less competent as an instrument for the provision of material goods, but when it "moves beyond welfare, it does not bring us the satisfactions of citizenship, but only vicarious participation, the illusion of a common life." This is because of the large size of modern liberal communities, which promotes the impersonal and therefore just administration of goods, but undermines the trust or friendship of citizens. Moreover, the large welfare state requires an "omnicompetent" bureaucracy, which becomes a source of social control or discipline, and tends toward paternalism. Above all, this modern state inevitably engenders "passive" and dependent citizens, who are merely spectators of a distant politics that they need not, and do not, understand. The liberal state culminates in "the voluntary passivity of enlightened men and women, their human desires recognized and (in part) gratified by the public authorities." Walzer wonders: "What more can we possibly ask?"[64]

Such citizens or subjects are easily "mystified by ideologies," says Walzer, and manipulated by "leaders whose purposes are not obvious"; or perhaps they are "tricked by parades and pageants, the rise and fall of political gladiators, the deaths of beloved chiefs." Thus, "There is a certain cynicism today about the symbolic expressions of American loyalty—perhaps because no one can imagine 200 million people celebrating the Fourth of July, simultaneously and together, in some way that isn't repellent to liberal sensibilities." And so, when liberal men and women are somehow engaged in support of a mysterious "national purpose," we can be confident that this purpose is not really a common purpose, because we know that liberal human beings are too dependent on the state, too isolated in their petty private worlds, to make common choices without the aid of propagandists and demagogues. The "patriotic communion" that is possible in the modern welfare state is always a "fraud": the liberal state is not a proper object of patriotic sentiments. So liberalism, which began as the honorable effort of free men to destroy the myth of organic community, threatens to culminate in a new and more dangerous nationalist ideology that will undermine liberal freedoms. Thus, says Walzer, the search for such national purposes beyond the welfare state "has nothing to do with socialism or with a meaningful com-

[63]Walzer, *Radical Principles*, 25, 68–69, 45.
[64]Walzer, *Radical Principles*, 44, 30, 35; see, generally, 23–39, 7–8, 59–60.

mon life"; ideologies of patriotism and community are too often the tools of wicked men.[65]

And yet, somehow, "socialists" remain "advocates of community," and even seek a "community of patriots." The "hard truth" about liberal individualism and pluralism is that they "make solidarity very difficult"; but human beings nevertheless have an ineradicable "longing for cooperative endeavor, for *amour social.*" Socialists argue, according to Walzer, "that mere private life . . . cannot sustain a significant human culture; that the family does not by itself provide an adequate arena for the human emotions; that man has both a mind and a passion for society; that he requires an active public life." The liberal project, of securing public peace so that individuals might pursue happiness in private, is therefore a hopeless one, from the beginning. Human beings cannot live happily, according to Walzer, when deprived of the joyful sense of community and even political community: the failure to accommodate this natural human aspiration is perhaps the fundamental defect of liberal politics.[66]

But how can Americans, today, satisfy their longing for community, especially given the terrible dangers that Walzer has recounted? First, says Walzer, we must now turn directly to politics for the pleasures of community: above all because our pluralist world is an exceptionally diverse one, so that many of the traditional forms of common life have now been greatly weakened; but also because Walzer does not share the neoconservative inclination to suppose that subpolitical communities might provide adequate compensations for our individualistic politics, even if they could somehow be sustained.[67] That is, our only common possession, now, is the "republic itself"; if we do not make a common life in politics, then we will inevitably be simply private men and women, and that is an unhappy fate. But, as we have seen, the attempt to achieve "social cohesion" from above, through political promotion of some national purpose, requires an "attack on the heterogeneity of liberal society" and gives rise to an "irrational and unreflective patriotism" that is not fit for free and equal citizens. A healthy communitarian politics today cannot be a politics of common purposes, because we are too different from one another to have common purposes; rather, it must be a politics of partic-

---

[65]Walzer, *Radical Principles*, 43–44, 56, 48; see, too, Walzer, *Obligations*, 93, 98. For a less temperate version of this argument, see Schaar, "The Case for Patriotism," 78–85.

[66]Walzer, *Radical Principles*, 12, 68–69, 39–40.

[67]Consider the reference to family life in the passage quoted in the previous paragraph. See, too, Plattner, "The Good Old Cause."

ipation, of common deliberation and action by men and women who
have "learned to think of themselves as individuals," and who therefore
disagree about important matters, and even about the purpose and nature of the community itself.[68]

What is required, then, is a socialist *"politics of politics"* to supplement the liberal "politics of welfare." The community that would emerge
from such a politics would *not* be a community of "warmth" or friendship, because socialist and liberal men and women do not love one another, at least not in politics, and only a demagogue or a tyrant could
make them fall in love. Rather, such a community would bring together
diverse (free, equal, rational) individuals who nevertheless seek to determine together, through common deliberations and actions, the "shape of
their common life":

> No, when we talk about community . . . it is not because we are eager for
> warmth. Politics, after all, is an experience of conflict and hostility as well
> as an experience of cooperation. We seek community for the sake of knowl-
> edge and self-management. . . . Our goal is not an ecstatic union of the
> faithful, or a band of brethren bound to some charismatic leader, or a hier-
> archy of benevolent masters and docile servants. Warmth can be had in all
> of these, but in none of them . . . do individual members share political re-
> sponsibility.

Indeed, political participation is the only way to patriotism in the liberal
world, as Walzer often says: "Politics is a school of loyalty, through
which we make the republic our moral possession and come to regard it
with a kind of reverence." "In a liberal world, patriotic feeling and political participation depend on one another." "Among people like ourselves, a community of patriots would have to be sustained by politics
alone." "All this is needed if patriotism is to be nourished, in the absence
of social and cultural cohesion, by what Mill calls 'artificial means,' political arrangements that foster activity and participation." And if that
patriotism is somewhat reserved when compared to the patriotism that is
possible in other sorts of community, that is no more than the price we
must pay for our liberal freedom, and for equality.[69]

Walzer concedes that this new participatory politics would "strain at
the limits" of what is "appropriate" in a liberal world; still, "that suc-

---

[68]Walzer, *Radical Principles*, 68–70, 48, 13; and see 55–57.
[69]Walzer, *Radical Principles*, 12–13, 72, 69–71.

cess is possible must be the socialist's faith, or better, the wager that sustains his commitment." Too much is at stake simply to concede that liberalism is incompatible with community. Thus, Walzer outlines a program for "expanding the possibilities for a participatory politics." Given the dangers of nationalist ideologies in the large modern state, what is required is "a politics of immediate self-government, a politics of (relatively) small groups"; only by restoring politics to a "human scale" will it be possible to place "power into the hands of ordinary citizens." That is not to say that the liberal state must be destroyed: we cannot do without the politics of welfare. The liberal welfare state must be "hollowed out," reduced to an "administrative shell" within which smaller groups can prosper, but we cannot permit it to "wither away"; above all, it must be "drained of whatever superfluous moral content and unnecessary political power it has usurped." Walzer suggests that the "most likely arenas of a democratic politics" include "all the local units of work, education and culture: cities and towns, factories, union locals, universities, churches, political clubs, neighborhood associations, theater groups, editorial boards, and so on." And he seems to deny that the "great functional organizations, labor unions, professional associations" can become "arenas of democratic decision making," because they are too readily integrated into the welfare state. Walzer also emphasizes the need for a "radical democratization of corporate government." Finally, he is confident that the "insurgency" that is necessary to bring power back to local communities (e.g. "wildcat strikes, welfare unions, student rebellions") will not merely express demands for greater benefits from the state, thus leaving the basic patterns of dependency unchanged, but will rather express "a demand that bureaucratic services make possible, instead of replacing, local decision making." Whether this vision describes a possible politics is a question that I want to set aside here. Instead, I want to suppose that such a community is possible, and ask whether this would be a healthy politics.[70]

In "Civility and Civic Virtue in Contemporary America," Walzer discusses what a good citizen is in America today. He argues that contemporary American citizens are expected to exhibit two sorts of virtue: liberal "civilities" and republican "civic virtues." These two sorts of virtue are less extreme versions of the liberal and republican citizenship and patriotism that I discussed above. More precisely, Walzer's "civic virtue" is the sort of republicanism that is possible for liberals. The lib-

---

[70]Walzer, *Radical Principles*, 69–70, 43–50, 53.

eral virtues include obedience to the laws and other kinds of social "good behavior," and tolerance. "Civility" is not always a virtue but can become a vice, according to Walzer, at least if obedience to the law becomes a pattern of social conformism. The republican virtues include activism or participation, and patriotism. But there is "a certain tension between civility and republican citizenship": the republican virtues require "zeal" and "make for excitement and tumult in public life"; but obedience to the laws and tolerance reduce the tensions of public life, and bring peace. Today, according to Walzer, Americans are more liberal than republican, "more civil and less civically virtuous." Walzer wants to help us move away from this "liberal balance," toward a more republican idea of citizenship.[71]

The difference between republicanism and liberalism can be seen clearly by comparing the effects of liberal tolerance and republican participation. Tolerance "makes for political peace" in a community of great diversity; this is an important liberal achievement (though not yet fully realized), "for the only alternative, if history has any lessons at all, is cruelty and repression." But liberal tolerance also leads us to be less passionate about our moral convictions, and gives rise to a "moral *laissez faire.*" Tolerance thus promotes a "general indifference toward the opinions" of fellow citizens, and surely makes us less inclined to turn to political action to engage in "group conflict"—partisan or sectarian strife. Tolerance "makes politics less dangerous and less interesting." But republican citizenship "demands precisely that citizens *be interested* in politics."[72]

Now consider the case of participation. Participation, and the patriotism that it promotes, gives rise to a certain "intolerance" and "zeal." Thus, "Militancy, righteousness, indignation, and hostility are the very stuff of democratic politics. The interventions of the people are not like those of the Holy Ghost. For the people bring with them into the arena all the contradictions of liberal society and culture." Indeed, "republican politics . . . is often more bitter and divisive than politics in other regimes"; it is surely more "tumultuous" than liberal politics. That is, the "pleasures of politics" are not idle pleasures, but are the "pleasures of power": politics is not only a place where human beings can experience the "joyful sense" of community; it is also, where power is unconstrained, a dangerous and frightening place, especially for moral and political strangers, who live in the community but are not "at home" there.

[71]Walzer, *Radical Principles,* 55–68; and see 31–39, 7–8.
[72]Walzer, *Radical Principles,* 62–64.

People participate in politics, "make the sacrifices and take the risks" that politics requires, only when the stakes are high, and only when their participation matters. But "if the issues are significant, if the conflict is serious, violence always remains a possibility"; Walzer almost regrets the passing of the "election riot, not uncommon in an age when party loyalties were considerably more intense."[73]

But liberals seek peace, and security: that is why liberal theorists tried to lower the stakes of political debate by removing fundamental ("interesting") questions from our common deliberations; and that is why liberals replace participation by representation, thus securing some distance between zealous and intolerant popular passions and "dangerous" political power. And so, if patriotism today requires robust republican participation, then liberals may wonder whether it is worth the price.

An uneasy tension between public moderation and private aspirations is at the core of liberal moral psychology. Private hopes and partisan enmities must remain behind closed doors in the liberal community; they have no place in the liberal public square. More precisely, to repeat, partisan ideas about justice and the good life have no place in that public square; and our public square is thus "naked."[74] That is as it should be, more or less. Liberals distrust great political enterprises, which are too often inspired by the partisan opinions about the common good that adorn the public squares of illiberal communities; these political enterprises crush opposing private aspirations, which are often more reasonable than the common hopes of citizens. Indeed, liberals distrust the very idea of citizenship, understood as common deliberation and common action in pursuit of the common good ("civic virtue"), because they worry that this idea will inevitably undermine peace ("civility") by engendering partisanship, and so tumult. Classical liberals, in short, are not participatory democrats or republican citizens; such liberals advocate limited government, which protects the privacy of individuals just so far as it is "limited" to the task of providing for "Peace and Safety," rather than the more tumultuous republican or participatory politics of civic virtue, which recognizes no such limits and thus emancipates those "great" parties that threaten the privacy of individuals.

But forgetful human beings, especially in apparently secure times, will be tempted to repudiate these limits of liberal politics, and to seek

---

[73]Walzer, *Radical Principles*, 66–71, 40, 49, 61; see, too, Plattner, "The Good Old Cause," 93–94.

[74]See Richard John Neuhaus, *The Naked Public Square*.

to revitalize the political passions of citizens, which liberals once sought to crush, and thereby to enlist the collective force of the community in the pursuit of controversial partisan ends: they will become communitarians, for it is "a common defect of men, not to take account of the storm during the calm."[75] And they will call this new partisanship "citizenship," because promising justice appears to be more public-spirited than does securing peace. Justice and happiness, after all, are more compelling goals, for most human beings, than is mere peace; only the reasonable judgment that we can achieve justice and happiness, if at all, only by following the road that leads to peace and civility, can moderate our passionate hopes for these greater goods. But this judgment is surely vulnerable to the ideologies and dogmas that it is meant to restrain, and so it is always necessary for liberals to cultivate habits of reasonable self-restraint ("liberal virtues"), which sustain our vigilance against partisans, as well as a certain sobriety about our own political hopes.

But the longing for a community of citizens seems to encourage and even to celebrate the tumult of public life that liberals seek to quiet, and it is therefore a threat to liberal civility. Today's advocates of a communitarian politics of the common good, who admire political activism and citizenship, do not often repudiate the reasonable individualism of liberalism (in the name, say, of a self-abnegating republican patriotism, like the patriotism of Rousseau's Geneva or Tocqueville's New England townships); rather, they typically repudiate the liberal moderation or self-restraint that I have been praising, in the name of citizenship, or of participatory communitarian politics. These imprudent critics seek the restoration of a politics of common deliberation about the common good, and common action on the basis of this deliberation: but now in a community populated by rational individuals, who seek their private good as well as (or more than) the public good, rather than in a community populated by loyal republican citizens. Today's communitarians often do not want to deny that individuals seek private goods, and that the community should be judged by its success in meeting these needs; that is, they do not want to affirm that individuals are subordinate parts of an organic whole, related to the community as the hand is related to the body, or that citizens ought to love their communities as they love themselves, or more. They thus risk a politics that unites the worst of republicanism with the worst of liberalism: the moralism and civil strife of republican politics, com-

[75]Machiavelli, *The Prince*, ch. 24.

bined with the selfishness and civic incompetence of liberal politics. That would surely be an unhappy politics.

In Chapter 7, on the "liberal virtues," I consider again a number of liberal doubts regarding republican or communitarian politics of the sort praised by Walzer. I conclude here by noting a certain similarity between the republican projects of Walzer and Barber. What distinguishes Walzer and Barber from, say, MacIntyre, is an unwillingness (clearest in the case of Walzer) to break with liberalism (Barber, at least, is prepared to break with its rationalism), since liberalism must be credited with notable achievements (above all, liberation, security, and welfare). So neither Barber nor Walzer quite pursues the republican argument to its illiberal end; both recognize the threat therein to valuable liberal freedoms, and both manifest a deep ambivalence regarding liberal politics. And yet, both Barber and Walzer embrace at least one aspect of MacIntyre's account of the failure of liberalism: that liberal *reason* cannot sustain community— or citizenship, or patriotism. (For further evidence of Walzer's argument on this point, see Chapter 8.) And so they are compelled to seek illiberal (republican) solutions to problems that might admit of more modest, and so safer, liberal solutions, as I argue here with respect to the case of patriotism, and in the previous chapter with respect to the case of citizenship. Here, then, is a further battleground in the contest between communitarians and liberals: can liberal reason sustain the moral life of a community? That is the principal business of the next two chapters.

7

The Liberal Virtues

Liberal politics is a politics of rationalism. The liberal virtues are reasonable virtues, as I have already argued with respect to the case of liberal tolerance, which has its origins in a reasonable quest for civil peace and not in a loving respect for creative idiosyncrasy (Chapter 3). As such, the liberal virtues are principally the humane virtues: we respect above all those qualities that belong to human beings simply on account of their common humanity; the liberal virtues are not only communal virtues ('we-intentions'), which ask so much more of fellow citizens and so much less of fellow human beings (Chapter 4). And liberal citizenship is the citizenship of reasonable human beings who seek a way of self-government and who have come to recognize that the ordinary vices of human beings must somehow be tamed by self-interest, properly understood; liberal citizenship is not the transformative, sentimental or passionate, republican citizenship of human beings who seek warmth in a common embrace of the community (Chapter 5). So, finally, liberal patriotism is more or less reasonable patriotism, the conditional love of grateful citizens for a liberal community that serves them well, and not the unconditional ("beyond rational criticism") love of those for whom loyalty to a particular community is the foundation of morality (Chapter 6). In this chapter and the next, I propose to discuss this liberal rationalism more directly: what is the relation between liberal community and liberal reason?

I

What, again, is a "public philosophy"?[1] A public philosophy is a common source of authoritative guidance on questions of political right; it

[1]See above, pp. 23–27.

teaches citizens their rights or prerogatives as well as their duties or responsibilities, in an authoritative (but not therefore authoritarian) way.
That is, a public philosophy somehow reveals the authoritative judgment
of the community about certain most important political matters—its
first principles of justice. Those who do not recognize the community's
authority in such matters are for that reason not quite members of the
community, but resident aliens-in-spirit. So, for example, Jefferson properly doubts that it would be prudent for republican America to receive as
citizens those who would not admit the truth of republican principles:
how could republicans and monarchists, he worries, live together peace-
fully? And so (in the same spirit), Jefferson reminds his partisan friends
and partisan enemies, in his remarkable First Inaugural, that the "ani-
mation of discussions" of the struggle just concluded could now give way
to "harmony and affection," since those partisan controversies were after
all not so fundamental: "Every difference of opinion is not a difference of
principle. We have called by different names brethren of the same principle. We are all Republicans, we are all Federalists." Where there are, to
borrow Tocqueville's formula, no "great parties" but only "small parties," political life is marked by the friendly disposition to suppress petty
disputes ("politics is the art of compromise") in order to preserve the
greater harmony. Small-party politics is boring, but peaceful: most folks
stay home.[2]

But some differences of opinion are, of course, differences of principle, and such differences will bring citizens out of their homes and into
the public square, as well as into the streets. Such moments—when love
of party is more powerful than love of community—are exciting.
Sometimes, though rarely, it is even just and honorable to set one's allegiance to party above one's loyalty to community. With respect to such
grave issues, as Lincoln said, "a house divided against itself cannot
stand." In such times, the breakdown of a public philosophy, which is
manifested as well in the emergence of "great parties," puts the preservation of the community as one community at risk: more or less open
civil strife is the unhappy but inevitable consequence. Civil strife surely
makes for an exhilarating politics, if it can be kept within some bounds,
and there are those communitarians who hope for a restoration of such
passionate and tumultuous politics, or of so-called "true" citizenship,

---

[2]Thomas Jefferson, *Notes on the State of Virginia,* in *Thomas Jefferson: Writings,*
211–12 (in Query VIII); and his First Inaugural, in the same volume, 492–96 (the quoted
passage is on 493); on "great" parties, see Tocqueville, *Democracy in America,* I.ii.2.

and who think that the liberal fear of such politics is cowardly. (Consider Walzer's praise of participatory tumult, discussed in Chapter 6.) In the absence of the homogeneity of opinion that constitutes the old-fashioned republican community of virtue (which does not tolerate diversity), a no-holds-barred participatory politics can emerge for us only where some fundamental questions are once again ripe for political debate, only where politics is as a result not limited, only where there is no public philosophy that settles the most important issues. But for the liberal, such times are fraught with peril, for they portend a restoration of the natural and ordinary state of war, now made more terrible by partisan doctrines.[3]

In America, an unfortunate disruption of our public philosophy of rights has had a baleful effect on our political debates, undermining civility. We can no longer distinguish between fundamental principles and partisan questions, and so we immoderately confuse fundamental principles and partisan questions in our public debates: every claim about "rights" is rejected by some party, and every mere interest is described by another party, with the help of friendly intellectuals, as a "right." As the public philosophy of rights has lost its vitality, rights can no longer be seen as "trumps" that end political controversies, revealing a nonpartisan or common agreement among the members of the community to recognize that a certain private claim is worthy of the community's respect and forbearance. At the same time, many private (or partisan) philosophies of rights are gaining a new vitality, as they fill the vacuum created by a combination of our enduring attachment to the term "rights" and our growing inability to assign a common meaning to that term. These private philosophies of rights, which flourish on both the Right and the Left, are now powerful weapons to be wielded by partisans during political controversies, precisely where no common understanding or agreement exists.

Thus, to mention one example among many, the activity of the Supreme Court can no longer quite be understood, even by the most generous observers, to be the judicious application of a public philosophy of rights, enacted in the Constitution, which expresses a common agreement among the American people about what is and is not a right. Indeed, it is now thought, in some quarters, to be laughable to suppose that the Constitution could have such a determinate meaning, as the expression of the com-

---

[3]On the case of the Civil War, and on the question at issue here more generally, see Harry V. Jaffa, "The Nature and Origin of the American Party System."

mon sense of the people about the public meaning of the idea of "rights." Rather, the Supreme Court is now often understood to be just another partisan institution, and the formerly respectable language of constitutional rights is now just another tool of partisans in the community; or perhaps the task of the Supreme Court is, in Dworkin's now famous formulation, to bring about a "fusion of constitutional law and moral theory"—that is, of public law and private philosophy. (Dworkin's "moral theory" is surely not a "public philosophy.") But, then, why should citizens respect the judgments of this Supreme Court, whether it is frankly partisan or merely enacts a certain private philosophy of rights?[4]

This situation—the absence of a public philosophy that expresses the common beliefs of citizens on fundamental questions of political right—inevitably engenders a dangerous new willingness to appeal to the coercive apparatus of the state to resolve debates between individuals and parties about fundamental principles. Indeed, it is now increasingly difficult to specify any limits to the legitimate exercise of political power, and the idea of limited government is thus increasingly difficult to explain. The idea of limited government is intelligible only where the distinction between fundamental principles and partisan questions remains viable: a limited government is prohibited from stepping beyond the boundaries set by whatever fundamental agreement constitutes the community; *within* those boundaries, anything goes, so to speak. That is, we now enter the political arena not just to press our interests, but also to vindicate our rights, in both cases as partisans. But it then becomes very difficult to distinguish between the vindication of a right and the pursuit of an interest—or why interests only, but not rights, should be subject to political judgment and compromise, and therefore ultimately to the will of the party with the greater force.[5] When the language of rights becomes so devalued, the real rights, as well as the ones that we have so facilely contrived, may be rendered vulnerable. It is therefore not surprising that some, including many communitarians, have even begun to doubt whether there really is such a thing as a "right" at all: perhaps "rights" are just interests in disguise.

---

[4]See Unger, *Critical Legal Studies*; and Dworkin, *Taking Rights Seriously*, 149. Cf. Sanford Levinson, "Law as Literature." See, too, Mansfield, "Constitutional Fideism," a review of Levinson's *Constitutional Faith*.

[5]On the question of partisanship in liberal politics, I am indebted to a number of essays by Mansfield on representation and party government: see "Hobbes and the Science of Indirect Government"; "Modern and Medieval Representation"; "Whether Party Government is Inevitable"; and "Party Government and the Settlement of 1688." See, too, Mansfield, "Social Science and the Constitution."

Not only the liberal polity, but any enduring polity, must be founded on the basis of a public philosophy that makes it possible to distinguish between fundamental principles and partisan questions, and that discourages political controversy—which is inevitably partisan controversy—regarding fundamental principles. A public philosophy quiets dissent by reminding dissenters and their partisan friends that they too somehow acknowledge the community's authority in this matter; a public philosophy reminds partisans that they are citizens first, as when one who despises flagburners or Nazis is reminded of his greater attachment to the First Amendment. If nothing is beyond partisanship, then there is no civil politics at all, but only a kind of war, where the greater force prevails. One might even say that this is the definition of a political community: an association in which agreement about fundamental matters makes possible peaceful controversy about all other matters. In this sense, the legitimate exercise of political power is "limited" by shared understandings in all political communities. On this point, the ancient regime does not greatly differ from the modern constitution: in different ways, both settle fundamental political disputes in order to make ordinary political controversy more civil. To be sure, the existence of a nonpartisan consensus, or a public philosophy, may often or always reflect the successful imposition of a partisan claim; a party may sometimes successfully secure a special legitimacy for its particular claims that is not matched by the justice of these claims.

Political life depends upon certain shared opinions about justice. In the absence of such agreement, human beings will quarrel, sometimes violently, about first principles. That is why it is necessary for a thoughtful citizen to be concerned with "public" philosophy, with agreement as well as truth. The idea of a public philosophy combines the elements of "reflection" and "choice" that the *Federalist* suggests are necessary for free government. A public philosophy is not merely an expression of popular will, because it aspires to be a kind of philosophy; but a public philosophy is also not simply reason, because it is chosen by the people, who must consent. American liberal society might once have had such a consensus, the core of which was expressed in our Declaration of Independence: an agreement that all citizens equally possess certain natural rights, given in a well-known enumeration; that the only legitimate government is a government of limited ends established by consent; and that citizens may justly revolt against illegitimate governments. But all of this seems almost irrelevant today: thoughtful citizens today are no longer confident that the argument for natural rights is true. Indeed, it is now

possible to dismiss the idea of natural rights as "discredited," almost
without an argument, because we now suspect, as Rorty says, that
human beings are historical "all the way through" and that there is no
such thing as human nature, much less a natural right.[6]

Liberal politics, then, is properly founded on reasonable agreement regarding first principles of justice. But prevailing ways of reconstructing
public philosophy forget either the reasonableness or the agreement, it
seems to me.

Political philosophy is now understood, by many communitarian theorists, to be the full articulation of our "shared moral horizons," not the
discovery of good reasons for adopting certain principles of political
right. Walzer is especially clear on this point in *Spheres of Justice*: "One
way to begin the philosophical enterprise—perhaps the original way—is
to walk out of the cave, leave the city, climb the mountain, fashion for
oneself (what can never be fashioned for ordinary men and women) an
objective and universal standpoint. . . . But I mean to stand in the cave,
in the city, on the ground. Another way of doing philosophy is to interpret to one's fellow citizens the world of meanings that we share." Or
again: "It is to these [shared] understandings that we must appeal when
we make our arguments—all of us, not philosophers alone; for in matters
of morality, argument simply is the appeal to common meanings." And
finally: "Justice is relative to social meanings. . . . A given society is just
if its substantive life is lived in a certain way—that is, in a way faithful to
the shared understandings of the members. . . . Every substantive account of distributive justice is a local account."[7] Philosophy is, on this account, nothing more than the interpretation of community values; this is
perhaps the most important sense in which much of contemporary political theory is "communitarian." (See Chapter 8 for a more thorough account of Walzer's way of doing moral philosophy.)

There is something discomfiting about the implications of this mode of
argument: the communitarian critique of liberalism apparently stands or
falls on the claim that its moral vision is more "American" than is the alternative, not that it is more true. The self-understanding of political philosophy today is in this respect profoundly conservative. The philosopher
is no longer the most radical or even revolutionary critic of conventional
opinion, a "gadfly" capable of liberating thoughtful citizens from the dis-

---

[6]See Rorty, *Objectivity*, 175–77. Cf. James H. Nichols, Jr., "Pragmatism and the U.S.
Constitution," on John Dewey's view that the Declaration of Independence is a mere "ideology." And see Becker, *Declaration of Independence*, 24–79, 224–79; cf. xviii.
[7]Walzer, *Spheres*, xiv, 29, 312–14.

abling orthodoxies of a particular time and place; he is rather a certain kind of apologist for the ruling ideas (not, of course, the partisan ideas of the political rulers, which are easily criticized even on the basis of "shared understandings," but the ideas of the spiritual or moral rulers, who hold sway over the minds of human beings, but who may not in a particular place also hold political power).[8] In any case, there is surely no reason to suppose that such "shared understandings" or common agreements will be reasonable.

"Justice is our critic, not our mirror," writes the liberal Dworkin against the communitarian Walzer.[9] It is the business of the thoughtful liberal citizen not only to understand who we are, as individuals and as a community, but also to try to discover who we ought to be. And this requires more than reflection about what human beings believe and desire here and now (or what they believed and desired here and then), since human beings often believe silly or contradictory things; it is also necessary to think about the origins of these beliefs and desires, and about how far these comport with whatever is written by nature into the hearts and minds of human beings. But we must also remind ourselves that "public" philosophy is not private philosophy, that principles agreed upon are probably not the principles of the philosophers or the intellectuals. I have already alluded to one of the forms that this problem takes in the case of Dworkin's liberal theory ("fusion of constitutional law and moral theory"). But even Rawls, who seems (in *Political Liberalism*, at least) to seek no more than an "overlapping consensus" uniting the prevailing moral doctrines in the community in defense of his "justice as fairness," overreaches: for we have no good reason to believe (on the classical liberal view) that free and equal individuals will be able to reach an agreement as substantial as that contained in "justice as fairness."

Here is the problem confronted in Rawls's most recent book, *Political Liberalism*: "a modern democratic society is characterized not simply by a pluralism of comprehensive religious, philosophical, and moral doctrines but by a pluralism of incompatible yet reasonable comprehensive doctrines." Since this is the natural (and honorable) consequence of free democratic politics, Rawls's justice as fairness must somehow be established on grounds capable of admitting this pluralism: "the problem of political liberalism is to work out a conception of political justice for a

---

[8]See "'Spheres of Justice': An Exchange"; see, too, *Spheres*, 9 (in the footnote), where Walzer admits the propriety of this distinction; and cf. 312–16.
[9]Dworkin, "To Each His Own."

constitutional democratic regime that the plurality of reasonable doctrines . . . might endorse." Thus, the task of *Political Liberalism* is to
show how citizens might be brought to affirm principles of justice in
common, without being required to renounce the various comprehensive
religious or philosophical doctrines that will naturally arise in democratic societies. Political liberalism is simply the public aspect of every "reasonable" comprehensive doctrine in a well-ordered society; unlike the
liberalisms of Kant and Mill, it is not itself a comprehensive doctrine but
rather "applies the principle of toleration to philosophy itself." There is
no liberal *community* but only an "overlapping consensus" among citizens who affirm in common (but for many different reasons) rules of
public reason and principles of justice suitable for a democratic society of
free and equal persons.

As Rawls himself notes, some will surely wonder whether any such
"abstract" project of political constructivism can really settle the quarrels
that arouse citizens of free democratic societies who are profoundly divided by more or less comprehensive moral and religious opinions.
Indeed, Rawls's new and welcome emphasis on the principle of "toleration as the origin of liberalism" does not reach far enough. *Political
Liberalism* may describe a theory of justice suitable for "reasonable" persons, who already somehow admit the conditions of "fairness" that are
modeled in Rawls's new and improved original position—even *this* surely
presupposes more "consensus" in our liberal community than really exists. But who needs to persuade *these* people to be tolerant and liberal? A
truly *political* liberalism must recognize the intractability of certain naturally intolerant partisan opinions, including 'unreasonable' and 'irrational' opinions, thus the necessity of meeting these threats to civility
with good (concrete) reasons that manifestly answer potent natural passions (fear of death, love of liberty, desire for comfortable security, and so
on through the "traditional" liberal list). Here is what classical liberals
doubt, regarding the project of "political liberalism": the naturally lawless and warlike passions that (as Hobbes says) "carry us to Partiality,
Pride, Revenge, and the like" will commonly inspire partisan opinions
("comprehensive doctrines") that are too deep and abiding to be tamed
by appeal to an idea of justice that is "constructed" by hypothetical
moral persons subject to "reasonable" constraints. What good reason is
there to agree to *that*? One may wonder, in short, whether Rawls has
really plumbed "the absolute depth of that irreconcilable latent conflict"
between comprehensive (religious) doctrines that inspired the liberal
project at the beginning. Even here in *Political Liberalism*, there is some-

thing notably apolitical about Rawls's way of doing political philosophy—as if the moral and political quarrels of liberal citizens might somehow be settled by philosophers or imaginary (rational and reasonable)
representatives.[10]

Classical liberalism seeks a more modest, yet still reasonable, agreement: (a "public philosophy") to seek peace together so that we will not
discover war as we go our separate ways. That is the least that might be
expected from reasonable human beings; but it is also, perhaps, the most.

II

In a recent essay, "Liberal Virtues," William A. Galston recounts the current state of play in an old and oft-repeated game: the debate about
whether liberal politics requires *virtue*, or not.[11] Galston argues that an
older tradition of thought about liberalism was "dominated by the belief
that the liberal polity does not rest on individual virtue," since liberal
principles are nothing more than "the articles of a peace treaty among individuals." As representatives of this older (1950s and '60s) interpretation of liberalism, Galston mentions Leo Strauss and C. B. Macpherson
on Locke; Martin Diamond and Gordon Wood on the "new science of
politics"; Robert Dahl and Theodore Lowi on liberal pluralism. This "in-
terest-based" interpretation of liberalism is now being supplanted by a
new view of liberalism, which understands that "liberal theory, institutions, and society embody—and depend upon—individual virtue." As
advocates of this new liberalism of virtue, Galston mentions, among others: Judith Shklar, Nathan Tarcov, Harvey Mansfield, Jr., James Q.
Wilson, and Thomas Spragens.[12]

Perhaps Galston somewhat overstates the novelty of (at least some versions of) the new liberalism; in any case, I argue that the reinterpretation
of liberalism offered by Galston and others renders liberalism unnecessarily vulnerable to attack from so-called "republicans" and "communitarians" (for example, J. G. A. Pocock, Michael Sandel, and Alasdair
MacIntyre, among others mentioned by Galston). For Galston imprudently concedes, it seems to me, what the communitarian critics of liberalism affirm: that it is not quite reasonable to be virtuous, even in the
liberal way of virtue. The liberal virtues, says Galston, are not always
"individually advantageous"; they are not "reducible to self-interest,

---

[10]For this paragraph, and the previous two, see Rawls, *Political Liberalism*, esp.
xvi–xviii, xxvi–xxviii, 4–11; and see, generally, 3–46, 89–129, 133–72.
[11]Galston, "Liberal Virtues," 1277–89.
[12]Galston, "Liberal Virtues," 1277–78.

even self-interest 'rightly understood.' "[13] He thereby deprives liberals of the most powerful liberal answer to the question, "Why be virtuous?" and so invites illiberal answers to this question. So far as the new liberals deny that it is reasonable to be virtuous, they are faced with an unhappy choice: they must somehow teach liberals not to be reasonable, or they must permit them not to be virtuous. If liberals are above all "rationalists of everyday life," then virtues thus understood are not "liberal" virtues. But let me now begin again.

Classical liberalism is not simply hostile to the idea of virtue. Locke and other classical liberals reinterpret virtue, duty, the law of nature, and the rest, but they do not suggest that liberal communities can do without virtue altogether, though they may be able to do without the name.[14] Galston argues that Strauss's account of Locke "stressed his effort to liberate individual acquisitiveness from traditional moral constraints."[15] And yet it does not follow from this understanding of Locke's moral project that there are no liberal or Lockean virtues: the individual, once liberated from unreasonable moral constraints, might now be "directed" (as Locke puts it) by a new and more reasonable law of nature; the old virtues and duties might be replaced by new virtues and duties, perhaps ones that would advance rather than inhibit the individual's acquisitiveness (broadly conceived as the pursuit of the individual's own well-being).[16]

More generally, even if liberal politics seeks to liberate the individual from traditional moral constraints, so that the individual might be able

[13]Galston, "Liberal Virtues," 1281.

[14]Whether this *name* is useful for liberals is largely a question of rhetoric. To answer this question, liberals must consider whether "virtue" has been defined, in a particular time and place, by the friends or enemies of liberalism; whether the language of virtue can be appropriated by liberals without imprudently distorting the meaning of liberal moral doctrines.

[15]Galston, "Liberal Virtues," 1277. Galston appears to suggest that Strauss, among others, argues that Locke's liberalism is "bereft of—if not hostile to—*any* conception of virtue," even the Hobbesian instrumental virtues that are the means of peace (cf. 1277 and 1279–80). See, too, Diamond's account of the thought of the framers in "Democracy and *The Federalist*: A Reconsideration of the Framers' Intent"; and cf. Diamond, "Ethics and Politics: The American Way."

[16]See, for example, Locke, *Second Treatise*, §57. See, too, Smith, *Wealth of Nations*, I.ii: "But man has almost constant occasion for the help of his brethren, and it is in vain for him to expect it from their benevolence only. He will be more likely to prevail if he can interest their self-love in his favour, and shew them that it is for their own advantage to do for him what he requires of them. . . . It is not from the benevolence of the butcher, the brewer, or the baker, that we expect our dinner, but from their regard to their own interest. We address ourselves, not to their humanity but to their self-love, and never talk to them of our own necessities but of their advantages."

to pursue his own happiness in his own way, it would not follow that a liberal community can do without virtue: for it is not possible to pursue happiness reasonably in the absence of habits of self-mastery that one might as well call virtues—for two reasons. First, happiness can be pursued only in a certain sort of political community, one that preserves peace and supplies (or protects) the prosperity and liberty that are the conditions of many pursuits of happiness. Second, even in one's private life, the reasonable pursuit of happiness requires the cultivation of certain virtues, which the prudent liberal will therefore cultivate, willy-nilly.

Strauss discusses the liberal idea of virtue in *Natural Right and History*. He discusses the new meaning of virtue more fully in his discussion of Hobbes than in his discussion of Locke.[17] Strauss argues that Hobbes attempted "the restoration of the moral principles of politics, i.e., of natural law, on the plane of Machiavelli's 'realism'": Hobbes is a natural-law philosopher, a teacher of morality. Like Machiavelli, and in the same "public spirited" way, Hobbes repudiated the classical teachings about virtue and substituted "merely political virtue" for "moral virtue": "Just as Machiavelli reduced virtue to the political virtue of patriotism, Hobbes reduced virtue to the social virtue of peaceableness." It is doubtless true that Hobbesian virtue is more modest than classical virtue: "if virtue is reduced to social virtue or to benevolence or kindness or 'the liberal virtues,' 'the severe virtues' of self-restraint will lose their standing."[18] So Strauss's Hobbes was a teacher of a new sort of virtue, and his Locke was in this respect a student of Hobbes.

The question, then, is not whether liberal politics requires virtue or not: it evidently does. The question is whether the liberal account of virtue, as opposed to another, more rigorous account, is true: whether the liberals are right that the most important virtues are reasonable; whether the liberals are right that these liberal virtues alone are sufficient to preserve the peace and to sustain a livable political community. Thus, Locke sought to destroy the old natural law, which was an obstacle to human happiness, in order to establish a new and more reasonable law of na-

---

[17]Strauss, *Natural Right*. But Strauss's discussion of Locke is explicitly based on the earlier discussion of Hobbes: see 166, 221, 227–31, esp. 229.

[18]Strauss, *Natural Right*, 177–79, 187–88. On Locke's similar view, see 229: "Locke's natural law teaching can then be understood perfectly if one assumes that the laws of nature which he admits are, as Hobbes puts it, 'but conclusions, or theorems concerning what conduces to the conservation and defense' of man over against other men. . . . The law of nature, as Locke conceives of it, formulates the conditions of peace or, more generally stated, of 'public happiness' or 'the prosperity of any people.' " See Galston, "Liberal Virtues," 1280, on Hobbes.

ture; this new law of nature or "law of reason" would serve as a kind of map, guiding our various pursuits of happiness.[19] Virtue, on the liberal and not only the liberal view, is the disposition or habit of restraining and ordering one's passions so that they submit to one's reason; thus to say that the liberal virtues are not simply reasonable is to repudiate this rationalist idea of virtue. The reasonable pursuit of one's self-interest, that is to say, *is* virtue, on this account of virtue. Only if virtue *must* mean something more than what it means for Locke and Hobbes could it be said that liberalism is bereft of virtue.

Liberalism is said to consist of the "articles of a peace treaty among individuals."[20] But it is necessary to be clear about what such a view really implies. For example, this interpretation of liberalism does not at all imply that liberal politics can dispense with virtue; one cannot reasonably rely on any peace treaty, especially a peace treaty with hostile rivals, and even more a peace treaty with unjust enemies, without practicing some virtues. One must, in the first place, "trust but verify": that is, one must possess those *virtues*, as well as reasonable opinions, that enable one to be vigilant and effective in the defense of one's own interests against the possible violators of the so-called peace treaty—here, the "social contract." One cannot simply rely on liberal institutions to preserve the peace.

This peace treaty contains, for example, certain articles that concern the execution of the laws against criminals, those "wild Savage Beasts, with whom Men can have no Society nor Security"; these provisions are necessary because the execution of the law in the state of nature is for various reasons unreliable—too vengeful here, too cautious there.[21] Liberal citizens must surely possess certain virtues if they are to do this job well. Above all, they must be able to restrain the powerful moral passions that tempt them to be either too angry or too compassionate when inflicting punishments, for both excessive harshness and excessive gentleness in the execution of the law can often threaten the security of individuals, and sometimes even undermine civil peace. Unnecessary harshness in the execution of the law, which may be an expression of the understandably powerful moral indignation of citizens, can threaten the security of individuals; but excessive gentleness, which may result from reasonable and compassionate doubts about the true moral responsibility of certain crim-

[19]Locke, *Second Treatise*, §§6–15, 57.
[20]Galston, "Liberal Virtues," 1277.
[21]Locke, *Second Treatise*, §§7–13.

inals, can deprive the community of an effective deterrent to crime, so that we are soon less secure against such criminals. The liberal legislator and the liberal juror must be able to recognize and restrain these angry or compassionate sentiments; thus, for example, a liberal juror has a *duty* to be dispassionate, and to set aside those qualms that spring from compassionate doubts about the moral responsibility of the criminal as well as those vengeful passions that spring from fear and anger. Such prudent restraint of one's passions is one of the liberal virtues. And the liberal institutions of criminal justice cannot operate well without such virtuous citizens.

Moreover, liberal citizens must also *promulgate* laws well, which requires them (among other things) to restrain the various passions and opinions (perhaps especially the religious ones) that might tempt them to make pernicious laws, since some laws would threaten rather than preserve the peace. The liberal Montesquieu, especially, teaches the importance, for a healthy liberal politics, of a certain kind of criminal-justice system that is possible only on the basis of certain liberal virtues of self-restraint—one that, for example, allows the people to resist their (more or less natural) temptations to punish heresies, or unnecessarily to restrict distasteful private practices, or to subordinate the security of individuals to the putative interests of the community, or to permit partisan considerations to corrupt the legal system, among many other vices. A liberal criminal-justice system must encourage liberal citizens to leave some of their moral, political, and religious passions at home and bring others with them, when they go on jury duty, or elect legislators, or respond to public-opinion pollsters. Or, consider another contentious problem of criminal justice: how far should liberals permit their understandable compassion for the victims of brutal crimes to undermine their good judgment that the protection of the rights of criminals is necessary for the security of all private citizens, even when that sometimes leads to grave injustices in particular cases? Only a certain kind of virtuous citizenry can restrain its present passion to avenge this crime, as well as its continuing passion that such crimes should always be avenged and their victims repaired, on the strength of a sound judgment that they thereby preserve the security of every citizen more fully.[22] In any case, the establishment and preservation of such a criminal-justice system is both gravely important for liberal communities and extremely difficult for many citizens: it

---

[22]On these liberal virtues, see Montesquieu, *Spirit*, bk. 12; and see Locke, *Second Treatise* §§6–13, 123–31.

requires not only good judgment about how best to achieve security through moderate laws and the judicious execution of those laws, but also the self-restraint (or virtue) necessary to prevent injudicious passions from undermining the effectiveness of law. The cultivation of such liberal virtues is only reasonable, for in their absence liberal citizens, like other citizens, are very likely to behave unreasonably.

Further, liberal citizens must be able to choose well the legislators who will make the laws and the judges who will apply them, and they must be willing to sacrifice the resources necessary to establish an effective criminal-justice system. The liberal peace treaty is also most secure where citizens possess the virtue of law-abidingness—that is, where they habitually obey the law, even when there is no policeman around the corner, and even where the law contravenes one's immediate or apparent interest. And it goes without saying that virtues—including even some measure of courage—are also necessary, among the contracting parties, to protect one another from enemies who are not parties to the peace treaty. These virtues, the "trust but verify" liberal virtues, are self-regarding as well as social virtues, for both sorts of virtue are necessary components of the foundation of the liberal peace treaty. A prudent human being will enter into a peace treaty (a "social contract") only with certain kinds of human beings, those who are capable of self-mastery and other liberal virtues, in the expectation that it will be necessary to cultivate certain kinds of virtues, in himself and in others, in order to secure the peace. Nor is it necessary to stop here: the liberal virtues, strictly speaking, are those virtues necessary to preserve the peace, thus virtues in which the liberal state might take an interest. But there are other liberal virtues, less strictly speaking, that are elements of the reasonable self-mastery necessary for the pursuit of happiness in one's private life.

Thus, as Galston argues, we must imagine a "liberal character"—not a "nation of angels," but some kind of "virtuous citizenry": "to an extent difficult to measure but impossible to ignore, the viability of liberal society depends on its ability to engender a virtuous citizenry."[23]

Two questions arise: What is virtue? And is virtue reasonable? Locke and other classical liberals can hardly be accused of failing to recognize the importance of virtue and duty in public life. But Locke argued that this

---

[23]Galston, "The Liberal Virtues," 1279. I should emphasize here that my disagreement with Galston concerns only the question whether liberals must abandon or sharply confine the language of self-interest properly understood. Galston's substantive account of the liberal virtues, and of the moral dimension of the liberal polity, is generally quite persuasive. See his admirable book, *Liberal Purposes*.

virtue, or obedience to the "law of nature," is reasonable, and can be made to appear so to reasonable human beings: indeed, the law of nature is a law of reason, Locke argues. From this point of view, one might argue that the decline of liberal virtues in our time is not the product of the corrosive effects of liberal rationalism on traditional (nonrational or irrational) understandings of virtue: that is, it is not a decline of virtue so much as it is a decline or failure in reasonableness. The Lockean liberal can easily admit the necessity of virtue for public life; he can further admit that contemporary life reveals a decline in the virtue that is necessary to sustain liberal institutions and principles; but he would then conclude that we are not sufficiently reasonable, not that we are *too* reasonable, or that our excessive reasonableness has undermined our capacity for liberal virtues. The new liberals, so far as they argue that the decline of liberal virtues is a consequence of the corrosive effect of liberal rationalism, lend support to those critics of liberalism who argue that liberalism is in principle defective because virtue is not rational. That is, the new liberals seem to concede the point of the critics of liberalism, that virtue requires a nonrational foundation; and they must then seek an inevitably unhappy middle course between liberal rationalism and more-than-rational virtue. The contemporary world has largely abandoned rationalism; those who have done so include communitarian critics of liberalism who suppose that morality is always founded on more-than-rational identification with one's community, as well as postmodern individualist critics of liberalism who view reason as an unwelcome intrusion into individual self-expression. So it is the task of liberals to defend virtue against the latter camp, without falling into the old-fashioned intolerances risked by the former camp.

III

In *Ordinary Vices*, Judith Shklar associates the liberal hatred of cruelty with Montesquieu and (above all) Montaigne. But her liberalism is also, I would say, a kind of Hobbesian liberalism: anger at cruelty is an altogether reasonable passion, rooted in the natural fear of violent death; such reasonable anger is surely a helpful sentimental support for the first law of nature—to seek peace. Here, I again argue that humanity is reasonable and cruelty unreasonable; that is, I offer a further account of "humanity" as a reasonable liberal virtue, against those who argue that there *are* no liberal virtues, and against those who argue that the liberal virtues are not simply reasonable. (In this, I continue the argument of Chapter 4.)

Hobbes defines "cruelty" as "little sense of the calamity of others . . . proceeding from Security of [one's] own fortune": the insecure, says Hobbes, are never cruel. But since security is almost always (in fact) uncertain, Hobbes can argue that cruelty is a manifestation of self-deluding "vain-glory, and contrary to reason": cruelty often betrays a false sense of security. Prudent liberals, whether they hate cruelty or seek peace above all, should therefore cultivate a true sense of the natural insecurity of human beings. Vainglorious cruelty, says Hobbes, gives rise to enmity or war and thereby threatens the peace—and so is "against the Law of Nature."[24] For the humane Hobbes, cruelty is unreasonable and is therefore a vice: human beings cannot reasonably be confident that their cruelty or contempt will not be answered by war or punishment; it is therefore prudent for human beings to cultivate in themselves and others a certain solicitous "sense of the calamity of others"—call it *humanity*. This moral truth is perhaps clear enough, to sober men, in the state of nature; but civil society, especially where it is most successful, makes possible a new kind of vanity, one that is almost unknown in the state of nature: only a very great fool, in the state of nature, would believe that he could somehow exempt himself from the state of war, but in peaceful society this is unhappily not true. The liberal state must therefore remind such fools, from time to time, of their (objective) insecurity, and this sometimes requires the liberal state to employ harsh measures. Indeed, a reasonable anger at those cruel and perverse human beings who bring about unnecessary calamities—above all, criminals at home and tyrants abroad—is surely a moral or sentimental corollary of the humane "sense of the calamity of others."

Here is an example of this sort of argument. Walter Berns argues that the case for the justice of capital punishment should not rest on the narrowly utilitarian argument that capital punishment deters crime; capital punishment is just, says Berns, because it reflects and even enhances the capacity for moral anger of citizens confronted by a certain kind of cruelty, and because it "remind[s] us of the moral order by which alone we can live as *human* beings." Capital punishment is just, above all, because

[24]For the definition of cruelty, which is also called "contempt," see Hobbes, *Leviathan*, ch. 6. Here is the sequel to the passage quoted in the text: "For, that any man should take pleasure in other mens great harmes, without other end of his own, I do not conceive it possible." On the law of nature and cruelty, see ch. 15; cf. ch. 6 on "vain-glory"; cf. ch. 15, on the similar case of "contempt" and the law of nature. Some deny that a Hobbesian liberalism is imaginable; indeed, Hobbes was no liberal. But I argue here that a Hobbesian moral psychology can serve well as a foundation for certain liberal virtues. Elsewhere in the book, I resist the temptation to rely too heavily on Hobbes, since the kinship between Hobbes and the classical liberals is a contentious question.

it is humane. My argument here is in the spirit, but in some measure against the letter, of Berns's argument, so far as Berns suggests that the Hobbesian account of crime and punishment relies too much on enlightened self-interest, and thereby undermines humane moral passions, including anger. But it seems to me that Berns's argument might be restated as the argument of a *liberal humanitarian*; a Hobbesian liberal should seek not only to instill fear in criminals (above all), but also to instill reasonable moral anger and a spirit of humanity in citizens, in order to secure more completely the peace that is the condition of a happy life. In short, I am not yet persuaded that "a nation of simply self-interested men will soon enough perish from the earth": that is—and here is the main point—if self-interest is understood reasonably.[25]

Still further, it follows that liberals must guard against the emergence, in themselves and others, of an unreasonable (but somewhat natural) pride, since that is the psychological root of cruelty and other vices, insofar as pride enables human beings to forget their natural insecurity. Thus, liberals should assiduously cultivate the humane sentiments that counterbalance this unreasonable pride, including above all a moral sense of human equality. Indeed, that is perhaps the chief liberal virtue: to admit the natural equality of other human beings in one's heart, so to speak, even when it seems perverse to ignore, as the liberal must to some extent, manifest inequalities.[26]

From the fact that humanity, moral anger, insecurity, and a moral sense of human equality are reasonable, it does not follow that their cultivation must only be by reasonable means, or that no elements of passion or sentiment should be permitted to corrupt the reasonable calculations of liberal citizens: some sentiments and passions are more reasonable than others. The liberal need not eschew certain more-than-rational aids in the cultivation of these liberal virtues. Indeed, each of the liberal sentiments or virtues mentioned above cuts against the grain for human beings, at least in some measure; prudent human beings, then, ought to cultivate those habits and sentiments that aid reason in its battle against unreasonable passions, which often do not cut against the grain. A Hobbesian virtue is simply a moral disposition to obey the laws of nature; such a disposition is or may be some combination of sentiment, habit, and good judgment. It

---

[25]Berns, *For Capital Punishment*. See, for example, 17–24, 132–42, 152, 172–76.

[26]See Hobbes, *Leviathan*, ch. 15, on the dangers of pride and arrogance, which are against the law of nature, and in defense of a kind of humility that cuts against the grain, as Hobbes here suggests: "*That every man acknowledge other for his Equall by Nature*" (emphasis in original). Cf. ch. 13, on natural equality.

is noteworthy that Hobbes presents, here and there in the *Leviathan*, a rather full liberal moral psychology, not just a reasonable juridical deduction of liberal principles of justice from the natural equality of human beings in the state of nature. This Hobbesian moral psychology shows the way toward a liberal moral education, or an education in the liberal "virtues." To be sure, Hobbes himself does not always speak in this way, though he sometimes does so.[27]

We liberals, Hobbes reminds us, must never become so complacent about the prosperity and freedom we now enjoy that we forget the "liberal virtues" (as well as the liberal sciences of politics and economics) that are the foundation of our way of life—or we will then be tempted to excuse or practice some of the vices or passions that would threaten it. A little insecurity or reasonable fear is politically salutary, according to the classical liberal philosopher. Hobbes shows, what we now have no reason to doubt, that human beings will find many motives for cruelty, for that is our nature. Great and small cruelties are everywhere—here too—inspired by religious and political fanaticisms, or by the simple desire for mastery, or by the desire for good things that others now enjoy, or even by a perverse delight in cruelty for its own sake, among other motives. In the face of evidence that inhumanity and cruelty are a natural part of the human condition, perhaps more natural and ordinary than liberal humanity and gentleness, Hobbes undertakes to answer the question: "Why not be cruel?" His answer—which is also the liberal answer—is that it is unreasonable to be cruel, because of the natural and ineradicable insecurity of human beings, and that human beings generally can be persuaded of this fact, by means of a moral education and political institutions that teach citizens and others, in various ways, that they too are vulnerable. Such reasonable fear, perhaps supported by moral anger, is what thwarts cruel passions and desires—not only in others (fanatics, criminals, tyrants, sadists), but even in ourselves. If we repudiate this answer, as Rorty does, we are still left with Hobbes's question.

Rorty proudly insists that "there is no answer to the question 'Why not be cruel?'" Yet Rorty is still (generally) a critic of cruelty, and a humane liberal.[28] That is, Rorty refuses to admit that cruelty is unreasonable by

---

[27]See Hobbes, *Leviathan*, esp. chs. 13–16, as well as ch. 6 and chs. 10–12, read in the light of the following chapters. See, too, ch. 15, on "the means of Peace," which are called the "*Morall Vertues.*"

[28]Rorty, *Contingency*, xv. There is significant ambiguity about the possible cruelties of the so-called "strong poet." Rorty's unmistakable fascination with Nabokov's Kinbote and his Humbert (as well as with Orwell's O'Brien) is notable; even the liberal ironist,

nature, or that a cruel human being cannot enjoy a secure happiness; but he is still somehow confident that his liberals can (what is perhaps most important) resist the many temptations to be cruel, as well as defend themselves against dangers posed by cruel adversaries and criminals. Perhaps such liberals can indeed defend their way of life against cruel or inhumane enemies, if a way of life that is justified by nothing deeper than contingent historical circumstance can nevertheless be worth dying for; and if Rorty's argument here—that there is no answer to the question "Why not be cruel?"—does not compel us, as it might seem to, to excuse and even to respect the cruelty of other ways of life. But what, absent Hobbes's sober and humane doctrine, is to prevent such unreasonable liberals from fighting cruelty with cruelty, or even from inflicting cruelty on innocent bystanders, finally forgetting the very distinction between cruelty and humanity? But that is nothing other than the restoration (more or less) of the very state of war that liberals used to abhor. Again: *why not be cruel?* Or are liberals alone somehow never tempted by the charms of cruelty? Rorty's easygoing liberalism without fear, which encourages a proud but false sense of security, is the opposite of the Hobbesian liberalism that never forgets, or permits others to forget, the weakness of humanity in a cruel world, as well as the cruel passions hidden in almost every human heart, which flourish in the absence of fear.

To be sure, not all fears are politically or morally salutary; thus, a certain kind of fear is the "principle" of despotism, according to Montesquieu. Shklar even argues that such "fear is the ultimately evil moral condition"; but Shklar too suggests that the liberal "fear of fear," or Montesquieu's "liberalism of fear" as opposed to the "liberalism of rights," contributes to the reasonable suspicious temper that arms humanity against cruelty.[29]

Cruelty is not the only vice, although it is perhaps the most dangerous, that emerges when human beings imprudently believe that threats to their own security are now surely at an end; a similar argument could be made in defense of many liberal virtues.[30] Indeed, insecurity, or reason-

---

who believes that "cruelty is the worst thing we do," is not altogether immune to the charms of cruelty (see Rorty, *Contingency*, 141–88). Of course, we may not choose to imitate those who charm us; but the good reasons for such self-restraint are not typically insuperable.

[29]Montesquieu, *Spirit*, 3.9, 4.3, 5.14; Shklar, *Ordinary Vices*, 241–42, 237–39; and Shklar, "Liberalism of Fear."

[30]See Galston, "Liberal Virtues," 1277–90. Galston is surely right to say that liberalism both requires and can sustain certain "liberal virtues." See, too, Galston, "Liberalism and Public Morality."

able fear, might be said to be the foundation of every liberal virtue, for it explains why civil society is necessary, and why liberal individuals should often obey the community or serve their fellows—that is, why they should be virtuous. So liberals today must remind themselves from time to time of the various harms that may come to them in the natural course of events, given the nature of human beings; and they must continue to cultivate the various virtues (among other qualities) that earlier liberals hoped would be fences against these dangers.

This is a great dilemma for partisans of liberalism, here understood as the reasonable pursuit of peace and security: liberal politics aims to make possible a reasonable confidence, here and now, about one's future security and even comfort or prosperity, by somehow vitiating the passions and consequent vices, like pride and cruelty among many others, that would undermine that security; but precisely if this liberal project somehow succeeds, as it happily has for us, peace and security and comfort and freedom may come to seem ordinary or natural, and their moral and political conditions may be forgotten. The liberal statesman and the liberal theorist must therefore, it seems to me, always seek to cultivate a certain prudent insecurity among liberal citizens, a reasonable understanding of the many (hidden) threats to our way of life and of the various liberal virtues necessary to preserve it: sober fear makes men reasonably virtuous. This is a task for partisans of liberalism, even, and especially, in the most secure times. And that is a liberal paradox: liberal statesmen must often seem to be crying wolf, so to speak, since the preservation of our humane way of life depends on our regarding it as always vulnerable, because of certain facts about human nature, even when it seems to be most secure.

Shklar describes Machiavelli as the "foremost teacher of cruelty"; it is "a great mistake," according to Shklar, "to read Machiavelli as another Hobbes—a bit wry, but wishing mankind well."[31] This view is misleading, it seems to me, since Machiavelli's praise of cruelty is also often humane. The so-called cruel are often "more merciful" than the so-called merciful, given the nature of human beings, says Machiavelli. He is, in important respects, among the "humane" philosophers who are critics of the classical idea of "virtue"; but he is perhaps concerned even more than Hobbes and others to remind human beings that their natural condition is one of permanent (more or less hidden) insecurity.[32] Thus, to mention

---

[31]Shklar, *Ordinary Vices*, 10, 207. So Hobbes wishes men well.
[32]See Machiavelli, *The Prince*, chs. 3, 7, 17. And see Sheldon Wolin, *Politics and Vision*, 195–238.

only one among a number of pieces of evidence that might be adduced here, Machiavellian *virtù* is much more flexible than the Hobbesian "Morall vertues," as is demanded by the greater uncertainty and insecurity in human affairs that Machiavelli observes.

8

Community and Philosophy

Here is the fundamental ground of the quarrel between classical liberals and their contemporary communitarian critics: the communitarian affirms, what the liberal denies, that human beings are so constituted by their communities that they "must exempt at least some fundamental structures of that community's life from criticism," so that (among other things) "patriotism has to be a loyalty that is in some respects unconditional." For the liberal citizen, on the contrary, "no limitations are or can be set upon the criticism of the social *status quo*."[1] The communitarian view of moral reasoning is a problem, for liberalism, because liberal citizenship is possible only if classical liberal philosophy is possible. Certainly, the liberal citizen is not a philosopher. And yet, a kind of freedom from the moral authority of the community must be possible, on the liberal view, for most human beings, if political freedom from authorities and the right to consent are to be meaningful.

Liberalism opposes authoritarianism. But this cannot mean merely that liberals seek freedom from the particular officeholders who hold political power, narrowly understood, here and now. Such freedom is indeed quite important from a certain point of view, but it is surely incomplete. The freedom from authority that liberals seek is not just freedom from this or that particular petty authority within a community or tradition. It is also, and more crucially, freedom from those greater authorities, the ruling orthodoxies in a community and the priestly interpreters of these orthodoxies. Thus, for example, Walzer's remarks on authority, and on the possibility of opposition, in *Interpretation and Social Criticism*, are mostly

[1] MacIntyre, *Is Patriotism a Virtue?* 12–13.

unsatisfying, because he is preoccupied with the question whether the communitarian view of philosophy leaves room for criticism of today's officeholders, but is more or less indifferent to the question whether it leaves room for criticism of the authority of tradition altogether.

Or again: liberalism is a doctrine of consent. But consent is an empty idea unless one can plausibly assert the existence of human beings of a certain kind: those who can constitute their own communities, and who are therefore not, or not wholly, constituted *by* their communities. Against the communitarians, the liberal must insist that our political judgments and obligations are in the most important cases chosen by us, and not given to us. Liberalism depends on the prevalence of autonomous men and women who choose their political principles, as well as their companions, on the basis of reason, and not because of a history or tradition that they can "neither summon nor command." But such reasonable freedom is finally possible only if something like what I have described as philosophy is possible—only if, as Strauss puts it, "there is something in man that is not altogether in slavery to his society." The deepest meaning of freedom, for the liberal as well as for the philosopher, is this freedom—of the mind to choose.[2] For this reason, I conclude here with a discussion of Walzer's account of the relation between community and philosophy.

I

What is the place of philosophy, or of social criticism, in the life of a political or moral community? Michael Walzer considers this question in *Interpretation and Social Criticism*, an impressive defense of the philosophical communitarianism that dominates contemporary political theory. Walzer here defends his "way of doing moral philosophy"—the "interpretation," or criticism from within, of a particular existing morality—against certain critics. He seems to be especially troubled by the suspicion that such interpretation is inherently conservative. According to certain liberal and radical critics, interpretation "binds us irrevocably to the status quo—since we can only interpret what already exists—and so undercuts the very possibility of social criticism."[3] But Walzer denies that interpretation is conservative; indeed, he argues that it is the true ground even of radical social criticism, because only those who share a moral or

[2]Strauss, *Natural Right*, 3.
[3]Walzer, *Interpretation*, 3; cf. Dworkin, "To Each His Own," a review of Walzer's *Spheres of Justice*, 4–6; and Sandel's review of the same book.

cultural horizon can engage in genuine moral argument. So our "experience of moral argument is best understood in the interpretive mode"; "in matters of morality, argument simply is the appeal to common meanings."[4] Not only when we apologize for existing social practices and institutions, but also when we criticize them, we must appeal to a shared moral horizon. Detached moral and political philosophers, including those liberals who remain at bottom Enlightenment rationalists, appeal to universal principles of justice rather than to particular shared values, and accordingly cannot be effective social critics. They cannot participate in the most important moral arguments: they will not be heard because they appear to be "enemies" and so "lack standing"; they will not be understood because they speak a strange and abstract moral language that seems to teach us nothing about the moral world that exists here and now. The classical liberal theorist in particular, who traces principles of political right to an imaginary state of nature, an unreal condition of solitude, cannot fathom our moral experience as rooted communal beings, and so has little to contribute to the moral argument.[5]

Walzer distinguishes three ways of doing moral philosophy. Some philosophers claim to "discover" objective moral truths that are revealed by God or found in nature; such a philosopher learns to see these truths by "wrench[ing] himself loose from his parochial interests and loyalties," or from his community. "There are natural as well as divine revelations, and a philosopher who reports to us on the existence of natural law, say, or natural rights or any set of objective moral truths has walked the path of discovery." Philosophical "inventors," by contrast, somehow create entirely new moral worlds without guidance from God or nature; they are guided at most by a "design procedure" that yields "agreement," as in the case of many neo-Kantian liberal theorists. But these inventions are still meant to provide a "universal corrective for all the different social moralities," because they are agreements not among actual human beings with particular prejudices, but rather among imaginary or ideal interlocutors behind a veil of ignorance or its equivalent. "Assume the death of God or the meaninglessness of nature—apparently painless assumptions in these latter days—and then we can say of these legislators that they invent the moral world that would have existed if a moral world had existed without their inventing it. They create what God would have created if there were a God." (But do the "Laws of Nature and of Nature's God" bind as

---

[4]Walzer, *Interpretation*, 21; and see 3; Walzer, *Spheres*, 29; see, too, xiv, 313–14.
[5]Walzer, *Interpretation*, 59, 78; and see 14, 35, 62–64.

well where there is no God or Nature?) Finally, some philosophers (or "poets") do not seek to flee the cave at all; rather, they offer "interpretations" of the particular moral tradition they share with other members of a community. Such a philosopher seeks to persuade by evoking shared aspirations, not universal principles: "[Moral] questions are pursued within a tradition of moral discourse—indeed, they only arise within that tradition—and they are pursued by interpreting the terms of that discourse. The argument is about ourselves; the meaning of our way of life is what is at issue."[6]

But it soon appears that the more fundamental distinction, for Walzer, is between philosophy or the "conventional view" of philosophy, including both discovery and invention, and interpretive social criticism. Philosophy is "detached" or "external" or "asocial" criticism; interpretation is "connected" or "internal" or "social" criticism. So after the opening pages of this book, Walzer routinely speaks without discrimination of "discovery and invention," which together constitute the "conventional view" of philosophy.[7] Indeed, Walzer suggests that interpretive social criticism is perhaps best understood not as a species of philosophy, but rather as "one of the more important byproducts of a larger activity—let us call it the activity of cultural elaboration and affirmation," which is the work of "priests and prophets" and "poets," among others, but not of philosophers. It is thus not surprising that Walzer's model social critic is the prophet Amos, a "connected critic" who is contrasted, in the final chapter of the book, with the "detached critic" Jonah. Walzer is a critic of philosophy, or of the conventional view of philosophy, in the name of interpretive social criticism and cultural affirmation; more precisely, he is an enemy of Enlightenment philosophy because he is a certain kind of partisan of moral community.[8]

Political philosophy, on the "conventional" or Enlightenment view, is the quest for universal and objective principles of political right, against which we might measure the justice or prudence of the principles and practices of any particular community, including our own. Philosophy thus understood seeks to provide a "universal corrective for all the different social moralities"; and this is true, again, whether philosophy proceeds by way of discovery or by way of invention (as Walzer recognizes).

[6]Walzer, *Interpretation*, 5, 12–13, 23; and see 9–10. And cf. Barber, *Conquest*, esp. 193–211.
[7]Thus, the differences between classical liberal discoveries and neo-Kantian liberal inventions, to which I have already alluded, are not critical, on this account.
[8]Walzer, *Interpretation*, 77, 69, 64, 35, 38–40, 50, 89–94; see 21, 36, 64. And see Rorty, *Objectivity*, 175–96; and Rorty, *Contingency*, 44–95.

Liberation from particularism is, on this account, a theoretical imperative: any possible philosophical method or "way of doing moral philosophy" will require radical intellectual and emotional detachment from one's own community, freedom from parochial ideas and affections that would only be obstacles to the search for universal truths. Such freedom of the mind is possible, on the Enlightenment view, only if our thoughts are not fundamentally determined by our historical circumstances, and only if our moral passions and attachments are not altogether constituted by the various communities into which we are born. It must be possible to love the truth more than we love our "home"; and there must be available to us a truth that summons us beyond this particular time and place. Philosophy, or moral freedom, is possible only if some part of our hearts and minds belongs to us as individual human beings and not simply as members of this or that historical community—to repeat, only if "there is something in man that is not altogether in slavery to his society." Thus, there is also a moral argument for the Enlightenment liberal account of philosophy: liberation from one's community is not only a theoretical imperative, the indispensable condition of any quest for universal truths; it is also itself a moral good. Only if it is possible to "step back" from the merely conventional prejudices and loves that belong to us as citizens, as sons and daughters, as faithful servants of God, and step toward the truths that are available to us as human beings simply, by nature, can one be truly free. The human being who is not a philosopher is a moral slave to his community.[9]

But Walzer argues that it is a mistake—both moral and theoretical, but especially moral—to seek in this way to "liberate" oneself "from the bonds of particularism." Walzer does not repeat the now commonplace objections to the very possibility of philosophy thus understood, although he is "tempted" by the view that "philosophical discovery and invention . . . are disguised interpretations." Walzer's temptation, however, is less interesting than his conviction that it is not necessary to decide this theoretical question: the issue between philosophy and community can be decided on moral grounds alone. Thus, Walzer argues (here in agreement with Rorty) that philosophical detachment is not a true liberation

[9]Walzer, *Interpretation*, 5–7, 13, 15, 36–38; and Strauss, *Natural Right and History*, 3 (only if "there is something in man that is not altogether in slavery to his society"); and 6. And see Sandel, *Liberalism*, 179: "to have character is to know that I move in a history I neither summon nor command." And recall the case of Lincoln, for an argument that moral freedom from community does not require disowning love for one's own community: but this love will be humane.

but an attempt to "escape" from moral life, from the particular community that has wholly constituted our "moral existence." This is, to repeat, probably a theoretical mistake, because there are no universal moral truths that are not "minimal." But it is also and more importantly a moral error: "existing morality . . . is authoritative for us because it is only by virtue of its existence that we exist as the moral beings we are." We owe allegiance to the existing morality, not because "God made it or because it is objectively true," but because it constitutes us as moral beings: "our categories, relationships, commitments, and aspirations are all shaped by, expressed in terms of, the existing morality." And we are doubtless obligated in this way not only as philosophers or social critics, but also as human beings and citizens. So the philosophic longing to liberate oneself from the bonds of particularism is a moral error, not wicked but pitiable: "escape" from one's community does not bring freedom from merely local prejudices, or from the arbitrary and unnatural constraints imposed on our various pursuits of happiness by law or convention; rather, it deprives a human being of his humanity, his "moral existence," his capacities for love and hope and virtue, which are wholly constituted by the existing moral world. Philosophy renders us homeless: it deprives us of the "moral comfort" of home; it cuts us off from all the moral attachments, aspirations, and excellences that make us fully human. Outside of his own moral world, a human being is "nobody, or at best a stranger or an outcast."[10]

This fundamental dispute between partisans of philosophy and partisans of community, which can be understood in moral terms as a choice between freedom and being "at home," gives rise to a secondary dispute about the nature of moral reasoning. What at first appears to be a theoretical dispute about method, about "ways of doing moral philosophy," is more precisely understood as a disagreement about the moral natures of human beings. Moral reasoning must begin, on Walzer's view, not with doubt about existing morality that points to our essential humanity, but rather with "cultural elaboration and affirmation," with the recognition that "we have to start from where we are" and that "where we are . . . is always *someplace of value*." Social criticism is only useful, and perhaps only possible, in the context of "some prior acknowledgment of the value of [existing] morality." Thus, the Enlightenment philosopher and the interpretive social critic stand in different moral postures toward

[10]Walzer, *Interpretation*, 12, 15, 20–25, 81; see also 6–7; and MacIntyre, *After Virtue*, 32 ("nobody, or at best a stranger or an outcast"). Cf. Rorty, *Consequences*, 164–66.

their communities. Philosophic doubt or detachment is not an abstract theoretical method but rather the consequence of a concrete moral experience: the experience of community morality as a prejudice, and as an arbitrary obstacle to the possession of good things—to "what any nature naturally pursues as good," in Glaucon's phrase. Cultural affirmation is similarly derived from a certain moral experience: the experience of community morality as a source of moral comfort, and even as the condition of virtue and happiness. The moral reasoning that is inspired by philosophic doubt is likely to be more radical than the moral reasoning that begins from cultural affirmation; this is the basis of the charge that interpretive social criticism is inherently conservative, as well as of the charge that philosophic criticism is inherently revolutionary.[11]

Certainly, it would be foolish to deny the power of either the love of freedom or the love of home. Human beings are almost always devoted to their own families and countries; there are of course countless cases of blind loyalty to family or country, "right or wrong." But human beings also, often enough, long to be liberated from their homes; from time to time, they even reject them as unjust and aspire to make them just. Perhaps our "experience of moral argument" is more ambiguous than Walzer suggests: we sometimes even find ourselves in rebellion against "common meanings." Conservatism and radicalism are both, so to speak, rooted in the nature of the human being. Social critics, whether philosophic or interpretive, will seek in various ways to combine, or to appear to combine, the moral satisfactions of philosophic doubt and cultural affirmation. Thus, as Walzer argues, on the conventional view the "philosopher emerges, like Descartes in his *Discourse*, as a separatist in thought, a conformist in practice": the propriety and even necessity of conformism can be seen above all in the example of Socrates, who "irritated" the Athenians and was killed by them. Philosophers, who are always radical thinkers but seldom radical social critics, were moved by the example of Socrates to adopt a politics that might resemble conservatism—"cultural affirmation" in public, moral freedom in private. Certainly, it is evident from the tradition of political philosophy that radical principles do not in every case sanction a radical politics: the zeal to apply universal principles of political right, here and now, is often tempered by a prudent awareness of the intractability of those particular

[11]Walzer, *Interpretation*, 40, 17 (emphasis in original); see 62. Plato, *Republic*, 359c; and "he pursues a thing dependent on truth and does not live in the light of opinion" (362a). See MacIntyre, *Is Patriotism a Virtue?* 8–11.

moral opinions that constitute particular communities, and that make it possible for human beings to feel "at home."[12]

But the author of *Radical Principles* seems to recommend another course, the opposite of Descartes's: conformism in thought, separatism in practice. Walzer's social critic aims to remain faithful in thought to the community (for it cannot be otherwise), but also to preserve enough "critical distance," enough freedom from prevailing community morality, to make it possible to repudiate the most constraining or disagreeable aspects of the community's way of life. That is, Walzer refuses to renounce the human "capacity for reflection and criticism," and he undertakes to defend the way of life of the radical social critic: it is usually better to be a radical, for some reason, than to be an apologist. The main task of *Interpretation and Social Criticism* is to show that the social critic can acknowledge the "authoritative" character of existing morality, but nevertheless preserve and even cultivate a certain freedom from the "authorities" here and now: "subversion is always possible." This union of philosophical conservatism and political radicalism is perhaps the most curious aspect of Walzer's thought.[13]

II

Walzer's account of the ways of doing moral philosophy—discovery, invention, and interpretation—is therefore somewhat misleading, chiefly because it distracts attention from the more fundamental distinction between cultural interpretation and Enlightenment philosophy. But there are other difficulties with this taxonomy. In particular, there are problems with the idea of invention: discovery is clearly a species of universal philosophy; interpretation is clearly a mode of moral reasoning about particular moral worlds. But what is *invention*?

Walzer tends to assimilate invention and discovery, in opposition to interpretation. But this, too, is misleading, in two ways. First, there is a "minimalist" version of philosophical invention, as Walzer acknowledges, which "runs close" to interpretive social criticism. In *Political Liberalism*, for example, John Rawls appears to make a "minimalist" or interpretive argument. There, he invents or constructs "an account or model of . . . existing morality"; his invention is guided by "the values (like liberty and equality) that we share." That is, the "inventiveness of the philosopher

---

[12]Walzer, "Philosophy and Democracy," 380. See my "Postmodern Liberalism and the Politics of Liberal Education."

[13]Walzer, *Interpretation*, 21–22; see 60; see, too, Walzer, *The Company of Critics*.

consists only in turning moral reality into an ideal type," and not in the construction of an "objective morality." Walzer's *Spheres of Justice* and Rawls's *A Theory of Justice* (as elaborated in *Political Liberalism*) both offer an account, or interpretation, of our particular moral community; neither author attempts to judge that world by reference to universal principles of political right. If that is so, then it is perhaps misleading to say, as Walzer does, that interpretation is today not "philosophically respectable": according to Walzer, the principal representative of the dominant contemporary school of political theory practices a way of doing moral philosophy that "runs close" to Walzer's own.[14]

Walzer is, of course, a critic of Rawls; but his fundamental disagreement with Rawls, although perhaps not with some of his "epigones," concerns how to think about existing morality from the inside, not *whether* to think about existing morality *only* from the inside. Rawls's inventive philosopher is surely as much a "local judge" as is Walzer's interpretive social critic: he just has a different theory of jurisprudence. Walzer argues, against Rawls, that the moral world "lends itself less to abstract modeling than to thick description," and that moral argument is less like the orderly "work of legal codification" than the more ambiguous "work of a lawyer or judge who struggles to find meaning in a morass of conflicting laws and precedents." Certainly, these controversies about the nature of our moral world have important practical consequences. Walzer denies that the moral world is as orderly as Rawls implies; he therefore also denies the possibility of a systematic model of existing morality that will provide unambiguous resolutions of important moral controversies in a community. Compare Walzer's discussion of Rawls's attempt to demonstrate the possibility of a "reflective equilibrium" among our often conflicting moral intuitions with Walzer's account of his own view of the problem of contradiction and incoherence in existing moral understandings. Walzer denies, against Rawls, that these contradictions within our shared moral horizon can be fully resolved on the level of the intuitions themselves. Such controversies cannot be settled by good reasons, but only by superior ("evocative") rhetoric or superior force.[15]

This theoretical difference has an important practical consequence: Rawls's philosopher is not detached from the community as a whole, but

---

[14]Walzer, *Interpretation*, 69, 16–19, 39; and see 13; see, too, Rawls, *Political Liberalism*, esp. 89–129; and cf. Rorty, *Objectivity*, 175–96.

[15]Walzer, *Interpretation*, 13, 39, 17–20, 28–30. Cf. Rorty, *Contingency*, 37.

he claims to be detached from any particular party in the community; Walzer's social critic is necessarily a partisan. It is impossible, according to Walzer, to "lift the discourse above the level of ideological confrontation." But Walzer and Rawls nevertheless agree on what might be the most important point: moral reasoning, to repeat, depends on "some prior acknowledgment of the value of [existing] morality"; all cultural interpretation or criticism rests upon a more fundamental cultural affirmation. Moral reasoning is therefore always a kind of interpretation. From the point of view of more ambitious understandings of philosophy as a search for universal truths, this might seem to be a relatively trivial intramural squabble.[16]

Walzer's account of invention is misleading in a second, more important, way. Speaking now of invention in the strong sense, he writes, "The point of an invented morality is to provide what God and nature do not provide, a universal corrective for all the different social moralities." That is, the philosophical inventor shares the aspiration of Enlightenment philosophers to teach universal truths; but unlike those philosophers, who claimed to discover truths that are revealed by God or manifest in nature, the inventor begins from the new knowledge that "God [is] dead, or mankind radically alienated from nature, or nature devoid of moral meaning." The task of philosophical invention, it appears, is to find a new foundation for the universal claims of traditional philosophy in the face of admittedly unanswerable objections to the metaphysical foundations of traditional philosophy. It is hard to see how this project can succeed.[17]

Perhaps the most powerful attack on the foundations of traditional moral philosophy was made by Nietzsche, who announced "the death of God" and who affirmed, so to speak, the "meaninglessness of nature." That is, in particular, he denied that there are any objective and universal moral truths that are manifest in nature or revealed by God: "Verily, men gave themselves all their good and evil. Verily, they did not take it, they did not find it, nor did it come to them as a voice from heaven. Only man placed values in things to preserve himself—he alone created a meaning for things, a human meaning." But for Nietzsche, this novel discovery that "values" are not revealed to human beings, but are created by them, leads to a renunciation of the universal pretensions of philosophy. Human beings give values to themselves; they constitute

---

[16]Walzer, *Interpretation*, 11, 17; see 62.
[17]Walzer, *Interpretation*, 13, 9.

their own moral worlds, freely or willfully, without guidance from God or nature, or in the absence of constraints imposed by God or nature. Nietzsche is therefore led to investigate the human origins of the values of the many particular peoples or communities, rather than their supposed divine or natural origins. He is a student of human creativity; he directs our attention to the creative peoples of past ages, as well as to those individual legislators or founders who, as Walzer says, "imitat[ed] God's creation rather than the discoveries of his servants." For these creators, who are poets and prophets but not philosophers, the invention of a "morality" or a "common life" is the unpredictable and mysterious expression of the unfettered human will. This is true even where human beings have understood themselves to be acting in obedience to God or nature: for God too is an unwitting creation of men. There are no, or very few, natural limits on what human beings can make of themselves; thus, there are no, or very few, universal and objective standards that might make it possible to judge the various historical creations of new kinds of human beings. Our choices of values, of which there have been, as Nietzsche says, "a thousand and one," more fully constitute us than anything that we possess by virtue of our common humanity; or, rather, there is no true or natural humanity but only an irreducible pluralism of cultures, each constituted by some unique decision about values. And so, Nietzsche teaches, philosophy should cease its vain quest for universal moral truths; without God or nature, serious thought and action must remain within the horizon of particular moral worlds or cultures, or create new worlds.[18]

Now it is possible that Walzer would agree with the Nietzschean criticism of old-fashioned philosophy that is here only adumbrated. He is certainly a partisan of pluralism and particularism; that is why he is an advocate of interpretation, a mode of moral reasoning that does not pretend to escape from shared values. It is therefore somewhat surprising that in his discussion of philosophical invention, Walzer explicitly dismisses "the existentialists," who are "committed to an invented morality," but "are of little help in the business of invention" because they do not begin with "method" or "design procedure." That is, Walzer's philosophical inventors are not philosophers like Nietzsche, who does not begin with a "discourse on method," but rather philosophers like Descartes and above all John Rawls. But Descartes was "really launched on a journey of discovery," as Walzer admits; as for Rawls, we are here

---

[18]Walzer, *Interpretation*, 9–10; and Nietzsche, *Thus Spoke Zarathustra*, 171.

considering a "caricature," since Rawls is, as we have seen, really engaged in "minimalist" invention, which is closer to interpretation than to universal philosophy. Walzer appears to believe that Habermas and Ackerman are true philosophical inventors, but he does not discuss them at any length. Ackerman, at least, probably fits Walzer's definition of invention in the strong sense. The problem with such invention can be clearly seen in an extraordinary and revealing remark in Ackerman's *Social Justice in the Liberal State*: "The hard truth is this: There is no moral meaning hidden in the bowels of the universe. . . . Yet there is not need to be overwhelmed by the void. We may create our own meanings, you and I."[19]

According to Walzer, philosophical invention begins with a "design procedure" that guarantees that "all of us" are represented in a way that can secure "agreement." I do not here want to consider whether such attempts to secure universal principles of justice can succeed; I share Walzer's doubts. But I want to argue that such invention will always really be a species of philosophical discovery; certainly, these philosophers do not really "assume the death of God or the meaninglessness of nature."[20]

According to the proponents of philosophical invention, if we can construct a design procedure that provides for "universal presence" and nevertheless yields agreement and not "cacophony," then the principles of justice that result will be universal principles. But how do we know that agreement is more important than, say, wisdom or creativity, in the constitution of a just and "livable" moral world—since justice or happiness or virtue, and not peace or equality, might be thought to be the end of political life? One cannot know how to go about "inventing" moral principles or constituting a moral community, unless one already knows something about the justice of the claims of consent ("all of us"), or of wisdom or creativity, to rule or "to invest their principles with the force of (moral) law," and this knowledge cannot itself be invented, at least not in the manner of Walzer's inventors. Walzer argues that any mode of invention that involves a wise and powerful legislator (as with Descartes and Rousseau) prematurely "settles a basic feature of the design—the just distribution of power." But does not the requirement of agreement imply a decision in favor of consent, or natural equality, as the first principle of justice? It should be noted that the issue here concerns the design procedure, and not the principles that are then adopted; it is therefore

---

[19]Walzer, *Interpretation*, 9–13; and Ackerman, *Social Justice*, 368.
[20]Walzer, *Interpretation*, 10–12; see 19.

possible that a method that elevates wisdom above consent might yield principles that require government by consent (and the reverse). Indeed, Walzer has argued elsewhere that such design procedures in contemporary theory are often less representative than despotic, or look less to consent than to wisdom, although they yield representative principles.[21]

Further, how do we know that the various constraints that must be imposed on the deliberations of "all of us" (the "veil of ignorance"), in order to ensure that the outcome of the conversation is not "cacophony" but agreement, are just? How do we *know* that all of the various particular or partisan claims about justice, like the claims of the rich or of the poor, or those of industrious or courageous or prudent human beings, are merely prejudices that must be set aside in moral deliberation? The answers to these questions will always include more or less explicit assumptions about nature and human nature. That is, any design procedure will depend upon some discovery that is more fundamental than the invention; too often, method is merely a mode of obfuscation that permits these assumptions to remain implicit and unexamined. Only in this way can invention, like discovery, be said to yield universal principles, rather than the pluralism that would surely result from unconstrained invention, or creation: for the universal truths are embedded in the design procedure from the beginning. Thus, *such* inventors do not really "imitate God's creation rather than the discoveries of his servants"; that is why Rawls and Ackerman are less "frightening" than Nietzsche. It is because Walzer believes that invention and even interpretation are constrained—naturally, so to speak—that he can make the otherwise extraordinary remark, to which Ackerman but not others would assent, that the "death of God or the meaninglessness of nature" are "apparently painless assumptions." In short, Walzer's account of invention distracts attention from the radical quality of a Nietzschean philosophy of culture; and it further enables Walzer to embrace interpretation without dwelling on the radical freedom of the interpreter, at least if interpretation is best understood in a Nietzschean manner.[22]

It is now possible to reconsider the dispute between conventional philosophy and interpretive social criticism. To repeat, Walzer insists that moral philosophy is properly nothing more than the "thick description" of a particular moral world. The task of thoughtful citizens here and now

---

[21]Walzer, *Interpretation*, 10–11, 19; and see 25; and Walzer, "Philosophy and Democracy," 388–89; see, too, Walzer's review of Dworkin's *Taking Rights Seriously*; and his review of Ackerman's *Social Justice in the Liberal State*.

[22]Walzer, *Interpretation*, 13, 8–9.

is to "struggle to find meaning" in the existing "moral morass," rather than to seek a "universal corrective for all the different social moralities," including our own. Like Nietzsche, Walzer can "see no way in which the pluralism [of moral cultures] might be avoided," and so he does not long to be "liberated from the bonds of particularism." It is therefore somewhat surprising that Walzer does not undertake a philosophical inquiry into the various ways in which human beings constitute or create their particular moral worlds, especially against the background of the meaninglessness of nature or the death of God. That is, Walzer does not, in general, ask how we came to possess our moral principles or values. He is more concerned with contemporary interpretations of the existing moral world than with its creation or founding. But this perspective is surely too narrow.[23]

Walzer suggests that any discovered, revealed or invented morality will require interpretation, from time to time. This is doubtless true. Concerning "every religious and moral reformation," Walzer remarks, "God is not present now in the same way as he was in the beginning"; but the same is surely true of founders and founding principles.[24] Besides, the memory of foundings fades in time. And so, when a Supreme Court justice interprets the Constitution, or when a pious scholar interprets God's decrees for his particular community, his task will very often require the exercise of a certain kind of judgment or prudence, where the tradition does not provide any strict guidance. Interpretation is a necessary part of moral reasoning, whether the moral world is constituted by principles or values that are revealed by God, or discovered and enacted by a philosophical legislator, or created and enacted by a poetic founder, or whatever.

So it appears that interpretation is an essentially derivative activity, always necessary but never fundamental. Someone must write the founding texts, so to speak; the author or founder of a moral world either discovers or invents the principles that he enacts, and thereby constrains those interpreters who are not themselves discoverers or inventors. Walzer is sometimes "tempted" by the more radical view that every so-called discovery or invention is really a "disguised interpretation": discoveries and inventions are never altogether novel, and so there are no true foundings but only traditions of interpretation that have no beginning. But this is an implausible view, as Walzer acknowledges. Above all,

---

[23]Walzer, *Interpretation*, 20, 12–13, 25.
[24]Walzer, *Interpretation*, 5.

it does not account for the manifest, even "dangerous," novelty of those whose speeches and deeds come, in time, to be interpreted as the authoritative beginning of an altogether new community.[25]

Thus, any interpreter must ask: what is the nature of the principles or values that I now interpret for my companions? Is our shared moral horizon constituted by self-evident truths, as Americans once thought? Or are our shared values given to us through a revelation from God? Or are they a human creation, the gift of a great poet or legislator, like Lycurgus or Homer? Or is our moral world simply the accidental product of a more or less unquestioned tradition? The answer to such questions will, to a very large extent, determine the specific character of the task of interpretation. Thus, for example, interpretation might take the form of a recovery or restoration of original principles that have been corrupted or forgotten. Or it might take the form of a reformation of one aspect of the tradition in the light of an admittedly more important aspect. Or it might take the form of an imaginative innovation, something wholly "new." But in any case, the faithful interpreter of any tradition must first of all understand the true nature of the moral principles that constitute his moral world, as well as the orthodox understanding of the nature of those principles. Only on the basis of an answer to these questions can he undertake, with full clarity about the nature of the project, either to imitate the discoveries or the inventions of his ancestors, or to rebel against them and against his tradition by making another choice.[26]

A simple example of this problem, as I have already suggested, is that of constitutional interpretation. Those interpreters who believe that the authors of the Constitution sought to embody in it universal or philosophic principles of political right are engaged in an altogether different inquiry from those interpreters (often on the Right) who believe that the Constitution enacts certain popular or unphilosophic moral or political principles into positive law, as well as those interpreters (often on the Left) who believe that the genius of the Constitution is its capacity to live or evolve with the changing moral commitments of the community.[27] The second and third modes of interpretation ignore as imaginary the supposed philosophic aspirations of some of the founders, who sought to constrain their interpreters by

[25]Walzer, *Interpretation*, 21.

[26]Walzer, *Interpretation*, 12, 5, 88–89, 30; see 9–10.

[27]For examples, see Robert H. Bork, *The Tempting of America*; and Sanford Levinson, *Constitutional Faith*.

revealing certain truths about political right; the first and last modes of interpretation are likely to deny the primacy of consent as the authorized mode of judging between competing interpretations; and more. Each of these competing modes of interpretation is intelligible; the point here is that interpretation must in any case be guided by a more fundamental judgment about the nature of the (constitutional) principles that are to be interpreted.

The idea of interpretation does not provide a middle way, or any kind of alternative, to discovery and invention. It is impossible to escape the confrontation, as Walzer aims to do, between the tradition of universal philosophy and the more "frightening" way of doing moral philosophy that was inaugurated by Nietzsche. In any case, interpretation is surely not enough. Something else—religion, philosophy, poetry—provides the foundation upon which the interpreter builds.

III

Political philosophy, on the conventional view (as Walzer calls it), is the search for true principles of political right. This search no doubt requires the critical examination of orthodox opinions, which are, often or always, vindications of partisan interests. Thrasymachus, for example, openly affirms this common suspicion about justice: what is called "just" is perhaps merely the "advantage of the stronger," or the ruling party. The philosopher Socrates's inquiry gives rise to even more radical doubts about the provenance of the various opinions about justice; he, too, brings to light the moral or interested motives that often lie at the foundation of foolish or partisan ideas. The *Republic* (Book I) suggests that the range of possible doubts about ideas of justice is much broader than what is implied by Thrasymachus or others, who see these ideas only as instruments of domination: justice sometimes appears to be derived from piety, and is rendered doubtful when that piety is challenged (Cephalus); justice sometimes appears to be directed toward the common good or common interests of fellow citizens, who are friends and have enemies, and is rendered doubtful where the value of community, or of a particular community, is questioned (Polemarchus); justice sometimes appears to be associated with the interests of the ruling party within any community, and therefore cannot command the assent of the disadvantaged (Thrasymachus). Today, the most common suspicion about justice is the last one, and even a rather narrow version of that doubt. But it is worth remembering that moral ("communitarian") motives, as well as more narrowly interested motives, can give rise to false opinions. The *Republic* suggests that piety and community, as well as the interest of the stronger, may also present a false story about justice.[28]

Moreover, even where the conventional opinions are more or less adequate, our understanding of them is imperfect, unless our opinions are transformed into knowledge. Thus, the political philosopher is always a social critic, a gadfly who annoys his fellows by reminding them of their vices and follies. But the philosopher sometimes appears to be *only* a critic: he is not a constructive critic, much less a "creative" critic, or a founder.[29] The social critic, on Walzer's view, must be more than a critic, and also a reformer or prophet or activist. The philosopher is notoriously querulous: always searching, questioning, doubting; never quite a partisan or a patriot. Philosophy, say its critics, is much more successful when it raises doubts about existing morality than when it attempts to constitute a new moral world; in any case, it rarely makes this attempt. This debunking quality of philosophy gives rise to the charge that the philosopher is not a good citizen, but an irresponsible and dangerous "enemy" of the decent human beings who love morality, or their homes, more than they love the truth. This charge is made, today, not primarily by reactionary partisans of tradition, but by "radical" partisans of community.[30]

Thus, the case for philosophy is sometimes said to depend on the more ambitious claim that the political philosopher does not merely seek but actually possesses knowledge of universal and objective truths about morality and politics, and that this knowledge can guide or even constitute a political community. Only if it is possible not only to raise doubts about orthodox opinions, but also to secure certain knowledge of truths about justice and the common good that can assist citizens and statesmen, can the philosopher be a useful member of the political community. The political philosopher is a good citizen, on the conventional view, because he possesses a kind of knowledge, of what is just and unjust and good and bad for human beings and communities, that the community requires if it is to govern itself well.

Such knowledge enables the philosopher to stand above the partisan disputes that agitate every political community; he can therefore serve as an impartial arbiter in the controversies that divide the parties in a community. He sees that the various partisans advance opinions about jus-

---

[28]Plato, *Republic*, 338c–339a.

[29]On the desirability of a creative and even programmatic interpretation of existing morality, see Unger, *Critical Legal Studies*, 114–17, on "transformative politics"; and cf. Walzer, *Interpretation*, 29–30, 82–83.

[30]Walzer, *Interpretation*, 59.

tice or the common good that are partial, in two senses: based on one-sided understandings of the nature of human beings, and designed to vindicate particular claims or interests. As Walzer says, characteristically speaking only of the ruling party, and only of the problem of interest: "every ruling class is compelled to present itself as a universal class"; "ideology" always speaks the language of justice or the common good, providing "particularist ambitions" with a "universalist disguise." But the philosopher's understanding, on the conventional view, is both comprehensive and impartial. He can therefore come to the aid of the disadvantaged: those whose opinions about justice are disfavored by the ruling ideas. The philosopher as philosopher is not a member of any political party: he is not a partisan of the rich or the poor, or of the courageous, industrious, or prudent; he is not even a partisan of aristocracy, or of democracy; still less is he a Democrat or a Republican. But the philosopher as citizen tries to teach each party, and especially the dominant party, the limitations of its partial perspective; he thereby reminds thoughtful citizens, at least, of the necessity of moderation not only in the prosecution of their private claims, but even in their advocacy of a vision of the common good.[31]

Further, knowledge of the true principles of political right enables the philosopher to raise doubts about those authoritative opinions that are a common possession of all the parties in a particular community, and that express the common sense of the community about justice. These orthodoxies are always more or less defective. No one but a blind or thoughtless patriot would deny that every political community falls short, in greater or lesser measure, of establishing perfect justice—and not only because of an inevitable failure to live up to its own principles. The philosopher, insofar as he is a lover of justice, can therefore never be altogether devoted to any particular community: Socrates could not be a simply loyal Athenian. It does not follow, of course, that the philosopher cannot be a helpful participant in political debates: the detached philosopher is by no means always an "enemy" of his political community; he will probably not even be a revolutionary. To repeat, any attempt to bring about the best politics that is possible here and now demands attention not only to true principles but also to intractable opinions and circumstances. Yet, the philosopher can, from time to time, be very useful to his community: he can remind the community, when it is tempted by this or that opportunity for zealous intolerance to-

---

[31]Walzer, *Interpretation*, 40–41.

ward strangers at home or abroad, that justice is not the same as law-fulness, or patriotism.[32]

Of course, political philosophers can also be a nuisance: a partisan or a patriot who is not annoyed by the scoldings of the philosopher will have ceased to be a partisan or a patriot. But on the conventional view, the occasional usefulness of the political philosopher to the political community more than compensates for his usual querulousness. This is true above all because if knowledge of the true principles of political right is not available, then the struggle of parties cannot be settled except by force or fraud. Only if there is something beyond ideology, only if political philosophy is possible, can there be any principled and peaceful resolution of these partisan struggles.

But Walzer argues that, on the contrary, philosophy is mostly useless in moral or political argument: it teaches only what we already know and does not teach what we need to know; objective moral principles are often or always like Nagel's principle that "we should not be indifferent to the suffering of other people." Walzer is not impressed: "I acknowledge the principle but miss the excitement of revelation. I knew that already." Such principles can surely be defended by "sane philosophy"; at least, Walzer does not seem to share the extreme skepticism of those who would deny the objectivity even of such "minimal" principles. But for Walzer, this is small consolation, because moral life requires more than obedience to such principles. And the stronger moral opinions that constitute communities are indeed vulnerable to the debunking skepticism of philosophy: "Love thy neighbor as thyself" is "unlikely to figure in the list of philosophical discoveries—if only because the question, Why should I love him *that* much? is not crazy."[33]

In this, Walzer argues, philosophical discovery is very different from divine revelation. God characteristically demands more of us than adherence to Nagel's "principle of minimal concern." "God's servants," or the "religious leaders," announce to the rest of us, at the beginning, the shape of a moral world that is "like a new continent": not just strange but also formidable. Thereafter, priests and prophets "rediscover" or "interpret" this moral world, which soon loses its novelty but always retains its moral potency, its "critical force." The injunction, "Love thy neighbor as thyself," may cease to seem novel, but it will always offer clear, strong, and challenging moral guidance to its adherents. Walzer sometimes sug-

[32]See Walzer, *Interpretation*, 59.
[33]Walzer, *Interpretation*, 6–8; see 47.

gests that the novelty of the principles that are revealed by God and brought to human beings by his servants is their "chief advantage" over rational principles, but what is more important is the "specificity" or "strength" of these moral demands. This emphasis on novelty undermines his general attack on the weakness of reason in moral matters (if the capacity of a morality to guide human beings and communities depends on its novelty, then religious morality, like rational morality, will rarely be adequate); but it contributes to his turn to interpretation as the most characteristic mode of moral reasoning (every morality, once discovered or revealed, soon requires interpretation). But "philosophical discovery is likely to fall short of the radical newness and sharp specificity of divine revelation": the philosopher "will not discover anything that isn't already there," or rather, "here"; further, rational moral principles are always too general or minimal to provide guidance for "everyday social practice." Indeed, moral life generally is constituted by opinions of a kind less likely to be discovered by philosophers than to be written in a "sacred book" and interpreted by priests and prophets. It is thus not surprising that Walzer's concluding chapter, in which he provides a "historical analysis of social criticism . . . in the interpretive mode," is a study of "biblical prophecy." Walzer is more interested in this interpretive prophecy than in the nature and origin of the sacred book that must in time be interpreted, but which we "first experience . . . through the medium of discovery," or rather, revelation.[34]

This is not to say that philosophy is altogether incapable of providing moral guidance; but the content of that guidance and the situations in which it will be useful are extremely limited. Thus, Walzer speaks of the possibility of "a kind of minimal and universal moral code," which provides "a framework for any possible (moral) life, but only a framework." These "moral understandings that do not depend upon communal life" are especially useful or common as "a kind of international law," governing relations among communities that do not share a fully articulated moral horizon but nevertheless share some (very limited) "moral knowledge." Thus, *Just and Unjust Wars* can be, or appear to be, an exercise in philosophical discovery of universal truths; but *Spheres of Justice* is, with very few exceptions, unavoidably an interpretation of a particular moral world constituted by moral "truths" that are local and traditional and thus cannot be known by philosophy.[35]

[34]Walzer, *Interpretation*, 3–9, 82–83; and see 48, 29, 69–70.
[35]Walzer, *Interpretation*, 24–25, 78, 89–90.

The exceptions to the rule that moral reasoning begins from particular shared understandings are very limited, for Walzer. First, the rules of war arise from individual rights, which are in this sphere "something like absolute values," but which may or may not be "natural."[36] Second, there are perhaps universal principles of justice that govern the threshold between international law and communal self-determination, and that limit the autonomy of communities in decisions that concern "membership" in the community.[37] Finally, there are perhaps universal, or "almost universal," principles of justice that provide the "basic prohibitions" that every community acknowledges; but even these are not really discovered in nature, but are "emergent prohibitions, the work of many years, of trial and error." Even in these three cases, Walzer is very reluctant to affirm that any principles of justice are truly universal and natural; he sometimes argues that these minimal principles only express very broadly shared moral understandings, or that there is in some sense a community of all, or almost all, human beings—but a community that remains particular and historically contingent, engaged in an "unfinished conversation."[38]

Walzer illustrates the problem by means of a "story" that he tells about the limits of philosophy. "Imagine," Walzer asks, a group of travelers from different moral cultures who speak different languages but must now adopt "principles of cooperation." Assuming that they succeed in finding principles to govern their lives together, is there any reason to think that they have a moral obligation to "carry those same principles with them when they go home"? "Men and women standing behind the veil of ignorance . . . will perhaps, with whatever difficulties, find a *modus vivendi*—not a way of life but a way of living." But such rules of accommodation, which are characteristic of liberalism if not of philosophy altogether, are as little the material of a "livable morality" as a hotel is like a home. Hotels are useful, if one's home is temporarily or permanently beyond one's reach, as it is for travelers and refugees. But we would still "long for the homes we knew we once had." Philosophy can perhaps discover or invent "a universal (if minimal) morality, or at least a morality worked out among strangers." But human beings—one

---

[36]See Walzer, *Just and Unjust Wars*, xvi; and see 54, "if they are not natural, then we have invented them, but natural or invented, they are a palpable feature of our moral world"; see, too, Pangle, review of *Just and Unjust Wars*.

[37]See Walzer, *Spheres*, 31–63, esp. 33–34, 40–41, 45, 51, 61–63; cf. xiv–xv; see, too, Rosenblum, review of *Spheres of Justice*.

[38]Walzer, *Interpretation*, 24–25.

is tempted to say, by nature—*"want"* something more: "a . . . home, a dense moral culture within which they can feel some sense of belonging," a "livable morality." Human beings cannot live together, cannot be happy, without embracing moral doctrines that are simply beyond the reach of human reason. "Sane philosophy," unlike divine and perhaps "crazy" revelation, cannot constitute a home, however useful it might be in the interpretation of existing homes; indeed, the moral principles that form the various communities are not true, strictly speaking, but are only "'true.'" Walzer is, for this reason, a critic of philosophy, and especially liberal philosophy, in the name of community morality. This is, it seems to me, the most important aspect of the contemporary communitarian criticism of liberalism.[39]

Philosophy is also sometimes dangerous, according to Walzer: "it presses its practitioners toward manipulation and compulsion." Knowledge of universal principles, if these principles make more than minimal claims, can give rise to a temptation to "intervene" in the political community and to " 'compel the people to an enforced awakening' " (quoting Gramsci). This "dangerous presumption" has led too often, especially among radical thinkers, to "one or another version of an unattractive politics." But according to Walzer, interpretation is not dangerous, but friendly, criticism; even radical interpretive critics share with the orthodox a commitment to the deepest values of the community. For this very reason, interpretation has appeared to be conservative, confined within the limits of a tradition. Walzer responds that moral and cultural traditions, including our own, are not as univocal as his critics imply. Every moral world contains ambiguity, complexity, and even "contradiction." We do not, it turns out, share as much as is suggested by the comforting picture of the community as a "home": we may differ as much as Marxists and liberals differ about the meaning of equality, or as much as the critic Amos and the apologist Amaziah differ about whether "justice" or "worship" is the "core value of the Israelite tradition." In such cases, there are only "minimal" standards to help the citizen who must choose between competing interpretations; it is not surprising that most will remain obedient to the ruling opinions.[40]

Ultimately, Walzer cannot escape the charge that interpretation is conservative, and even illiberal, because the contest between critic and apol-

---

[39]Walzer, *Interpretation*, 14–16, 25, 8, 90; and see Rorty, *Contingency*.
[40]Walzer, *Interpretation*, 62–64, 21, 88–89; and see 7–8, 18–23, 28–32, 39–44, 48–49, 52, 58–61, 65, 75, 80–83, 89–91.

ogist remains an argument about the meaning of an authoritative tradition. Their dispute takes the form of claims to orthodoxy and charges of heresy, rather than appeals to what is reasonable or just. The interpretive social critic may oppose those authorities who actually wield power, but the authority of the tradition altogether can never be doubted. Liberalism teaches that real criticism requires a standpoint from which to question the authority of tradition, however interpreted. But Walzer argues that the existing moral world "is authoritative for us because it is only by virtue of its existence that we exist as the moral beings we are": for Walzer, the moral world is authoritative merely because it is ours. This argument virtually concedes the charge of conservatism, it seems to me; and it yields too much to the various authorities, intellectual and other, that have accidentally or historically secured power in particular communities.[41]

For the same reason that Walzer's position is conservative it is also itself potentially dangerous. Interpretive social critics can be no more than partisans, since the critic cannot claim to be more objective than the apologist; and there are no judges between them, even in principle, but the members of the community themselves. When the argument is about which prejudice will be the reigning prejudice, "there is no definitive way of ending the disagreement." Or rather, there is no principled way to end the disagreement; civil war is surely a definitive way to settle the quarrel (as Walzer himself suggests, by making the French Revolution the outcome of an interpretive struggle). Interpretation is no less dangerous than philosophy, and it deprives the citizen of the chance to oppose orthodoxy in the name of true principles of justice, and not mere prejudice or taste.[42]

---

[41]Walzer, *Interpretation*, 20–22; see 17–18, 60–62.
[42]Walzer, *Interpretation*, 28, 42n.5; and see 26–30, 37, 44–45, 49–50, 60, 65, 88.

9

Conclusion

In the world of political philosophy today, the partisans of the idea of community urge liberal democrats to renounce their sober rationalism. They thus invite an immoderate or slavish politics, for where human beings are denied reasonable grounds on which to endorse or repudiate the prevailing principles and practices of their own political community, they are compelled either to embrace that community thoughtlessly, or to rebel against it thoughtlessly.

Today's advocates of "community" teach us to identify with our community: for identification with one's own community is now said to be the foundation of any truly moral way of life. But in politics, identification with one's community—if the true lineaments of that construct can even be perceived—may give rise to blind patriotism, or to ethnocentrism, an intolerance of moral strangers at home and away from home. And in philosophy, identification with one's community deprives one of moral freedom, which requires that the mind be liberated from the authoritative prejudices of a particular time and place.

Political communities are constituted on the basis of certain shared opinions about fundamental principles—a "public philosophy." For the liberal, the "public philosophy" in a just community must be the product of a reasonable agreement, or consent: for a politics that is based on force or fraud or fashion is a slavish, mindless politics. And so, the liberal seeks to enlighten citizens, to teach them the fundamental law of nature, so that they will be able to choose for themselves, on the basis of good reasons and sound reasoning, as they pursue their "proper interest" through the establishment of a peaceful, prosperous political community.

But if community, of whatever passing form, is the only ground of our moral and political opinions, then it is not possible to judge the prevailing orthodoxies or the way of life of our particular community on the basis of good reasons that are *not* given us by our community. Thus there is no law of nature we can appeal to; there are only the transient laws of the community. And where that is so, partisan political disputes (about the meaning of our way of life, or about what the laws of the community should say) can be resolved only by more or less illicit means—by the various modes of force and fraud that over time induce citizens to adopt new orthodoxies and new ways of life, or to retain the traditional ones. And so, the contest between the apologists for today's practices and principles and the visionaries who propose new practices and principles admits no basis for resolution in principle. Citizens who must choose between apologists and visionaries cannot ask the contestants for good reasons, but must be content with pleasing poetry. Thus situated, they are distracted from the liberal task of reflection and choice about the purpose of their political community; they are not free and intelligent agents, but rather slavish adherents of the old order, or creative partisans of the new. Such passionate controversies are often settled by wars; only "calm reason" keeps the peace, says the liberal.[1]

The politics of community is, in any case, likely to be a rather "tumultuous" politics. Since reason cannot be brought to bear on the fundamental questions of politics, says the partisan of community, citizens should judge for themselves, unconstrained by self-evident truths or other good reasons. Liberals seek peace; but communitarian citizens, having forgotten the stark lessons of the past, seek the excitement and tumult of a public life, where such questions are routinely debated, and where citizens undertake common enterprises on the basis of these common deliberations. But if every fundamental agreement among the citizens in a community is up for grabs, and if even the most important issues cannot be settled on the basis of good reasons (since they are matters of mere taste), then a communitarian politics will produce only the (insecure) rule of the party with the greatest force (or the winning poem).

The great achievement of liberalism has been to make possible a political community that is not only peaceful, prosperous, and relatively just, but also the product of the (more or less) reasonable choices of free (and

---

[1]On the connection between war and the idea of community, see Bloom, *The Closing of the American Mind*, 141–240, esp. 154–56, 187–90, 194–216. "Nietzsche was a cultural relativist, and he saw what that means—war, great cruelty rather than great compassion" (202).

free-minded) individuals. Democratic politics was once thought to depend upon extraordinary civic virtue: the self-abnegating virtue of citizens who somehow love their country more than they love themselves. Such virtue could be brought into being only on the strength of poetry and religion; it could not be made to seem reasonable. Liberal political communities have now revealed that a democratic politics can be established on the basis of "reflection and choice," by human beings who follow only this law of nature: "Be reasonable." It is not surprising that the liberal politics of rights is more selfish and vulgar (but also more moderate) than the republican politics of virtue. Perhaps our hopes from reason were too great; but that is surely not a sound basis for abandoning reason, or for repudiating the many victories of reason over the forces of prejudice.

The idea of community is, finally, an attack on a certain kind of human being: the solitary. Human beings, it is said, are not made to live alone. Solitude (in spirit, or mind) is the lonely condition of "moral strangers" in the world, and their loneliness is surely incompatible with happiness or virtue. But perhaps we should *not* speak of solitude as loneliness; perhaps we should, rather, affirm that solitude is a kind of liberation, that the solitary human being is content as a "rugged individualist." However that may be, it seems to me that the dispute between communitarians and liberals today is not only a dispute about politics. It is also a dispute about these ways of life: the way of life of the solitary, the moral stranger, the rugged individualist, as opposed to the way of life of the citizen, the partisan, the comrade.

The communitarian critics of solitude deny that thought is a lonely activity. Is thought the activity of the solitary thinker, the philosopher, who undertakes the difficult but pleasing task of liberating himself from the reigning orthodoxies of a particular community? Or is thought always in the service of some party, or some community? If the latter, then in our time it is democratic public opinion, not solitary thought, that is the source of whatever "truth" is available to human beings. Further, the critics of solitude now argue that as individuals we owe some gratitude to our "parents," so to speak—that is, to those benefactors who constitute our moral world, who nourish and educate us and provide us our home. But is "home" above all a source of meaning and comfort for human beings in an unfriendly world, so that it is not only imprudent, but also ungrateful, to seek to leave home—figuratively or otherwise— and explore that world? Or is "home," in some sense, a kind of tyranny, an obstacle to the greater happiness that is available only to those human beings who overthrow their spiritual masters? And is the community in better hands with those who stay at home, or with those who habitually look beyond?

For the partisans of individualism, human beings are indeed, in the most important respects (if not also in certain petty respects) made to live alone. For these rugged liberal individualists, "home" is (sometimes) a nice place to visit, but no place to live.

References Cited

Ackerman, Bruce A. *Social Justice in the Liberal State*. New Haven: Yale University Press, 1980.

——. "Why Dialogue?" *Journal of Philosophy* 86 (1989): 5–22.

Ambler, Wayne. "Aristotle's Understanding of the Naturalness of the City." *Review of Politics* 47 (1985): 163–85.

Aristotle. *Nicomachean Ethics*. Trans. Martin Ostwald. Indianapolis: Bobbs-Merrill, 1962.

——. *Politics*. Trans. Carnes Lord. Chicago: University of Chicago Press, 1984.

Barber, Benjamin R. *The Conquest of Politics*. Princeton: Princeton University Press, 1988.

——. "Letter from America." *Government and Opposition* 26 (1991): 34–43.

——. "Neither Leaders nor Followers: Citizenship under Strong Democracy." In *Essays in Honor of James MacGregor Burns*, ed. Michael R. Beschloss and Thomas E. Cronin. Englewood Cliffs, N.J.: Prentice Hall, 1989.

——. *Strong Democracy*. Berkeley: University of California Press, 1984.

——. "The Undemocratic Party System: Citizenship in an Elite/Mass Society." In *Political Parties in the Eighties*, ed. Robert A. Goldwin. Washington: American Enterprise Institute, 1980.

Baumann, Fred E. "Historicism and the Constitution." In *Confronting the Constitution*, ed. Allan Bloom. Washington: American Enterprise Institute, 1990.

Becker, Carl L. *The Declaration of Independence*. New York: Random House, 1942.

Beer, Samuel H. "The Idea of a Nation." *New Republic* (19 & 26 July 1982): 23–29.

——. "Liberalism and the National Idea." *Public Interest* 5 (1966): 70–82.

Beiner, Ronald. *Political Judgment*. Chicago: University of Chicago Press, 1983.

Bellah, Robert N., Richard Madsen, William M. Sullivan, Ann Swidler, and Steven M. Tipton. *Habits of the Heart*. New York: Harper & Row, 1986.

Berkowitz, Peter. "Liberal Zealotry." Review of Stephen Holmes, *The Anatomy of Antiliberalism. Yale Law Journal* 103 (1994): 1363–82.

Berman, Paul, ed. *Debating P.C.* New York: Dell, 1992.

Berns, Walter. "Does the Constitution 'Secure These Rights'?" In *How Democratic Is the Constitution?* ed. Robert A. Goldwin and William A. Schambra. Washington: American Enterprise Institute, 1980.

——. *For Capital Punishment.* New York: Basic Books, 1979.

——. *In Defense of Liberal Democracy.* Chicago: Regnery Gateway, 1984.

——. "Taking Rights Frivolously." In *Liberalism Reconsidered*, ed. Douglas MacLean and Claudia Mills. Totowa, N.J.: Rowman & Allanheld, 1983.

——. *Taking the Constitution Seriously.* New York: Simon & Schuster, 1987.

Bloom, Allan. *The Closing of the American Mind.* New York: Simon & Schuster, 1987.

——. "Justice: John Rawls vs. the Tradition of Political Philosophy." *American Political Science Review* 69 (1975): 648–62.

Bork, Robert H. *The Tempting of America.* New York: Free Press, 1990.

Burke, Edmund. *Selected Letters of Edmund Burke.* Ed. Harvey C. Mansfield, Jr. Chicago: University of Chicago Press, 1984.

Churchill, Winston. "The Scaffolding of Rhetoric." In *Winston S. Churchill*, by Randolph Churchill, vol. I, *Companion*, Part II, 1896–1900. London: Heinemann, 1967.

Cox, Richard. *Locke on War and Peace.* Oxford: Oxford University Press, 1960.

Cuomo, Mario. "Keynote Address." Delivered at the Democratic National Convention, 17 July 1984. *Vital Speeches of the Day* (15 August 1984): 646–49.

Dannhauser, Werner J. "Ancients, Moderns, and Canadians." Review of *Technology and Empire*, by George Grant. *Denver Quarterly* 4 (1969): 94–98.

Diamond, Martin. "Democracy and *The Federalist*: A Reconsideration of the Framers' Intent." *American Political Science Review* 53 (1959): 52–68.

——. "Ethics and Politics: The American Way." In *The Moral Foundations of the American Republic*, ed. Robert H. Horwitz. Charlottesville: University Press of Virginia, 1986.

Diggins, John Patrick. *The Lost Soul of American Politics.* New York: Basic Books, 1984.

Douglass, Frederick. "The Meaning of July Fourth for the Negro" [5 July 1852]. In *The Life and Writings of Frederick Douglass*, vol. 2. Ed. Philip S. Foner. New York: International Publishers, 1950.

——. "Oration in Memory of Abraham Lincoln" [14 April 1876]. In *The Life and Writings of Frederick Douglass*, vol. 4. Ed. Philip S. Foner. New York: International Publishers, 1955.

DuBois, W. E. B. *The Souls of Black Folk.* New York: Library of America, 1990.

Dworkin, Ronald. *A Matter of Principle.* Cambridge: Harvard University Press, 1985.

——. " 'Spheres of Justice': An Exchange" [between Dworkin and Michael Walzer]. *New York Review of Books* (21 July 1983): 43–46.

———. *Taking Rights Seriously*. Cambridge: Harvard University Press, 1977.

———. "To Each His Own." Review of *Spheres of Justice*, by Michael Walzer. In *New York Review of Books* (14 April 1983): 4–6.

———. "What Is Equality? Part 1: Equality of Welfare." *Philosophy and Public Affairs* 10 (1981): 185–246.

———. "What Is Equality? Part 2: Equality of Resources." *Philosophy and Public Affairs* 10 (1981): 283–345.

Elshtain, Jean Bethke. "Don't Be Cruel: Reflections on Rortyian Liberalism." In *The Politics of Irony*, ed. Daniel W. Conway and John Evan Seerey. New York: St. Martin's Press, 1992.

Epstein, David F. *The Political Theory of "The Federalist."* Chicago: University of Chicago Press, 1984.

Etzioni, Amitai. *The Spirit of Community*. New York: Crown, 1993.

Fowler, Robert Booth. *The Dance with Community*. Lawrence: University Press of Kansas, 1991.

Fox-Genovese, Elizabeth. *Feminism without Illusions*. Chapel Hill: University of North Carolina Press, 1991.

Galston, William A. "Community, Democracy, Philosophy: The Political Thought of Michael Walzer." *Political Theory* 17 (1989): 119–30.

———. "Liberalism and Public Morality." In *Liberals on Liberalism*, ed. Alfonso J. Damico. Totowa, N.J.: Rowman & Littlefield, 1986.

———. *Liberal Purposes*. Cambridge: Cambridge University Press, 1991.

———. "Liberal Virtues." *American Political Science Review* 82 (1988): 1277–89.

———. "Moral Personality and Liberal Theory: John Rawls's 'Dewey Lectures.'" *Political Theory* 10 (1982): 492–519.

Genovese, Eugene. "Pilgrim's Progress." Review of *The Papers of Martin Luther King Jr.*, vol. 1, ed. Ralph E. Luker and Penny A. Russell. *New Republic* (11 May 1992): 33–40.

Gill, Emily R. "Liberty, Equality, and Liberal Toleration." Manuscript, paper delivered at the 1994 Annual Meeting of the American Political Science Association.

Glendon, Mary Ann. *Rights Talk*. New York: Free Press, 1991.

Gutmann, Amy. "Communitarian Critics of Liberalism." *Philosophy and Public Affairs* 14 (1985): 308–22.

Hamilton, Alexander, James Madison, and John Jay. *The Federalist Papers*. Ed. Clinton Rossiter. New York: New American Library, 1961.

Herzog, Don. "Up toward Liberalism." *Dissent* 36 (1989): 355–59.

Hobbes, Thomas. *Leviathan*. Ed. Richard Tuck. Cambridge: Cambridge University Press, 1991.

Holmes, Stephen. *The Anatomy of Antiliberalism*. Cambridge: Harvard University Press, 1993.

Hughes, Robert. "Art, Morals, and Politics." *New York Review of Books* (23 April 1992): 21–27.

Hunter, James Davison. *Culture Wars*. New York: Basic Books, 1991.

Jaffa, Harry V. "The Nature and Origin of the American Party System." In *Political Parties, U.S.A.*, ed. Robert A. Goldwin. Chicago: Rand McNally, 1964.

Jefferson, Thomas. *Thomas Jefferson: Writings*. Ed. Merrill D. Peterson. New York: Library of America, 1984.

Kautz, Steven. "Liberalism and the Idea of Toleration." *American Journal of Political Science* 37 (1993): 610–32.

———. "Postmodern Liberalism and the Politics of Liberal Education." *Social Philosophy and Policy* 13 (1996, forthcoming).

———. "Privacy and Community." In *The Legacy of Rousseau*, ed. Nathan Tarcov and Clifford Orwin. Chicago: University of Chicago Press, forthcoming.

Kristol, Irving. *On the Democratic Idea in America*. New York: Harper & Row, 1972.

———. *Two Cheers for Capitalism*. New York: Basic Books, 1978.

Lasch, Christopher. "The Communitarian Critique of Liberalism." *Soundings* 69 (1986): 60–76.

———. *The True and Only Heaven*. New York: W. W. Norton, 1991.

Levinson, Sanford. *Constitutional Faith*. Princeton: Princeton University Press, 1988.

———. "Law as Literature." *Texas Law Review* 60 (1982): 373–413.

Lincoln, Abraham. *Abraham Lincoln: His Speeches and Writings*. Ed. Roy P. Basler. New York: Da Capo Press, 1990.

Locke, John. *A Letter Concerning Toleration*. Ed. James H. Tully. Indianapolis: Hackett, 1983.

———. *Two Treatises of Government*. Ed. Peter Laslett. Cambridge: Cambridge University Press, 1991.

Macedo, Stephen. *Liberal Virtues*. Oxford: Oxford University Press, 1990.

———. "Liberal Virtues, Constitutional Community." *Review of Politics* 50 (1988): 215–40.

Machiavelli, Niccolò. *The Discourses*. Ed. Bernard Crick (using the translation of Leslie J. Walker). New York: Penguin, 1988.

———. *The Prince*. Trans. Harvey C. Mansfield, Jr. Chicago: University of Chicago Press, 1985.

MacIntyre, Alasdair. *After Virtue*. Notre Dame: University of Notre Dame Press, 1981.

———. *Is Patriotism a Virtue?* The Lindley Lecture, University of Kansas, 26 March 1984. Lawrence: University of Kansas, Department of Philosophy, 1984.

Mansfield, Harvey C., Jr. "Constitutional Fideism." Review of *Constitutional Faith*, by Sanford Levinson. *Yale Journal of Law and the Humanities* 1 (1988): 181–86.

———. "Dewey, All-Out Democrat." *Times Literary Supplement* (24 January 1992): 26.

———. "Hobbes and the Science of Indirect Government." *American Political Science Review* 65 (1971): 97–110.

———. "Modern and Medieval Representation." *Nomos X: Representation*, ed. J. Roland Pennock and John W. Chapman. New York: Atherton Press, 1968.

———. "Party Government and the Settlement of 1688." *American Political Science Review* 58 (1964): 933–46.

———. "The Revival of Constitutionalism." In *The Revival of Constitutionalism*, ed. James W. Muller. Lincoln: University of Nebraska Press, 1988.

———. "Social Science and the Constitution." In *Confronting the Constitution*, ed. Allan Bloom. Washington: American Enterprise Institute, 1990.

———. *The Spirit of Liberalism*. Cambridge: Harvard University Press, 1978.

———. *Taming the Prince*. New York: Free Press, 1989.

———. "Whether Party Government Is Inevitable." *Political Science Quarterly* 80 (1965): 517–42.

Marcuse, Herbert. "Repressive Tolerance." In Robert Paul Wolff, Barrington Moore, Jr., and Herbert Marcuse, *A Critique of Pure Tolerance*. Boston: Beacon Press, 1965.

McWilliams, Wilson Carey. "Democracy and the Citizen: Community, Dignity, and the Crisis of Contemporary Politics in America." In *How Democratic Is the Constitution?* ed. Robert A. Goldwin and William A. Schambra. Washington: American Enterprise Institute, 1980.

———. *The Idea of Fraternity in America*. Berkeley: University of California Press, 1973.

Melzer, Arthur. *The Natural Goodness of Man*. Chicago: University of Chicago Press, 1990.

———. "Tolerance 101." *New Republic* (1 July 1991): 10–12.

Mill, John Stuart. *On Liberty and Other Essays*. Ed. John Gray. Oxford: Oxford University Press, 1991.

Montesquieu. *The Spirit of the Laws*. Trans. Anne M. Cohler, Basia Carolyn Miller, and Harold Samuel Stone. Cambridge: Cambridge University Press, 1989.

Nathanson, Stephen. "In Defense of 'Moderate Patriotism.' " *Ethics* 99 (1989): 535–52.

Neuhaus, Richard John. *The Naked Public Square*. Grand Rapids, Mich.: W. B. Eerdmans, 1984.

Nichols, James H., Jr. "Pragmatism and the U.S. Constitution." In *Confronting the Constitution*, ed. Allan Bloom. Washington: American Enterprise Institute, 1990.

Nietzsche, Friedrich. *Thus Spoke Zarathustra*. In *The Portable Nietzsche*, trans. Walter Kaufmann. New York: Viking Penguin, 1954.

Orwin, Clifford. "Civility." *American Scholar* 60 (1991): 553–64.

———. "Democracy and Distrust: A Lesson from Thucydides." *American Scholar* 53 (1984): 313–25.

———. "Welfare and the New Dignity." *Public Interest* (1983): 85–95.

Orwin, Clifford, and James R. Stoner, Jr. "Neo-Constitutionalism? Rawls, Dworkin, and Nozick." In *Confronting the Constitution*, ed. Allan Bloom. Washington: American Enterprise Institute, 1990.

Pangle, Thomas L. "The Liberal Critique of Rights in Montesquieu and Hume." *Tocqueville Review* 13 (1992): 31–42.

——. *Montesquieu's Philosophy of Liberalism*. Chicago: University of Chicago Press, 1973.

——. "Patriotism, American Style." *National Review* (29 November 1985): 30–34.

——. Review of *Just and Unjust Wars*, by Michael Walzer. In *American Political Science Review* 72 (1978): 1393–95.

——. *The Spirit of Modern Republicanism*. Chicago: University of Chicago Press, 1988.

Plant, Raymond. "Community: Concept, Conception, and Ideology." *Politics and Society* 8 (1978): 79–107.

Plato. *Apology of Socrates*. In *Four Texts on Socrates*, trans. Thomas G. West and Grace Starry West. Ithaca, N.Y.: Cornell University Press, 1984.

——. *The Republic*. Trans. Allan Bloom. New York: Basic Books, 1968.

Plattner, Marc F. "American Democracy and the Acquisitive Spirit." In *How Capitalistic Is the Constitution?* ed. Robert A. Goldwin and William A. Schambra. Washington: American Enterprise Institute, 1982.

——. "Capitalism." In *Confronting the Constitution*, ed. Allan Bloom. Washington: American Enterprise Institute, 1990.

——. "The Good Old Cause." Review of *Radical Principles*, by Michael Walzer. *Public Interest* (1981): 89–97.

——. "The Welfare State vs. the Redistributive State." *Public Interest* (1979): 28–48.

Pocock, J. G. A. *The Machiavellian Moment*. Princeton: Princeton University Press, 1975.

——. *Virtue, Commerce, and History*. Cambridge: Cambridge University Press, 1985.

Rawls, John. "Justice as Fairness: Political not Metaphysical." *Philosophy and Public Affairs* 14 (1985): 223–51.

——. *Political Liberalism*. New York: Columbia University Press, 1993.

——. *A Theory of Justice*. Cambridge: Harvard University Press, 1971.

Raz, Joseph. *The Morality of Freedom*. Oxford: Oxford University Press, 1986.

——. "Multiculturalism: A Liberal Perspective." *Dissent* 41 (1994): 67–79.

Reagan, Ronald. "Acceptance Speech." Delivered at the Republican National Convention, 17 July 1980. *Vital Speeches of the Day* (15 August 1980): 642–46.

——. "The Inauguration Address." Delivered 21 January 1985. *Vital Speeches of the Day* (1 February 1985): 226–28.

——. "State of the Union: 1986." Delivered to Congress, 4 February 1986. *Vital Speeches of the Day* (1 March 1986): 290–93.

Rorty, Richard. *Consequences of Pragmatism*. Minneapolis: University of Minnesota Press, 1982.

——. *Contingency, Irony, and Solidarity*. Cambridge: Cambridge University Press, 1989.

——. "Education without Dogma." *Dissent* 36 (1989): 198–204.

——. *Essays on Heidegger and Others.* Cambridge: Cambridge University Press, 1991.

——. *Objectivity, Relativism, and Truth.* Cambridge: Cambridge University Press, 1991.

——. "The Philosophy of the Oddball." Review of *In Quest of the Ordinary*, by Stanley Cavell. *New Republic* (19 June 1989): 38–41.

——. "Posties." Review of *Der Philosophische Diskurs der Moderne*, by Jürgen Habermas. In *London Review of Books* (3 September 1987): 11–12.

——. "Science as Solidarity." In *The Rhetoric of the Human Sciences*, ed. John S. Nelson, Allan Megill, and Donald N. McCloskey. Madison: University of Wisconsin Press, 1987.

——. "Taking Philosophy Seriously." Review of *Heidegger et le Nazisme*, by Victor Farias. *New Republic* (11 April 1988): 31–34.

——. "That Old-Time Philosophy." *New Republic* (4 April 1988): 28–33.

——. "Thugs and Theorists: A Reply to Bernstein." *Political Theory* 15 (1987): 564–80.

Rosenblum, Nancy L., ed. *Liberalism and the Moral Life.* Cambridge: Harvard University Press, 1989.

——. Review of *Spheres of Justice*, by Michael Walzer. *World Politics* 36 (1984): 581–96.

Rousseau, Jean-Jacques. *Emile.* Trans. Allan Bloom. New York: Basic Books, 1979.

——. *The First and Second Discourses.* Trans. Victor Gourevitch. New York: Harper & Row, 1986.

——. *On the Social Contract, with Geneva Manuscript and Political Economy.* Ed. Roger D. Masters. Trans. Judith R. Masters. New York: St. Martin's Press, 1978.

Sandel, Michael J. "Democrats and Community." *New Republic* (22 February 1988): 20–23.

——. *Liberalism and the Limits of Justice.* Cambridge: Cambridge University Press, 1982.

——. "Moral Argument and Liberal Toleration: Abortion and Homosexuality." *California Law Review* 77 (1989): 521–38.

——. "Morality and the Liberal Ideal." *New Republic* (7 May 1984): 15–17.

——. "The Procedural Republic and the Unencumbered Self." *Political Theory* 12 (1984): 81–96.

——. Review of *Spheres of Justice*, by Michael Walzer. *New York Times Book Review* (24 April 1983): 1.

Schaar, John. "The Case for Patriotism." *American Review* 17 (1973): 59–99. New York: Bantam Books.

Shklar, Judith N. "The Liberalism of Fear." In *Liberalism and the Moral Life*, ed. Nancy L. Rosenblum. Cambridge: Harvard University Press, 1989.

——. *Montesquieu.* Oxford: Oxford University Press, 1987.

——. *Ordinary Vices.* Cambridge: Harvard University Press, 1984.

Smith, Adam. *An Inquiry into the Nature and Causes of the Wealth of Nations.* Ed. R. H. Campbell, A. S. Skinner, and W. B. Todd. Indianapolis: Liberty Press, 1981.

Spinoza, Benedict. *A Theologico-Political Treatise.* Trans. R. H. M. Elwes. New York: Dover, 1951.

Storing, Herbert J. "The Case against Civil Disobedience." In *On Civil Disobedience*, ed. Robert A. Goldwin. Chicago: Rand McNally, 1968.

———, ed. *The Anti-Federalist: Writings by the Opponents of the Constitution.* Chicago: University of Chicago Press, 1985.

———, ed. *What Country Have I? Political Writings by Black Americans.* New York: St. Martin's Press, 1970.

Stout, Jeffrey. "Liberal Society and the Languages of Morals." *Soundings* 69 (1986): 32–59.

Strauss, Leo. *Natural Right and History.* Chicago: University of Chicago Press, 1953.

———. "On the Intention of Rousseau." *Social Research* 14 (1947): 455–87.

Sullivan, William M. *Reconstructing Public Philosophy.* Berkeley: University of California Press, 1986.

Tarcov, Nathan. "American Constitutionalism and Individual Rights." In *How Does the Constitution Secure Rights?* ed. Robert A. Goldwin and William A. Schambra. Washington: American Enterprise Institute, 1985.

———. *Locke's Education for Liberty.* Chicago: University of Chicago Press, 1984.

———. "Locke's *Second Treatise* and 'The Best Fence Against Rebellion.' " *Review of Politics* 43 (1981): 198–217.

———. "A 'Non-Lockean' Locke and the Character of Liberalism." In *Liberalism Reconsidered*, ed. Douglas MacLean and Claudia Mills. Totowa, N.J.: Rowman & Allanheld, 1983.

Taylor, Charles. "Atomism." In *Philosophy and the Human Sciences* 2, 187–210. Cambridge: Cambridge University Press, 1985.

———. *Multiculturalism and the "Politics of Recognition."* Princeton: Princeton University Press, 1992.

Thucydides. *The Peloponnesian War.* Ed. T. E. Wick (using translation of Richard Crawley). New York: Modern Library, 1982.

Tocqueville, Alexis de. *Democracy in America.* Ed. J. P. Mayer. Trans. George Lawrence. Garden City, N.Y.: Doubleday, Anchor Books, 1969.

Unger, Roberto Mangabeira. *The Critical Legal Studies Movement.* Cambridge: Harvard University Press, 1986.

———. *Knowledge and Politics.* New York: Free Press, 1984.

Walzer, Michael. *The Company of Critics.* New York: Basic Books, 1988.

———. "The Courts, the Elections, and the People." *Dissent* 28 (1981): 153–55.

———. "Flight from Philosophy." Review of *The Conquest of Politics*, by Benjamin Barber. *New York Review of Books* (2 February 1989): 42–44.

———. "From Contract to Community." Review of *Liberalism and the Limits of Justice*, by Michael J. Sandel. *New Republic* (13 December 1982): 35–37.

———. *Interpretation and Social Criticism.* Cambridge: Harvard University Press, 1987.

———. *Just and Unjust Wars.* New York: Basic Books, 1977.

——. "Liberalism and the Art of Separation." *Political Theory* 12 (1984): 315–30.

——. *Obligations.* Cambridge: Harvard University Press, 1970.

——. "Philosophy and Democracy." *Political Theory* 9 (1981): 379–99.

——. "Pluralism in Political Perspective." In *The Politics of Ethnicity*, ed. Stephan Thernstrom. Cambridge: Harvard University Press, 1982.

——. *Radical Principles.* New York: Basic Books, 1980.

——. Review of *Social Justice in the Liberal State*, by Bruce A. Ackerman. *New Republic* (25 October 1980): 39–41.

——. Review of *Taking Rights Seriously*, by Ronald Dworkin. *New Republic* (25 June 1977): 28–31.

——. *Spheres of Justice.* New York: Basic Books, 1983.

——. " 'Spheres of Justice': An Exchange" [between Ronald Dworkin and Walzer]. *New York Review of Books* (21 July 1983): 43–46.

Wills, Garry. *Explaining America: The Federalist.* Garden City, N.Y.: Doubleday, 1981.

Wolff, Robert Paul. *The Poverty of Liberalism.* Boston: Beacon Press, 1968.

Wolin, Sheldon. *Politics and Vision.* Boston: Little, Brown, 1960.

Index